Operational Research

T. A. Burley

and

G. O'Sullivan

MACMILLAN

First published 1986 by
THE MACMILLAN PRESS LTD
Houndmills, Basingstoke, Hampshire RG21 2XS
and London
Companies and representatives
throughout the world

ISBN 0–333–39618–9

A catalogue record for this book is available
from the British Library.

Printed in Malaysia

13 12 11 10 9 8 7 6
03 02 01 00 99 98 97 96 95

Contents

Preface

Our purpose in writing this book is to convey an understanding of the methods of operational research. It has been developed out of many years of teaching this subject on professional-stage accountancy courses and second-year degree and BTEC higher national courses. We have sought to provide a significant descriptive input in addition to numerical and algebraic aspects.

The book assumes an algebraic facility of about 'O' level standard. It also assumes a familiarity with such ideas of probability and statistics as are covered in the foundation stage of professional accountancy courses or in the first-year 'quantitative methods' units on degrees in business studies, accountancy and economics or on BTEC higher national courses in the business area. The use of an electronic calculator will be found helpful for a number of the exercises.

The first chapter provides an overview of the subject of operational research and an introduction to model building. This is followed by a further twelve chapters each of which is based on a particular area of operational research. Each chapter has a flowchart detailing the links between the topics, and an introductory section which is followed by a progression of examples and exercises. Full answers to the examples are given in the text. Where student exercises require numerical solutions these are given in Appendix 1. Solutions are not given for exercises requiring descriptions, tables and diagrams. We have found this arrangement of material to be the basis of a popular and successful teaching method over a number of years.

In order to provide a 'rich feast' of examples and exercises we have referred to a number of past examination questions set by ACCA and ICMA. The permission of these bodies to use their questions is gratefully acknowledged elsewhere. We believe that the book will be very useful to students studying for the professional-stage examinations of these bodies as well as to second-year students on degree courses in business studies, accountancy and economics or on BTEC higher national courses in the business area.

After the attempt in Chapter 1 to explain the scope of operational research and set the subject in its historical and practical context, the remainder of the book is largely devoted to consideration of particular OR models. This is to say we concentrate on the modelling of fairly simple situations, solving the models and interpreting the results. We hope that the reader in working through the book will not get lost in the 'trees' of detail of particular techniques and lose consciousness of the operational research 'wood' of which they are part. However, we believe that a thorough understanding of these techniques is a major objective of most people who will use this book. We also believe that this is the aspect of operational research most suited to textbook treatment. Issues of definition and data collection for substantial problems are better dealt with through project work, and the political and administrative issues associated with implementation can be fully appreciated only through experience in the practical situation.

In Chapters 2, 3 and 4 we look at models based on the ideas of linear programming. Chapter 2 treats linear programming explicitly from both graphical and algebraic viewpoints. Chapter 3 deals with the transportation problem, which is a particular kind of linear programming problem for which special methods of solution are available. Then Chapter 4 looks at the theory of games, for which the general problem can be solved using the standard linear programming methods of Chapter 2.

Chapter 5 looks at networks as a method for scheduling complex projects involving a number of activities. Different types of network diagram are considered, as well as aspects such as manpower deployment, and in the last section probabilities are used to deal with projects where activity durations are not known with certainty.

Chapter 6 considers stock control and is a particularly good example of the modelling process at work. We begin by considering a model which is very simple indeed and look at the solutions it offers. We then move to models which offer progressively closer approximation to reality, including the use of probabilities to take account of variable demand.

Chapter 7 looks at queuing models, beginning with a very simple model for which features such as average queue-length and average waiting-time are calculated.

Results for slightly more complex models are then quoted and used in the solution of problems.

Chapter 8 concerns simulation and the example on queuing simulation when contrasted with the approach in Chapter 7 provides a good illustration of the distinction between mathematical and simulation models.

Chapter 9 introduces dynamic programming. This is an approach to problems involving sequences of decisions or other activities by working *recursively*. That is to say, we start by looking at the final subsystem and work back from a solution to that to a solution for the system as a whole.

Chapter 10 considers replacement problems, looking at how decisions on scale and frequency of replacement are taken in the light of probabilities derived from past experience.

Chapters 11 and 12 look at major applications of matrix algebra in input-output analysis and in Markov processes.

Finally, Chapter 13 considers forecasting methods, beginning with a simple forecasting model and progressing as far as multiple regression models.

We hope that the reader will be helped to gain a clearer insight into what is covered in the remaining units by consideration of the introduction in Chapter 1 to the philosophy and approach of operational research, the variety of its techniques and the versatility of its applications.

Department of Mathematics and Statistics,   T. A. B.
City of Birmingham Polytechnic, February 1986   G. O'S.

Acknowledgements

We acknowledge with thanks the permission given by the following professional bodies to reproduce past examination questions set by them:

The Association of Certified Accountants (ACCA);
The Institute of Cost and Management Accountants (ICMA).

Where such questions are used as examples and exercises they are acknowledged by a statement at the end of the question of the initials of the body concerned and of the part of the examination in which they appeared. All answers to examples and solutions to exercises are completely our own and do not depend in any way on model answers produced by or on behalf of the professional bodies.

We also acknowledge the help of colleagues and students of the City of Birmingham Polytechnic who have helped us in the development and refining of the material presented in this book.

To our wives
Judith and Eleanor

1 Introduction

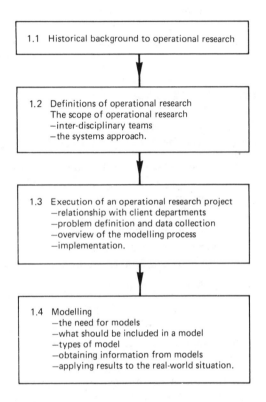

| 1.1 Historical background to operational research |
| 1.2 Definitions of operational research
The scope of operational research
—inter-disciplinary teams
—the systems approach. |
| 1.3 Execution of an operational research project
—relationship with client departments
—problem definition and data collection
—overview of the modelling process
—implementation. |
| 1.4 Modelling
—the need for models
—what should be included in a model
—types of model
—obtaining information from models
—applying results to the real-world situation. |

1.1   Historical Background

The concept of operational research as it is currently understood was mainly developed in World War II. The name operational research (or operations research as it is called in the American literature) arose because the concern in the war context was research on (military) operations. Although the concept was largely developed during the war the subject has advanced very greatly since that time. The immediate post-war years saw the recognition of operational research as an identifiable and respected area of study through the formation of the Operational Research Society and the establishment of departments of operational research in a number of universities. Then from the mid-nineteen-sixties onwards the practice of operational research has expanded greatly through the rapid development of computer technology, making possible the application of ideas which could previously be appreciated only at a theoretical level. Also in the post-war era, the primary area of operational research use has shifted from the military (where it remains, however, very important) to the area of industrial, commercial and governmental organisations. It is used by multinationals, nationalised industries, large-scale chemical producers and many private companies.

Operational research in the business context represents the further development of a phenomenon which has been present for a long time. With the industrial revolution and the advent of large-scale business enterprises it became more difficult for one individual to control all aspects of a business and specialist functional areas such as production, finance, personnel and marketing grew up. However, not all problems arising in a business could be isolated into particular functional areas and it became necessary to have some facility for dealing with problems spanning several areas. This led to the formation of management services facilities which would include operational research and also such things as computer services and O & M. Operational research departments are available to look at problems within any of the functional areas of a business, and many methods have been developed which can be applied in particular functional areas, and to problems spanning different functional areas.

1.2 Definitions and Scope

Tying down operational research to a concise definition is by no means easy. In 1962 the UK Operational Research Society formulated the following definition:

> Operational research is the application of the methods of science to complex problems arising in the direction and management of large systems of men, machines, materials and money in industry, business, government and defence. The distinctive approach is to develop a scientific model of the system, incorporating measurements of factors such as chance and risk, with which to predict and compare the outcomes of alternative decisions, strategies or controls. The purpose is to help management determine its policy and actions scientifically.

The definition of comparable standing which is used in the United States is as follows:

> Operations research is concerned with scientifically deciding how to best design and operate man-machine systems, usually under conditions requiring the allocation of scarce resources.

Both the above definitions emphasise the problem-solving aspect of operational research and the provision of a quantitative basis for management decisions. As another example, however, Sir Maurice Kendall has defined operational research in the following way:

> Operational research is a branch of philosophy; an attitude of mind towards the relationship between man and the environment; a body of methods for the solution of problems which arise in that environment.

This definition takes a wider view of operational research, as an approach to thinking about the world as well as looking at various techniques for problem solving.

One way in which operational research attempts to take the wider view of problems is by advocating the use of teams of specialists from a variety of disciplines to work together on problems from right across the organisation. Thus in practice operational research does tend to conform more to the problem-solving definition of the Operational Research Society than to the wider definition. In principle, the ever-increasing range of computer software available for operational research work should reduce the need for extensive mathematical ability. However, the availability of so much material increases the need for an ability to critically assess its effectiveness. Also, operational research workers are commonly called upon to be very proficient computer programmers. For these reasons operational research is likely to continue to attract more mathematically fluent personnel.

Another way in which operational research attempts to take a wider view of problems is by its use of the system approach. This approach assumes that it is necessary to regard a problem in the context of the whole system of which it is part, seeking a solution which is best for this system as a whole. Let us consider a very simple example to illustrate this. Imagine a firm with a production department and a distribution department where the former transfers items to the latter at a certain transfer price. Suppose the production department called in the operational research section to ask for advice on how much they should be producing in order to maximise their profit. The operational research workers would be reluctant to comply with such a request if varying the production output for this purpose could cause disastrous losses in other areas and consequent damage to the overall financial position of the firm. The concern must be to find the optimum production level for the business as a whole rather than to 'sub-optimise' by finding what is best for one part. However, it is again necessary to say that operational research in its practical outworkings is not always as broad in its scope as it might be. Many problems which operational research workers are asked to deal with are tactical rather than strategic and are concerned with a particular part of the business such as operations planning, stock control or storage location. The Operational Research Society has prepared a most useful introductory booklet entitled *Operational Research* (see Appendix 2).

1.3 The Steps in an Operational Research Project

The operational research department in a company is responsible to the management of the company. It is necessary for the department to have credibility with other departments of the company in order that they will call it in when a problem is perceived to exist. Typically, work done by operational research workers will be charged to the departments for which it is done, and these departments will be prepared to pay only if they have confidence in the effectiveness of the service they will get.

Having been called in, the operational researchers must identify the problem to be tackled. This is certainly not a trivial matter and normally needs substantial consultation with the managers of the department concerned. It may also emerge that the real problem is not quite the one which the people who asked for help thought it was.

An example of this occurred in the steel industry when stock costs were considered to be very high and operational research workers were called in to find by how much stock should be reduced in order to save money. It was found eventually that higher stock levels were needed in order to provide improved service to customers with resulting financial savings.

Having agreed a problem specification, the operational research workers need to plan the overall strategy for the project, including estimation of the time required and the costs involved. They can then embark on the core of their task, which begins with a careful gathering of all necessary data relating to the situation being considered.

The next phase is concerned with modelling that situation. Modelling is a substantial topic and section 1.4 is devoted to considering it. At this point we content ourselves with an overview of the modelling process as shown in Fig. 1.1. It involves constructing a suitable representation of the problem specified, obtaining a solution for that representation, and interpreting the solution in terms of the real situation. It may be possible to obtain a precise solution using some laid-down rules or *algorithms* (e.g. linear programming). However, it may often be necessary to proceed by *heuristic* methods. This means basically playing hunches in a trial-and-error approach aimed at improving the situation through a sequence of iterations, each involving solution, testing and improvement until a 'good enough'

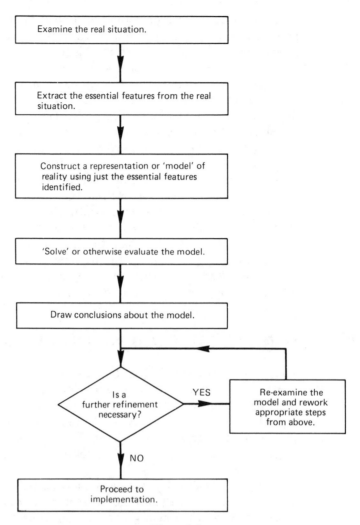

Examine the real situation.

↓

Extract the essential features from the real situation.

↓

Construct a representation or 'model' of reality using just the essential features identified.

↓

'Solve' or otherwise evaluate the model.

↓

Draw conclusions about the model.

↓

Is a further refinement necessary? —— YES —→ Re-examine the model and rework appropriate steps from above.

NO ↓

Proceed to implementation.

Figure 1.1

solution is reached. There is in these cases no attempt to identify 'the solution'.

When the modelling process is complete and conclusions are drawn as to what needs to be done it is necessary to set about implementation. Where possible it is desirable to carry out a pilot implementation of the proposed changes on part of the system. Experience has shown this to be a more efficient method than attempting to run a proposed new method on the whole system in parallel with an existing method. If the pilot is successful, then the new method can replace the existing one for the whole system. At all stages of implementation it is necessary that all operators are given clear, printed instructions on how to operate the new system.

Once a new system has been implemented as proposed by the operational research department it is that department's responsibility to monitor the early stages of its operation in order to help with teething troubles and iron out any unforeseen problems. The purpose of operational research is not to produce elegant reports but to propose practical ways of modifying real situations in order to achieve specific objectives. Whether a proposed course of action is implemented is a responsibility of management. They must be convinced that it is useful, cost-effective and will not lead to insurmountable trade-union resistance. They are also responsible for considering human elements such as the welfare of workers. Because the ultimate decision on implementation is in the hands of the managers, it is important that the operational research workers try to keep them in touch with what is going on throughout the duration of the project.

1.4 Modelling

From the definitions given in section 1.2 above we see that operational research aims to provide a scientific approach to management problems. Opinions differ as to whether it is truly a science, but certainly it seeks to use the scientific method. It tries to objectively compare the possible outcomes of suggested decisions, taking account quantitatively of the chances and risks involved.

It is rarely possible for direct experimentation to be used in operational research, because of the disruption which would be caused to the business. Thus a major characteristic of operational research is that it builds models of the system and experiments with those.

We now consider the individual steps in the modelling process as it is outlined in Fig. 1.1.

We begin with the real-world situation which is to be investigated with a view to solving some problem which has arisen or to otherwise improving that situation. The first step in the modelling process is to extract from the real-world situation the essential features to be included in the model. This is a very important step, as it is essential to include enough factors to make the model a meaningful representation of reality, while not creating a model which is impossibly difficult to use through the inclusion of a multitude of variables having only a very minor effect on the behaviour of the actual situation. Some of the factors to be included will be ones over which management has control while others will be external factors beyond the control of the business. For the factors which are included it will be necessary to make certain assumptions about their behaviour. There is again a balance to be struck between, on the one hand, a model which is realistic enough to be useful and, on the other, a model which is manageable.

Having decided what are the essential features to include in a model in terms of which factors to use and what assumptions are to be made about them, we must proceed to actually construct the model.

There are various different types of model available. One possible method is to construct some physical representation of the system. Examples of this approach would be the use of a model railway to study the behaviour of a real railway or use of scale models to study a plant layout design. These are examples of what are called iconic models. They are models in the most commonly understood sense of the word. However, this physical modelling approach is rarely used in practice.

A second type of model which is not very far removed from the iconic model is the analogue model. Here some other entities are used to represent directly the entities of the real model. A well-known example of such a representation is the analogue computer, where the magnitudes of electrical currents flowing in circuits can be used to represent quantities of material or people, say, moving around in a system.

The model one step removed from these two, and one commonly used in practice, is the simulation model. Simulation is the subject of Chapter 8 and we restrict ourselves here to only the briefest introduction to it. A simulation model attempts to do the same sort of thing as an iconic model or an analogue model, but instead of entities being represented physically they are represented by sequences of random numbers subject to the assumptions of the model. Simulation models are always in practice set up on computers and there are many computer packages available to facilitate this. The simulation model is used in the same way as an iconic model in that it is run on the computer and the behaviour as indicated by the computer is noted.

All three model types considered so far are descriptive in that they seek to give a representation of the system which can be run to allow us to observe or describe how the system will behave. The fourth main type of model is the mathematical model where the factors and assumptions included in the model are used to set up equations and inequalities which can be manipulated, again almost always by computer. Where such a model is available the hope will be that it can be treated by analytical methods to give 'the solution' — that is, a prescription as to how the system should be operated to ensure best results.

As a very simple example of a mathematical model suppose it has been observed that revenue from sales is always approximately equal to ten times what was spent on advertising in the period concerned. Then a forecasting model for future sales could be

$$\text{sales revenue} = 10 \times \text{advertising expenditure}$$

Careful analysis of future markets would be required and also care would have to be taken to consider the range of output or advertising expenditure figures to which the model was to be applied.

More realistic and important examples to be seen later are linear programming and transportation in Chapters 2 and 3 where we have a number of variables subject to certain mathematical constraints and we want to know how to achieve some objective, subject to those constraints. Similarly, in the stock-control and queuing models of Chapters 6 and 7, equations can be solved to determine such things as the best order-size or the average waiting-time in the queue.

Having constructed the model, we must set about obtaining useful information from it. This has already been touched upon and we just summarise here. In the case of an analogue or simulation model we have to run the model and measure what happens. So, for example, if we have a simulation of a queuing situation where two servers are employed we can run this for several hundred customers passing through the system and obtain such things as the average length of the queue and the average waiting-time per customer. We can then run it again with three servers, say, and see what new values are obtained for these measures.

Many such runs can be carried out making different changes to the structure and assumptions of the model. In the case of a mathematical model we essentially have to solve a set of equations of some kind. Thus for linear programming we have to solve a set of constraints as simultaneous equations and in stock control we have to deduce expressions for such quantities as best reorder quantity and best reorder level. The simulation method is a flexible one in that changes to the model can readily be made between runs or even, in the case of some computer systems, within a run. For mathematical models the solubility of the equations may depend on somewhat restrictive assumptions and this can lead to the use of over-simplified models. Where mathematical models are appropriate they are usually beneficial as they may be expected to be less demanding of computer power than simulation models.

Having solved our mathematical model or evaluated some simulation runs, we are in a position to draw some conclusions about the model. For example, if we have the average queue-length and average waiting-time for a queuing situation modified in various ways, we can use this in conjunction with information on such matters as the wage-rates for servers and the value of time lost in the queue to arrive at decisions on what seems to be the best way to service the queue.

Finally, we need to try to use our conclusions about the model to draw some conclusions about the original real-world situation. The validity of such conclusions will depend on how well our model actually represented the real situation.

The first attempt at modelling the situation will almost certainly lead to results which are at variance with reality. It is then necessary to go back and look at the assumptions in the model and adjust these. The construction of the model must then be reworked and new results obtained for comparison with reality. Usually, a large number of iterations of this type will be required before a basically acceptable model is obtained. When what seems an acceptable model has been arrived at it is necessary to test the *sensitivity* of that model to possible changes in circumstances to see whether it will continue to be useful if conditions change from those prevailing when it was established. This involves asking 'what if?' questions, e.g.

What if demand increases by 10 per cent?
What if material costs increase by 5 per cent?

and seeing what effect these changes have on the policy recommendations or profit forecasts or whatever that are produced by the model.

The modelling process can be considered for practical purposes to be 'complete' when it is decided that the model is representing the real world sufficiently well for conclusions drawn from it to be a useful guide to action.

Exercises

1.1 Discuss the methodology of operational research and describe the main stages involved in carrying out an operational research project. (*ICMA Prof. 1*)

1.2 'Model building is central to the Operational Research (OR) methodology. The models used in OR are usually of a mathematical form, although examples of iconic and even analogue models do occur. With relatively simple or standardised models, analytic "solutions" are sometimes possible, often based on appropriate algorithms or heuristics. In many situations, however, such solutions are either impossible or inappropriate and, as a consequence, a simulation approach would invariably be used. This type of model often tends to be of a descriptive rather than normative (or prescriptive) nature.'

Required:

(a) Describe mathematical, iconic and analogue models, giving an example of each type. (6 marks)
(b) Explain how the use of a mathematical model to simulate a particular situation differs from an analytic approach to problem solving. Use as a foundation for your answer the basic net-present-value model of capital investment appraisal. (6 marks)
(c) Explain the meaning of the terms 'algorithm' and 'heuristic' in the context of problem solving in OR. (4 marks)
(d) Using relevant examples, explain the distinction between a 'descriptive' and a 'normative' model. (4 marks)
(Total: 20 marks)
(*ACCA Prof. 2*)

2 Linear Programming

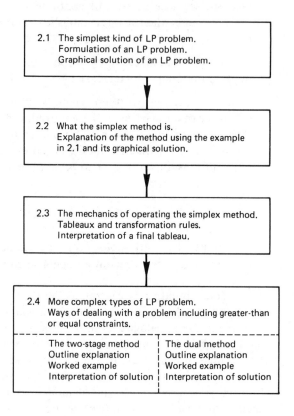

2.1 The simplest kind of LP problem.
Formulation of an LP problem.
Graphical solution of an LP problem.

2.2 What the simplex method is.
Explanation of the method using the example
in 2.1 and its graphical solution.

2.3 The mechanics of operating the simplex method.
Tableaux and transformation rules.
Interpretation of a final tableau.

2.4 More complex types of LP problem.
Ways of dealing with a problem including greater-than
or equal constraints.

The two-stage method	The dual method
Outline explanation	Outline explanation
Worked example	Worked example
Interpretation of solution	Interpretation of solution

2.1 Graphical Linear Programming

The most basic problem with which linear programming is concerned relates to a production situation where items of various kinds are to be made. Each of these different types of item needs different quantities of certain limited resources. The problem is to decide how many units of each kind of item to make, subject to constraints on the resources, in order to achieve some objective such as maximisation of profit or maximisation of revenue.

Problems of this kind which involve just two types of item can be solved graphically. We begin by considering such a simple problem graphically, and then proceed in section 2.2 to use the same example to explain the more general approach to linear programming problems.

Example 2.1.1

A company machines and drills two castings, X and Y. The times required are:

Casting	Machine hours per casting	Drilling hours per casting
X	4	2
Y	2	5

8

There are two lathes and three drilling machines, and the working week is 40 hours. Variable costs for both castings are £6 per unit, and total fixed costs amount to £50 per week. The selling price of casting X is £15 per unit, and that of Y is £18 per unit. How many of each of X and Y should be made in order to maximise profit?

ANSWER

Suppose the company makes x of casting X and y of casting Y.
Then the constraints are:

$$4x + 2y \leqslant 80 \text{ (machine hours)}$$
$$2x + 5y \leqslant 120 \text{ (drilling hours).} \qquad (x, y \geqslant 0)$$

(The requirements $x \geqslant 0$ and $y \geqslant 0$ are referred to as non-negativity constraints and apply to all variables in LP problems. So fundamental are such constraints that they are often taken for granted and not written out explicitly in problem formulations.)

The objective is to maximise the weekly profit. This is P, where

$$P = 9x + 12y - 50,$$

since each casting X makes a contribution of £15 − £6 = £9,
while each casting Y makes a contribution of £18 − £6 = £12
and the fixed costs are £50 per week.

Figure 2.1 is a graph showing the lines $4x + 2y = 80$
$2x + 5y = 120$.

From this graph we see that pairs of values for x and y allowed by the resource constraints lie in the area indicated by the shading, or on its boundary; this area is called the feasible region.

To solve the problem of maximising profit we need to find the point inside or on the boundary of the feasible region where $9x + 12y - 50$ is as large as possible.

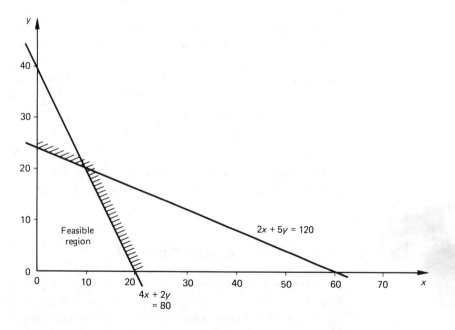

Figure 2.1

9

It is impossible for the maximum value to be achieved at any point strictly inside the feasible region because it will always be possible to move from there to another point inside where x and y are both larger and hence where $9x + 12y - 50$ is larger.

Also, if we look at a point along an edge of the feasible region it will usually be possible to move along the edge to another point where the objective will be larger. (The exception to this would be a case where the objective function line was parallel to a side of the feasible region, in which case all points along the side, including the corners at both ends, would be equally good.)

Thus we see that the maximum value for the objective function will always be found at a corner of the feasible region. Hence the graphical solution to the problem can be found by evaluating the objective function at each corner of the feasible region. The best production policy will be given by the values of x and y at the best corner and the maximum value of the objective function will be the value at that corner.

In our present example the feasible region has four corners:

where $x = 0$ and $y = 0$ we have $9x + 12y - 50 = 0 + 0 - 50 = -50$

where $x = 20$ and $y = 0$ we have $9x + 12y - 50 = 180 + 0 - 50 = 130$

where $x = 10$ and $y = 20$ we have $9x + 12y - 50 = 90 + 240 - 50 = 280$

where $x = 0$ and $y = 24$ we have $9x + 12y - 50 = 0 + 288 - 50 = 238$

The largest weekly profit is obtained by making <u>10 of casting X</u> and <u>20 of casting Y</u>.

The value of the maximum weekly profit is £280.

Exercise 2.1.1

The Harry Handle Manufacturing Company Limited makes two types of shelving unit, the Assault and the Dandy. The Assault has a unit manufacturing cost of £240 and a selling price of £300 while the Dandy has a unit manufacturing cost of £290 and a selling price of £360. Weekly fixed costs are estimated at £500 per week.

Both types of unit have to go through machining and assembly processes, in which the times required and the availabilities are as shown in Table 2.1.

Table 2.1

	Hours needed per unit of Assault	Hours needed per unit of Dandy	Hours available per week
Machining	8	6	98
Assembly	6	9	105

Use graphical linear programming to find the number of Assault and the number of Dandy that should be made per week in order to maximise profit.

2.2 Explanation of the Simplex Method

Problems involving the production of just two items clearly have a restricted use. It is not uncommon, indeed, for people to be interested in solving linear programming problems having hundreds of variables and large numbers of constraints. Hence it is necessary to move beyond the graphical method to an algebraic method which can be used as the basis of a computer program. The algebraic method for solving linear programming problems is called the simplex method.

In this section the simplex method will be explained using example 2.1.1, and the following sections will be concerned with executing the simplex method for a variety of slightly larger problems.

The formulation of the problem in example 2.1.1 was as follows:

$$4x + 2y \leqslant 80$$

$$2x + 5y \leqslant 120.$$

Maximise $\qquad P = 9x + 12y - 50.$

The feasible region was as shown in Fig. 2.2.

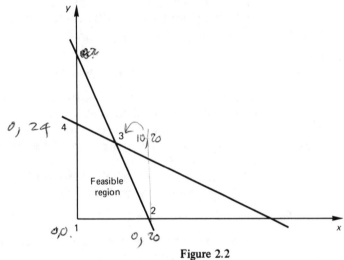

Figure 2.2

The simplex method moves from one corner to another, better, one until it arrives at the corner where the objective function has its best value.

The first step in the simplex method is to make the constraints into equations by introducing into each one a slack variable. This represents the amount of the resource left unused.

For this example we have

$$4x + 2y + S_1 = 80$$

$$2x + 5y + S_2 = 120.$$

Maximise $\qquad P = 9x + 12y - 50.$

A corner of the feasible region is a place where all variables are zero except one (for each constraint. In this case there are two constraints so there will be two non-zero variables at each corner.

The non-zero variables are called basic variables and the zero variables are called non-basic variables.

Referring to the labels on the corners in Fig. 2.2, we have the following:

At corner 1 $\qquad x = 0, y = 0, S_1 = 80, S_2 = 120.$

$\qquad\qquad\qquad S_1, S_2$ are basic; x, y are non-basic.

At corner 2 $\qquad x = 20, y = 0, S_1 = 0, S_2 = 80.$

$\qquad\qquad\qquad x, S_2$ are basic; S_1, y are non-basic.

At corner 3 $\qquad x = 10, y = 20, S_1 = 0, S_2 = 0.$

x, y are basic; S_1, S_2 are non-basic.

At corner 4 $\qquad x = 0, y = 24, S_1 = 32, S_2 = 0.$

S_1, y are basic; x, S_2 are non-basic.

Going from one corner to another means changing from one set of basic variables to a different set.

At each step we

(a) write the objective in terms of non-basic variables;
(b) write the basic variables in terms of the non-basic variables;
(c) move to a corner giving a better value for the objective.

We stop when there is no better corner to go to.

Usually the easiest place to start is the corner where all the slack variables are basic (i.e. the origin). Hence, initially take point 1: $x = 0, y = 0, S_1 = 80, S_2 = 120$.

(a) $P = 9x + 12y - 50$;
(b) $S_1 = 80 - 4x - 2y, \qquad S_2 = 120 - 2x - 5y$.

This is not best because x and y have positive coefficients here in the expression for P, and so having them equal to zero is not good. If they were positive we could increase P from its current value of -50.

So let us increase one of them. Which one? Choose y, since it has the larger coefficient (i.e. $12 > 9$).

(c) How much shall we increase it? Until we come to the first corner. We see from Fig. 2.2 that this is at point 4 (i.e. when $S_2 = 0$).

At corner 4 $\qquad x = 0, \quad y = 24, \quad S_1 = 32, \quad S_2 = 0.$

(a) Write the objective in terms of non-basics (i.e. x and S_2).
(b) Also express basics in terms of non-basics.

This means we need to proceed as follows:
Solve for y and S_1 in terms of other variables:

$$4x + 2y + S_1 = 80, \qquad (1)$$

$$2x + 5y + S_2 = 120. \qquad (2)$$

$(1) - \frac{2}{5} (2)$ gives: $\qquad (4 - \frac{4}{5})x + S_1 - \frac{2}{5}S_2 = 80 - 48$

$$\frac{16}{5} x + S_1 - \frac{2}{5}S_2 = 32$$

$$\underline{S_1 = 32 - \frac{16}{5}x + \frac{2}{5}S_2.}$$

From (1), $\qquad y = 40 - \dfrac{S_1}{2} - 2x$

$$y = 40 - \frac{1}{2}\left(32 - \frac{16}{5}x + \frac{2}{5}S_2\right) - 2x$$

$$\underline{y = 24 - \tfrac{2}{5}x - \tfrac{1}{5}S_2.}$$

$$P = 9x + 12\left(24 - \tfrac{2}{5}x - \tfrac{1}{5}S_2\right) - 50$$

$$\underline{P = 238 + \tfrac{21}{5}x - \tfrac{12}{5}S_2.}$$

This is still not the best because x has a positive coefficient in the expression for P. Increase x until we come to the next corner. This will be corner 3.

At corner 3: $\qquad x = 10, \quad y = 20, \quad S_1 = 0, \quad S_2 = 0.$

So x, y basic and S_1, S_2 non-basic.

Solve constraints for x and y in terms of S_1, S_2:

$2 \times (2) - (1):\quad 8y + 2S_2 - S_1 = 160$

$$y = 20 + \frac{S_1}{8} - \frac{S_2}{4}.$$

Putting in (1):$\quad x = 20 - \frac{1}{2}\left(20 + \frac{S_1}{8} - \frac{S_2}{4}\right) - \frac{S_1}{4}$

$$x = 10 - \frac{5S_1}{16} + \frac{S_2}{8}.$$

$P = 90 - \frac{45}{16}S_1 + \frac{9}{8}S_2 + 240 + \frac{3}{2}S_1 - 3S_2 - 50$

$P = 280 - \frac{21}{16}S_1 - \frac{15}{8}S_2.$

Because the coefficients of S_1 and S_2 are negative, this is optimal. It is no use increasing S_1 or S_2.

Thus we have arrived at the answer we had when solving the problem graphically in section 2.1.

The best policy is to make 10 casting X and 20 casting Y per week, giving a maximum weekly profit of £280.

2.3   Execution of the Simplex Method

In carrying out the manipulation of equations needed for the simplex method, as explained in section 2.2, it is usual to set out the calculations in the form of so-called simplex tableaux. These are tables showing the coefficients in the equations for the constraints (after insertion of slacks) and for the objective function. Movement from one corner of the feasible region to another is carried out by means of a set of rules called transformation rules. These have the effect of giving the sets of coefficients for the equations as they appear at the various different corners, as seen in section 2.2.

For example 2.1.1 the problem, after insertion of slacks, can be written as follows:

$$4x + 2y + S_1 = 80$$
$$2x + 5y + S_2 = 120.$$

Maximise P where
$$P - 9x - 12y = -50.$$

The expression of the objective function may seem a little strange but it has the algebraic merit of causing every line to have the same form, namely an equation with all variables on the left and all values on the right.

The initial simplex tableau then corresponds to the first solution considered in section 2.2 where the actual variables are all zero and the slack variables are basic. Shown below (Table 2.2) is the complete set of tableaux for solving this problem. We set it out in this way because it represents the whole manipulative part of solving the problem. It is the part which would in practice be done for you by a computer. Following the tableaux, we consider their content, the transformations between them and the interpretation of the final tableau by comparison with section 2.2.

Across the top of the table are listed the names of all the variables and the headings 'Basic' and 'Value'. For this example, involving two constraints plus the objective function, the first three lines below the heading constitute the initial tableau.

Table 2.2

Basic	x	y	S_1	S_2	Value
S_1	4	2	1	0	80
S_2	2	5*	0	1	120
P	-9	-12	0	0	-50
S_1	$\frac{16}{5}$*	0	1	$-\frac{2}{5}$	32
y	$\frac{2}{5}$	1	0	$\frac{1}{5}$	24
P	$-\frac{21}{5}$	0	0	$\frac{12}{5}$	238
x	1	0	$\frac{5}{16}$	$-\frac{1}{8}$	10
y	0	1	$-\frac{1}{8}$	$\frac{1}{4}$	20
P	0	0	$\frac{21}{16}$	$\frac{15}{8}$	280

Listed down the basic column are the basic variables at the first corner of the feasible region and the name of the objective to be maximised, in this case the profit, P. Then, under the respective variable headings we have the coefficients of the variables in the formulation of the problem when the slacks are included. Finally, in the right-hand column we have the values of the basic variables and for the objective function in the initial solution, point 1 of Fig. 2.2. These coefficients correspond to what we saw for point 1 in section 2.2.

Having obtained the initial tableau, we must decide whether it represents the solution to the problem. The way we decided this kind of thing in section 2.2 was to look at the coefficients of the non-basic variables in the expression for P and see whether any of them had positive values. If they did, then the value of P could be made larger by increasing any of those variables from their current zero value. In view of the way the objective row is written in the simplex tableau, the equivalence here of that procedure is to see whether any non-basic variable has a NEGATIVE coefficient in the objective row. The value of the objective can be made larger by increasing that variable from zero. In this case both x and y have zero values, so increasing either of them would be useful. As y has the coefficient of larger magnitude we choose to make y basic, as this will increase P at a faster rate than if we make x basic.

Having decided to make y basic, the next issue is to decide which of the current basic variables should be made non-basic in order to make room for it. In section 2.2 we found the answer to this question to be S_2, because as y increases it is S_2 which reaches zero first. It becomes zero when y reaches 24 while S_1 would not become zero until y reached 40 (see Fig. 2.1.) In terms of the numbers in the simplex tableau we arrive at this conclusion by considering for each of the currently basic variables:

$$\frac{\text{the figure in the value column}}{\text{the figure in the } y \text{ column}}.$$

The one to be made basic is the one for which this ratio is smallest. (If several have equal values for this ratio, any of them may be used). For the example here, we have $\frac{80}{2} = 40$ and $\frac{120}{5} = 24$, so the smaller ratio corresponds to S_2 and this is the variable we must make non-basic.

Having decided to make y basic and S_2 non-basic, we have decided to move from point 1 to point 4 and so must solve the equations as in section 2.2 so as to express S_1, y and P in terms of S_2 and x. The row transformations needed in the simplex tableau to achieve this are equivalent to the usual method for solving a set of simultaneous equations. They can be conveniently expressed as a set of transformation rules.

Central to these rules is the number in the column of the variable to be made basic (the y column here) and in the row of the variable to be made non-basic (the S_2 row here). This number is called the *pivot* of the transformation and it is marked by an asterisk in our initial tableau above. The row which contains the pivot is called the pivot row and the column which contains the pivot is called the pivot column.

The new tableau (lines 4 to 6 of Table 2.2) is set up by listing the new set of basic variables, putting y in the position of the variable S_2 which it has replaced. The rules which give the numbers in the new tableau are then as follows:

(a) Put 1s and 0s in the columns of the new basic variables. (The 1 goes where the row label and column label are the same.)
(b) Divide through the pivot row by the pivot.
(c) Divide through the pivot column by *minus* the pivot and put the results in the new non-basic column.
(d) Transform all other values using the rule:

$$\text{new value} = \text{old value} - \frac{(\text{value in pivot row}) \times (\text{value in pivot column})}{\text{the pivot}}.$$

You should confirm that carrying out these operations on the figures in our initial tableau gives the second tableau shown. Note also that the numbers in the second tableau are, apart from their signs, the same as the coefficients found for the variables in section 2.2 when we solved the equations for point (corner) 4. The differences in sign simply reflect the fact that in the tableaux we keep all variables on the left-hand sides of the equations.

Having arrived at the second tableau, we treat it exactly as we treated the initial tableau. We first look at the objective row coefficients to see if any are negative. As x has a negative coefficient we conclude that this is not the solution to the problem and that the value of P can be made larger if we increase x from zero. To then decide which of the currently basic variables should be made non-basic we need to look at the ratios:

$$\frac{32}{\frac{16}{5}} = 32 \times \tfrac{5}{16} = 10 \text{ and } \frac{24}{\frac{2}{5}} = 24 \times \tfrac{5}{2} = 60.$$

Since the former is the smaller ratio, it is S_1 which must be made non-basic and $\frac{16}{5}$ is the pivot of the transformation.

Carrying out the four transformation steps above then leads to the third tableau shown (lines 7 to 9 of Table 2.2). Again the reader should work through the transformations on all the elements in the second tableau and confirm that the third tableau is the result. Note that the numbers in the third tableau are the same, apart from their signs, as the coefficients when the equations in section 2.2 were solved at point 3.

The third tableau can be identified as the solution to the problem here because none of the coefficients in the objective row is negative.

From the final tableau we can see immediately that the solution to the problem is obtained by taking $x = 10$ and $y = 20$, giving a maximum value for P of 280.

That is, make 10 of casting X and 20 of casting Y, giving a maximum weekly profit of £280.

Furthermore, the objective-row coefficients themselves in the final tableau also have an important interpretation. To understand this interpretation it is best to again think about the final objective row as a full equation.

It is
$$P + \frac{21}{16}S_1 + \frac{15}{8}S_2 = 280,$$

which can be written, as in section 2.2,

$$P = 280 - \frac{21}{16}S_1 - \frac{15}{8}S_2.$$

In the solution we have $S_1 = 0$: we are on the constraint line $4x + 2y = 80$, which means that all the available machine time is being used. If S_1 were made equal to $+1$ we should reduce P by $\frac{21}{16}$, have $4x + 2y = 79$ and move strictly inside the feasible region. Profit would be lower and some machine time would be unused.

However, if S_1 were made equal to -1 we should increase P by $\frac{21}{16}$, have $4x + 2y = 81$ and move outside the feasible region. Profit would be higher but a constraint would be violated. We should need an hour of machine time more than is actually available. Thus if we could increase available machine time by one hour the profit would be increased by £$\frac{21}{16}$. Hence £$\frac{21}{16}$ is called the shadow price of extra machine time — it is the most that it would be worth paying per hour for extra machine time. Similarly, £$\frac{15}{8}$ is the shadow price of extra drilling time.

Exercise 2.3.1

A company manufactures three products, tanks, trays and tubs, each of which pass through three processes, X, Y and Z.

Table 2.3 gives the time required for each product in each process and, for a certain production period, the total process time available. The contributions to profit of each product are £2, £3 and £4 per unit respectively.

Table 2.3

	Process hours per unit			
Process	Tanks	Trays	Tubs	Total process hours available
X	5	2	4	12 000
Y	4	5	6	24 000
Z	3	5	4	18 000

You are required to:

(a) ascertain how many of each product should be produced to make the maximum profit and to state the profit figure;
(b) state how much slack time, if any, is available in the processes;
(c) interpret the shadow prices.

(ICMA Part IV)

As has been mentioned, the mechanics of the simplex method would normally be carried out by a computer. There are many packages available which require simply insertion of the coefficients in all the constraints and the objective function and which will then produce the final simplex tableau. Thus from a practical point of view the more important skills associated with linear programming are the ability to formulate problems and the ability to interpet a final tableau. We conclude this section with an example and an exercise which emphasise these points.

Example 2.3.1

(a) The following details are taken from the forecasts for 1979 of XYZ Limited.

Sales demand:

	Thousands of units per annum, maximum
Super De Luxe model, x_1	500
De Luxe model, x_2	750
Export model, x_3	400

Production Two production facilities are required, machining and assembly, and these are common to each model.

Capacity in each facility is limited by the number of direct labour hours available (Table 2.4).

Table 2.4

	Direct labour: total hours available (millions)	Direct labour hours per unit for each model		
		x_1	x_2	x_3
Machining, x_4	1.4	0.5	0.5	1.0
Assembly, x_5	1.2	0.5	0.5	2.0

Contributions are estimated to be:

Model	Amount per thousand units
x_1	£1500
x_2	1300
x_3	2500

You are required, using the above information, to set up the first tableau of a linear programme to determine the product mix which will maximise total contribution and then to complete the first iteration only.

(b) Interpret the accompanying tableau (Table 2.5), given that it is the final solution to the above problem. The s variables (s_1, s_2, s_3, s_4, s_5) relate to the constraints in the same sequence as presented in (a) above.

(ICMA Prof. 1)

Table 2.5

x_1	x_2	x_3	s_1	s_2	s_3	s_4	s_5	b_{ij}
1	0	0	1	0	0	0	0	500
0	0	0	0.25	0.25	1	0	−0.5	112.5
0	0	1	−0.25	−0.25	0	0	0.5	287.5
0	0	0	−0.25	−0.25	0	1	−0.5	487.5
0	1	0	0	1	0	0	0	750
0	0	0	−875	−675	0	0	−1250	−2 443 750

ANSWER

(a) Let x_1, x_2, x_3 be the numbers of units produced in thousands.

Formulation:

$$x_1 \leqslant 500 \quad \text{(maximum demand for Super De Luxe)}$$
$$x_2 \leqslant 750 \quad \text{(maximum demand for De Luxe)}$$
$$x_3 \leqslant 400 \quad \text{(maximum demand for Export)}$$
$$0.5x_1 + 0.5x_2 + x_3 \leqslant 1400 \quad \text{(machining-time constraint)}$$
$$0.5x_1 + 0.5x_2 + 2x_3 \leqslant 1200 \quad \text{(assembly-time constraint)}.$$

Maximise: $P = 1500x_1 + 1300x_2 + 2500x_3$ (contribution function).

$$x_1 \qquad\qquad + s_1 = 500$$
$$x_2 \qquad + s_2 = 750$$
$$x_3 + s_3 = 400$$
$$0.5x_1 + 0.5x_2 + x_3 + s_4 = 1400$$
$$0.5x_1 + 0.5x_2 + 2x_3 + s_5 = 1200$$
$$P - 1500x_1 - 1300x_2 - 2500x_3 = 0.$$

The first tableau is given in Table 2.6 and the first iteration in Table 2.7.

Table 2.6	Basic	x_1	x_2	x_3	s_1	s_2	s_3	s_4	s_5	Value
	s_1	1	0	0	1	0	0	0	0	500
	s_2	0	1	0	0	1	0	0	0	750
	s_3	0	0	1*	0	0	1	0	0	400
	s_4	0.5	0.5	1	0	0	0	1	0	1 400
	s_5	0.5	0.5	2	0	0	0	0	1	1 200
	P	−1 500	−1 300	−2 500	0	0	0	0	0	0

Table 2.7		x_1	x_2	x_3	s_1	s_2	s_3	s_4	s_5	
	s_1	1	0	0	1	0	0	0	0	500
	s_2	0	1	0	0	1	0	0	0	750
	x_3	0	0	1	0	0	1	0	0	400
	s_4	0.5	0.5	0	0	0	−1	1	0	1 000
	s_5	0.5	0.5	0	0	0	−2	0	1	400
	P	−1 500	−1 300	0	0	0	2 500	0	0	1 000 000

(b) The interpretation of the given final tableau is as follows.

Make 500 000 Super De Luxe, 750 000 De Luxe and 287 500 Export.

This means making 112 500 less Export than the maximum forecast. This policy leaves 487 500 of the available machining hours unused. The shadow price of an extra hour of assembly time is £1.25. The marginal increase in profit per additional Super De Luxe model made is 87.5p. The marginal increase in profit per additional De Luxe model made is 67.5p. The profit resulting from the proposed policy is £2 443 750.

Exercise 2.3.2

C Limited produces container cases for sale to toiletry producers. It has four product lines: cases for talcum powder, shaving foam, hair spray and deodorant. The given data are presented in Table 2.8.

Table 2.8	x_1 Talcum powder	x_2 Shaving foam	x_3 Hair spray	x_4 Deodorant	Total process hours available per week
Contribution per 1000 cases (£)	80	70	95	90	
Process times for manufacture (hours per 1000 cases)					
Production (x_5)	5.0	5.0	4.0	4.0	450
Finishing (x_6)	1.0	1.0	1.0	1.0	120
Printing (x_7)	2.0	2.5	3.5	3.5	280
Packaging (x_8)	0.5	0.5	0.5	0.5	80
Maximum expected weekly demand (1000 cases) (x_9 to x_{12})	30	40	20	25	

You are required to:

(a) formulate the information in Table 2.8 to give either the initial equations or the first tableau of a linear programme to maximise the total contribution which may be earned:
(b) interpret the accompanying tableau (Table 2.9) which is the solution to the problem of (a).

Table 2.9	x_1	x_2	x_3	x_4	x_5	x_6	x_7	x_8	x_9	x_{10}	x_{11}	x_{12}	b_{11}
	0	1	0	0	0.2	0	0	0	−1	0	−0.8	−0.8	24
	0	0	0	0	−0.2	1	0	0	0	0	−0.2	−0.2	21
	0	0	0	0	−0.5	0	1	0	0.5	0	−1.5	−1.5	2.5
	0	0	0	0	−0.1	0	0	1	0	0	−0.1	−0.1	30.5
	1	0	0	0	0	0	0	0	1	0	0	0	30
	0	0	0	0	−0.2	0	0	0	1	1	0.8	0.8	16
	0	0	1	0	0	0	0	0	0	0	1	0	20
	0	0	0	1	0	0	0	0	0	0	0	1	25
	0	0	0	0	14	0	0	0	10	0	39	34	8230

(ICMA Prof. 1)

2.4 Problems Involving Greater-than-or-equal-to Constraints

All the examples and exercises so far have been problems where all constraints have been of the 'less-than-or-equal-to' type. These are the easiest to deal with the simplex method and hence it is appropriate for the initial explanation to be in terms of them. If a computer package is used to solve a linear programming problem, the user is required to specify for each constraint whether it is a greater-than-or-equal-to or a less-than-or-equal-to constraint and the program then sorts out any complications arising from constraints of the former type being present. In this section we explain two major methods for coping with greater-than-or-equal-to constraints. These are

(a) the two-stage method.

(b) the dual method.

Before looking at them in detail in an example, we give an outline of each method and consider their relative merits.

The basic problem with a greater-than-or-equal-to constraint is that in order to make it into an equation a slack variable has to be introduced with a *minus* sign in front of it. This means that the initial simplex tableau cannot be written down with the slacks as basic and the other variables non-basic. (Graphically the problem is that the origin is not in the feasible region.) So what is done in the two-stage method to obtain an initial tableau is to introduce not only the slacks but also a second set of extra variables called artificial variables. One of these is put with a positive sign into each of the constraint equations where the slack variable has a negative sign. An initial tableau can then be written down using slacks as basic where they have positive signs and the artificials as basic in the other cases. The artificial variables have no real meaning in terms of the problem to be solved and so the first stage in the two-stage method is to make the artificials non-basic, regardless of the effect on the objective function. Once they have been made non-basic they can be totally disregarded. When all the artificials have been made non-basic and dismissed from the problem, it is possible to proceed to the second stage, which is to obtain the required best value of the objective function. In problems involving greater-than-or-equal-to constraints it is often a *minimum* value for the objective which is being sought. In such a case the solution tableau is identified as the one where all the objective row coefficients are *less than or equal to zero*. If a tableau contains any positive objective row coefficients then a further transformation must be carried out.

The two-stage method can be lengthy in view of the need to carry out two sets of transformations and to deal, at least in the early stages, with fairly large tableaux even for small problems. However, it is easy to understand and is necessary if there is a mixture of greater-than-or-equal-to and less-than-or-equal-to constraints in the problem. Interpretation of the final tableau is exactly as for the simplex method as described in section 2.3.

A further point to be made about the two-stage method is that it can be used to deal with *equality* constraints. Suppose, for example, we had a constraint:

$$7x + 9y + 3z = 20.$$

This could be expressed in a form suitable for an initial simplex tableau by introducing two slacks and one artificial variable, generating two rows of tableau. The constraint is equivalent to

$$7x + 9y + 3z \geqslant 20$$

and
$$7x + 9y + 3z \leqslant 20.$$

Hence we can write

$$7x + 9y + 3z - S_1 + A_1 = 20$$
$$7x + 9y + 3z + S_2 = 20.$$

20

These can be entered into a simplex tableau with A_1 as the basic variable in the first constraint and S_2 as the basic variable in the second constraint.

The dual method is a rather slicker approach which can be used for minimisation problems where *all* the constraints are greater than or equal to constraints. It involves taking the actual problem, called in this context the primal problem, and writing down a different linear programming problem called the dual problem. If the primal problem is a minimisation problem with all greater-than-or-equal-to constraints then the dual will be a maximisation problem with all less-than-or-equal-to constraints. The dual problem can thus be solved by the simplex method as explained in section 2.3. Having solved the dual we can then interpret its solution tableau in terms of the primal problem. This interpretation requres noting a correspondence between pairs of variables in the primal and dual problems. The values of variables in the dual solution then give the shadow prices of the corresponding variables in the primal solution and the objective-row coefficients in the dual solution give the values of the corresponding variables in the primal solution. Also, the maximum value of the dual objective function is equal to the required minimum value of the primal objective function.

The dual method generally involves less manipulation than the two-stage method but is not useful where there is a mixture of constraints. Rather more thought is required in the interpretation of the final tableau and also the mathematics behind the method, which essentially involves working on the transpose of the tableaux for the primal problem, is not quite so obvious as for the two-stage method.

To see how a dual problem is formulated from a given primal problem consider the following example:

$$3x + 4y + 7z \geqslant 9$$
$$2x + 19y + 15z \geqslant 8.$$

Minimise
$$C = 11x + 28y + 18z$$

Because the primal problem involves two constraints, the dual will involve two variables. Let these be called u and v.

Because the primal problem involves three variables, the dual will involve three constraints. A constraint in the dual problem is obtained by taking all the coefficients relating to one variable in the primal problem and applying these to the variables in the dual problem to set up a less-than-or-equal-to constraint. The variable x has coefficients 3 and 2 in the primal constraints and coefficient 11 in the primal objective function.

Thus the dual constraint corresponding to this variable is $3u + 2v \leqslant 11$.

Similarly, for the variable y we have $4u + 19v \leqslant 28$,

while for the variable z we have $7u + 15v \leqslant 18$.

The objective function for the dual problem is obtained by taking the right-hand sides of the primal constraints and using these as coefficients for the dual variables.

Thus the objective function here is seen to be $P = 9u + 8v$. We now have a maximisation problem which can be solved using the methods of section 2.3.

Use of both approaches to problems with greater-than-or-equal-to constraints and interpretation of the resulting final tableau are demonstrated in the following example.

Example 2.4.1

A pension-fund manager is considering investing in two shares, A and B. It is estimated that:

(a) share A will earn a dividend of 12 per cent per annum and share B one of 4 per cent per annum;
(b) growth in the market value in one year of share A will be 10 pence per £1 invested and in B 40 pence per £1 invested.

He requires to invest the minimum total sum which will give:

dividend income of at least £600 per annum; and
growth in one year of at least £1000 on the initial investment.
   You are required to:

 (i) state the mathematical formulation of the problem;
(ii) compute the minimum sum to be invested to meet the manager's objectives; using the simplex method.

(ICMA Prof. 1)

ANSWER

 (i) Suppose the manager invests £a in share A and £b in share B. Then the mathematical formulation of the problem is as follows.

$$0.12a + 0.04b \geqslant 600$$

$$0.10a + 0.40b \geqslant 1000.$$

Minimise $\qquad z = a + b.$

(ii) We give two solutions to the problem by the simplex method. Solution I uses the two-stage method and solution II uses the dual method.

SOLUTION I

Consider first the solution by the two-stage method. Introducing slacks, we have:

$$0.12a + 0.04b - S_1 = 600$$

$$0.10a + 0.40b - S_2 = 1000.$$

Minimise z where $\qquad z - a - b = 0.$

We note the negative signs on the slacks and observe that we cannot therefore use them as basic variables in an initial tableau. So we introduce a further set of variables, the artificials. This gives the following:

$$0.12a + 0.04b - S_1 + A_1 = 600$$

$$0.10a + 0.40b - S_2 + A_2 = 1000.$$

Minimise z where $\qquad z - a - b = 0.$

We can now write down an initial tableau using A_1 and A_2 as basic and go through simplex manipulations in order to make them non-basic. These steps are carried out in the set of tableaux shown in Table 2.10.

The third tableau (lines 8 to 10) actually gives the final solution to the problem because the artificial variables have been eliminated and also the

Basic	a	b	S_1	S_2	A_1	A_2	Values
A_1	0.12*	0.04	-1	0	1	0	600
A_1	0.10	0.40	0	-1	0	1	1000
z	-1	-1	0	0	0	0	0
a	1	0.3333	-8.3333	0		0	5000
A_2	0	0.3667*	0.8333	-1		1	500
z	0	-0.6667	-8.3333	0		0	5000
a	1	0	-9.09	0.909			4545
b	0	1	2.27	-2.727			1364
z	0	0	-6.818	-1.818			5909

Table 2.10

objective row coefficients are negative. Therefore we have the required minimum value for z. In this case it has not been necessary to carry out a proper second stage in the two-stage process because the steps in the first stage have left us with a tableau which is the answer without further manipulation.

The answer for the pension-fund manager is to invest £4545 in share A and £1364 in share B, a total investment of £5909. This is the minimum amount that can be invested to meet the stated requirements.

To interpret the objective-row coefficients in the final tableau let us consider this row written out in full as an equation:

$$z - 6.818S_1 - 1.818S_2 = 5909,$$

i.e.

$$z = 5909 + 6.818S_1 + 1.818S_2.$$

Thus if S_1 were made equal to 1, then z would increase by 6.818. To obtain a marginal increase in dividend income would require an increase in total investment of £6.82 per £1 increase in dividend income. Similarly, if S_2 were made equal to 1, then z would increase by 1.818. To obtain a marginal increase in growth would require an increase in total investment of £1.82 per £1 increase in growth.

SOLUTION II

Next, consider the solution by the dual method. Taking the formulation at the beginning of the answer as the 'primal' problem, we can set up a *dual* problem as follows:

Primal	*Dual*
$0.12a + 0.04b \geqslant 600$	$0.12u + 0.10v \leqslant 1$
$0.10a + 0.40b \geqslant 1000.$	$0.04u + 0.40v \leqslant 1.$
Minimise $z = a + b.$	Maximise $P = 600u + 1000v.$

Introducing slacks into both problems and writing in standard form we obtain:

$$0.12a + 0.04b - S_1 = 600 \qquad 0.12u + 0.10v + t_1 = 1$$
$$0.10a + 0.40b - S_2 = 1000. \qquad 0.04u + 0.40v + t_2 = 1$$
$$z - a - b = 0. \qquad P - 600u - 1000v = 0.$$

The dual problem can now be solved by the simplex method as in section 2.3.

23

This is carried out below. However, before doing this we consider the correspondence between pairs of variables associated with the same set of numbers, which are taken as corresponding. Hence we have the following:

Primal variables: a b S_1 S_2.

Dual variables: t_1 t_2 u v.

For example, a and t_1 are both associated with the numbers 0.12, 0.10 and 1 while S_1 and u are both associated with the numbers 0.12, 0.04 and 600.

The simplex solution to the dual problem is shown in the accompanying tableaux (Table 2.11).

Table 2.11

Basic	u	v	t_1	t_2	Value
t_1	0.12	0.10	1	0	1
t_2	0.04	0.40*	0	1	1
P	−600	−1000	0	0	0
t_1	0.11*	0	1	−0.25	0.75
v	0.1	1	0	2.5	2.5
P	−500	0	0	2500	2500
u	1	0	9.09	−2.27	6.818
v	0	1	−0.909	2.727	1.818
P	0	0	4545	1364	5409

In the final tableau (lines 8 to 10), t_1 has objective row coefficient 4545 so this is the value of the corresponding variable a in the solution to the primal problem. £4545 should be invested in share A.

The variable t_2 has objective row coefficient 1364 so this is the value of the corresponding variable b in the solution to the primal problem. £1364 should be invested in share B.

The maximum value for P is 5409 and this will be the minimum value for z.

The minimum total investment that can achieve the requirements is £5409.

The variable u has value 6.818 in the dual solution, so the corresponding variable S_1 has objective row coefficient 6.818 in the primal solution. As explained in the interpretation of the two stage solution, this means additional total investment of £6.82 is needed per £1 additional investment income if a marginal increase in investment income is required.

Similarly, v has value 1.818 in the dual solution, so the corresponding variable S_2 has objective row coefficient 1.818 in the primal solution. Additional total investment of £1.82 is needed per £1 additional growth if a marginal increase in growth is required.

We conclude this chapter with an exercise involving greater-than-or-equal-to constraints. We suggest that you solve this problem twice, using first the two-stage method and then the dual method.

Exercise 2.4.1

A company possesses two manufacturing plants, each of which produces three products from a common raw material. However, the proportions in which the products are produced are different in each plant and so are the plants' operating costs per hour. Data on production and costs are summarised in Table 2.12, together with the current orders on hand for each product.

Table 2.12	Product I (units)	Product II (units)	Product III (units)	Operating (£/hour)
Plant A	2	4	3	9
Plant B	4	3	2	10
Orders on hand (gal)	50	24	60	

You are required to.

(a) use the simplex method to find the number of production hours needed to fulfil the orders on hand at minimum cost;
(b) interpret the main features of the final solution.

(*ICMA Prof. 1*)

Further Exercises

2.1 TE Limited is investigating the investment opportunities of the expected new leisure era. Initially TE Limited is analysing markets in certain major conurbations for setting up:

(a) mini-golf courses.
(b) indoor sports-centres.

The capital costs and total returns are estimated as in Table 2.13.

Table 2.13	Capital costs		Total net income (over a 10-year period)
	Year 1	Year 2	
Mini-golf courses (per unit)	£80 000	£60 000	£180 000
Indoor sports-centres (per unit)	60 000	90 000	210 000

Capital available for investment is £980 000 in year 1 and £1 050 000 in year 2.

(*Note:* A discounted cash flow assessment should *not* be attempted.)

You are required to:

(a) formulate the investment opportunities open to TE Limited as a linear programme to maximise total return;
(b) solve the linear programme using a *graphical* analysis *only* and state the solution results;
(c) assume a further £120 000 capital became available in the first year and solve with a new graphical analysis the new linear programme incorporating this extra sum;
(d) evaluate the change between situations (c) and (b) brought about by the introduction of more capital in year 1.

(*ICMA Prof. 1*)

2.2 The manufacturer of three products tries to follow a policy of producing those which contribute most to fixed costs and profit. However, there is also a policy of recognising certain minimum sales requirements; currently these are:

Product	Units per week
X	20
Y	30
Z	60

There are three producing departments. The product times in hours per unit in each department and the total times available each week in each department are shown in Table 2.14.

Table 2.14

		Time required per product (hours)			Total time available (hours)
		X	Y	Z	
Department	1	0.25	0.20	0.15	420
	2	0.30	0.40	0.50	1048
	3	0.25	0.30	0.25	529

The contributions per unit of products X, Y and Z are £10.50, £9.00 and £8.00 respectively. The company has scheduled 1558 units of X, 30 units of Y and 60 units of Z for production in the following week.

You are required to state:
(a) whether the present schedule is an optimum one from a profit point of view and, if it is not, what it should be;
(b) the recommendations that should be made to the firm about their production facilities (following the answer to (a) above).

(*ICMA Part IV*)

2.3 A firm manufacturing agricultural feedstuffs has been asked to produce a feed containing at least 300 grams of protein per kilo, 300 grams of carbohydrate per kilo and 450 calories per kilo. It has three basic ingredients, A, B and C, which contain protein, carbohydrate and calories as follows:

	A	B	C
Protein (g kg^{-1})	60	5	25
Carbohydrate (g kg^{-1})	40	60	40
Calories (cal kg^{-1})	50	10	70

The costs per kilo of A, B and C respectively are 20p, 10p and 30p. Use the dual method to find what quantities of A, B and C should be used in order to make the requested feed at minimum cost. Also state the minimum cost.

2.4 Part of a company's operations involves producing separately and then selling in combination two items X and Y. The two items require, respectively, production times per unit of 4 hours and 1 hour and the total time available for producing them is 62 hours per week. Item Y is bulky and so it is desirable not to have to hold too many of these in stock. Hence there is a rule that the number of Y produced in a week must not exceed the number of X by more than 20. Revenue obtainable from the items is £12 per unit from X and £18 per unit from Y, while the variable costs are £1 per unit for X and £16 per unit for Y.

Given that weekly production from the operation is required to have revenue value of at least £216, find the numbers of units of X and Y to produce in order to maximise contribution to profit, using the simplex method. Interpret the main features of the final simplex tableau.

3 Allocation and Transportation

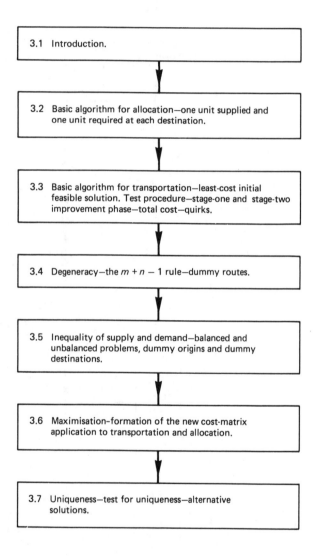

3.1 Introduction.

3.2 Basic algorithm for allocation—one unit supplied and one unit required at each destination.

3.3 Basic algorithm for transportation—least-cost initial feasible solution. Test procedure—stage-one and stage-two improvement phase—total cost—quirks.

3.4 Degeneracy—the $m + n - 1$ rule—dummy routes.

3.5 Inequality of supply and demand—balanced and unbalanced problems, dummy origins and dummy destinations.

3.6 Maximisation—formation of the new cost-matrix application to transportation and allocation.

3.7 Uniqueness—test for uniqueness—alternative solutions.

3.1 Introduction

The area of allocation and transportation is fundamentally concerned with the process of planning an optimal allocation of resources. In a typical starting-point we require a specification of the resources available and their location, and the resources required and their destination, in addition to the cost of transporting a unit from each of the initial locations to each of the final destinations.

It will help to consider the following practical example. Three depots have ambulances available, and there are five hospitals requiring varying numbers of ambulances to attend to patients' needs. Information is available concerning the time taken for the various journeys involved, also the costs involved. In an emergency situation we may require an optimal plan to transfer patients in the shortest possible time. In a non-emergency situation we may instead use the criterion of minimum total cost for formulating the plan. Figure 3.1 shows the relationship

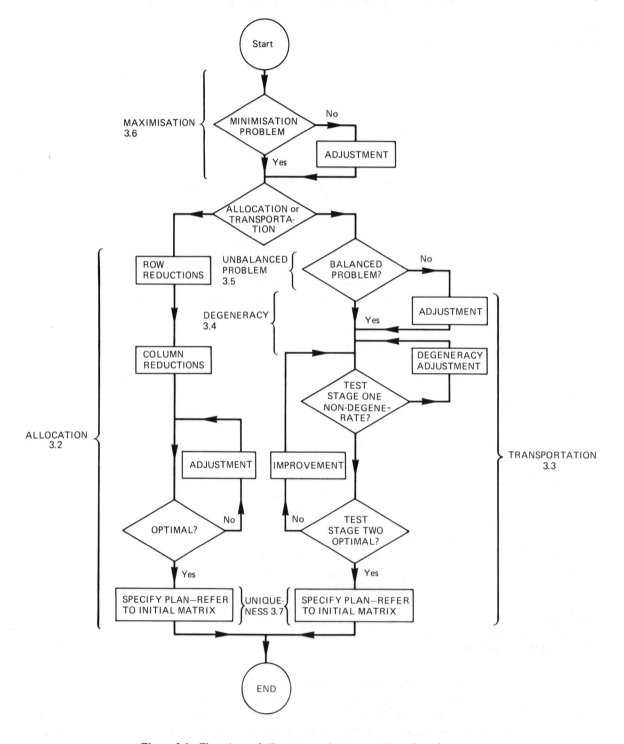

Figure 3.1 Flowchart of allocation and transportation algorithms

between variants on the basic theme. Normally the problem would be the minimisation of a balanced problem but with suitable modification an unbalanced and/or a maximisation problem may be solved.

If only one unit is available at each origin and only one unit is required at each destination then the allocation algorithm is used. Both algorithms involve an 'iterative' procedure. This involves a process of testing whether an arrangement is optimal: if it is, we stop; if it is not, we adjust the plan. We shall also consider whether a plan is unique or not. This is useful in practical situations as a minimum-cost requirement may be met, yet still allow a degree of management flexibility.

Notation

In order to record data relating to the units available and required, the unit costs of transporting and a particular plan, a special notation is introduced. The question will usually give the cost information in a table, with each particular row indicating the cost of transporting a unit from each particular origin to the various destinations. This table is sometimes known as a 'cost matrix' or a 'performance matrix' as it is a rectangular array of numbers.

Matrices are introduced with more detail in Chapter 11. It is convenient to specify a particular plan, by showing the number of units to be transported between an origin and a destination in a grid of horizontal and vertical lines. Each cell in the grid may be referred to as a letter and a number. For example a cell in row C, column II, may be referred to as CII. Each cell may also contain the unit transportation costs in a small box in the top left-hand corner, although as you develop an improved facility this may be omitted. In this chapter the costs are included in the grid only when they are of particular significance.

3.2 Allocation Algorithm

The objective of the allocation algorithm is to determine the best plan of pairing the item in each row with a specific column so that the overall cost is minimised.

Initially row reductions are made. Then the column reductions are followed by a testing and improvement iterative procedure until the allocation is made. The process is described on the left-hand side of Fig. 3.1.

Example 3.2.1

It is necessary to allocate persons A, B, C and D to tasks I, II, III and IV. A plan is required which will give the lowest overall value, i.e. the sum of the four pairings selected has to be minimised. The performance matrix is given here (Table 3.1) with the highest skill graded 1 and the lowest skill graded 9.

Table 3.1

	I	II	III	IV
A	8	5	2	1
B	5	8	6	2
C	6	9	5	3
D	2	4	1	5

ROW REDUCTIONS

We find the minimum value of the first row 8, 5, 2, 1, i.e. 1, and then subtract this value from each element of that row which now gives 7, 4, 1, 0.

Next we do this for row B, which transforms 5, 8, 6, 2 to 3, 6, 4, 0 as 2 is the lowest element and is therefore subtracted from the initial four values.

Row C changes 6, 9, 5, 3 into 3, 6, 2, 0 as 3 is the lowest value and similarly 2, 4, 1, 5 is changed to 1, 3, 0, 4 as 1 is the lowest value. We now obtain a new table (Table 3.2) consisting of the four rows we have found.

Table 3.2

	I	II	III	IV
A	7	4	1	0
B	3	6	4	0
C	3	6	2	0
D	1	3	0	4

COLUMN REDUCTIONS

We now reduce the values by considering them as four separate columns. The first column, column I, has values $\begin{smallmatrix}7\\3\\3\\1\end{smallmatrix}$, with the lowest value 1, and so each element of the column is reduced by 1. This will give a new first column of $\begin{smallmatrix}6\\2\\2\\0\end{smallmatrix}$. The second column, column II, has values $\begin{smallmatrix}4\\6\\6\\3\end{smallmatrix}$, with the lowest value this time 3, and the old column is reduced by 3 , giving a new column of $\begin{smallmatrix}1\\3\\3\\0\end{smallmatrix}$. The third column, column III,

has minimum value 0, and also the fourth column, column IV, has three occurences of the minimum value 0. Hence column III and column IV both remain unchanged, as subtracting 0 from each value leaves them unaltered. So we now obtain our new table by writing out the four columns we have just found (Table 3.3).

Table 3.3

	I	II	III	IV
A	6	1	1	0
B	2	3	4	0
C	2	3	2	0
D	0	0	0	4

The test is to check whether we are ready to pair persons to tasks. We would attempt to pair where we have a zero. However, although each row must now have a zero and also each column must have a zero, these are insufficient. We carry out the test by drawing vertical and horizontal lines so that each zero is covered, but we must draw the lines so as to have the minimum number possible.

Consider row D, a row with three zeros. A horizontal line through row D will cover three zeros at once. This will just leave three zeros in column IV. So we put a vertical line through column IV. In this case, just two lines were required to cover all the zeros. The result is shown in Table 3.4.

Table 3.4

	I	II	III	IV
A	6	1	1	0
B	2	3	4	0
C	2	3	2	0
—D—	0—	0—	0—	4

CONCLUSION OF TEST

The conclusion of this test is that the zeros do not give us an optimal allocation. As we have *four* rows and *four* columns, we require the minimum number of lines that have to be used to be *four*. In general, an $n \times n$ set of values requires n lines. As we do not have an optimal solution an improvement is required.

IMPROVEMENT

To improve the situation we need a new arrangement of the zeros. We obtain the rearrangement by noting that we have three categories in the previous 4×4 table. *Nine* entries have *no lines* through them, the *six* zeros all have just *one line* passing through them, while the 4 in the lower-right corner has *two lines* through it. Each category now has a special role. First we find the minimum value of the nine un-covered entries. This is 1 as we note the entries in row A column II and column III. This value 1 is important, for we now *reduce each of the nine uncovered* entries by 1, and we increase the single entry with two lines through by the same value 1. All other entries, that is those with one line passing through them, remain unchanged. This gives Table 3.5.

Table 3.5

	I	II	III	IV
A	5	0	0	0
B	1	2	3	0
C	1	2	1	0
D	0	0	0	5

We have now completed the improvement and note the two new zeros which occur in row A, column II and column III, so we now carry out a further test.

THE SECOND TEST

This test will proceed as the first, as we again seek the minimum number of lines to cover all the zeros. First we draw a line through row D. Next, we draw a line through column IV. Each of these lines is 'efficient', as six zeros have now been covered. The two zeros which remain are in row A, so a single line through this row ensures all the zeros are now covered, as shown in Table 3.6.

Table 3.6

```
          I   II  III  IV
        ┌─────────────────┐
   —A—5—0—0—0—
    B   1   2   3   0
    C   1   2   1   0
   —D—0—0—0—5—
        └─────────────────┘
```

The conclusion of this test is that we still do not have an optimal arrangement of the zeros as all the zeros can be covered with three lines. Our requirement is that four are needed for optimality, so we carry out a second improvement.

THE SECOND IMPROVEMENT

Six entries are now left without lines passing through them, and the minimum value is again 1 (in fact we note it occurs three times). So we proceed as before. Each of the *six* uncovered elements are reduced by 1. Each of the *two* elements (top-right and bottom-right) with two lines passing through them are increased by 1. All of the remaining *eight* elements with a single line passing through them are unchanged. This gives us Table 3.7.

Table 3.7

	I	II	III	IV
A	5	0	0	1
B	0	1	2	0
C	0	1	0	0
D	0	0	0	6

We are now ready for the third test and we note that although the last improvement produced three extra zeros, one zero in row A, column IV, became 1.

THIRD TEST

Try as we may, it is not possible to draw vertical or horizontal lines through all the zeros *unless* we use four lines. This is good news as we now have an *optimal arrangement* of the zeros and so we may now carry out the pairing process using the cells with a 0.

THE ALLOCATION

If we now examine each row and each column of Table 3.7 we find a minimum of two zeros and in some cases three zeros. To start the allocation process we can choose one of the zeros. Let us put an asterisk in row A, column II, to show a planned pairing. Next we pair row B with column I, shown again by an asterisk. We are now left with rows C and D and columns III and IV. A close inspection shows that row C is paired with column IV and row D is paired with column III. The plan is shown in Table 3.8.

Table 3.8

	I	II	III	IV
A		0*	0	
B	0*			0
C	0		0	0*
D	0	0	0*	

The value of our allocation is found by referring to the *initial* performance matrix:

Person	Task	Performance
A	II	5
B	I	5
C	IV	3
D	III	1
	Total	14

It may be noted that other combinations of starred zeros representing other optimal solutions are possible. For example A with III, B with IV, C with I and D with II, which gives the same minimum total of 2 + 2 + 6 + 4 = 14. If only one allocation plan can be determined, then it is a unique plan. This phase is shown in Fig. 3.1.

Exercise 3.2.1

Firms A, B, C and D each submit tenders for four contracts (I, II, III and IV) for which bids were invited. The bids are indicated in Table 3.9. Given that each firm is to be allocated one contract, obtain a plan to minimise the total cost.

Table 3.9

	I	II	III	IV
A	16	14	17	12
B	18	12	11	18
C	14	14	17	15
D	16	17	15	16

3.3   Transportation Algorithm

The objective of the transportation algorithm is to determine the best plan of assigning the units from each origin to specific destinations so that the overall plan of transporting the goods minimises the total cost. As with allocation there is an initial procedure but this time it will be a 'first feasible solution'. It will be followed by an iterative process of testing and improving until the plan is optimal. Figure 3.1 shows the components of the process and our initial example conveniently avoids the need for the extensions to the algorithm which are considered towards the end of this section.

Example 3.3.1

Obtain the optimal plan of transporting combine harvesters from four depots, A, B, C and D, to four farms, I, II, III and IV. The availabilities at A, B, C and D are 3, 4, 5 and 8 units respectively and the requirements at I, II, III and IV are 9, 5, 4 and 2 units respectively. The costs of the transportation of the combine harvesters between the depots and the farms are given in Table 3.10.

Table 3.10

	I	II	III	IV
A	8	5	2	1
B	5	8	6	2
C	6	9	5	3
D	2	4	1	5

ANSWER

FIRST FEASIBLE SOLUTION

In obtaining the first feasible solution, we are seeking a plan to send all the combine harvesters from the depots to the farms. We do not expect it to be immediately optimal. However, it will help to use a least-cost method of assignment. This involves allocating as many units as possible to the cheapest route and the next cheapest route and so on until a plan is found. To record the proposed plan we first complete a grid, linking each depot with each farm as shown in Table 3.11.

Table 3.11

	I (9)	II (5)	III (4)	IV (2)
A (3)				
B (4)				
C (5)				
D (8)				

To select the first route we see from the costs table that the minimum value is 1 which occurs in row A, column IV, and row D, column III. The maximum we can send in row A, column IV, is 2 units limited by column IV. We note this in our initial table (see Table 3.12). The maximum we can send in row D, column III, is 4 units, limited by column III.

Table 3.12

	I 9	II 5	III 4̸ 0	IV 2̸ 0
A 3̸ 1				2
B 4				
C 5				
D 8̸ 4			4	

We see above that the availabilities of A and D have been reduced to 1 unit and 4 units respectively, also that the requirements at III and IV have been satisfied. The next lowest cost is found in row D, column I. We send 4 units over this route as D has 4 units left and column I will hence obtain 4 units and will now require only 5 units. We now compare the costs of the six routes in rows A, B and C and columns I and II as they are the only units remaining unassigned. Equal-lowest costs are found in row A, column II, and row B, column I, i.e. 5. The maximum number of units conveyed will be 1 and 4 respectively. We now have the situation shown in Table 3.13.

Table 3.13

	I 9̸ 5̸ 1	II 5̸ 4	III 4̸ 0	IV 2̸ 0
A 3̸ 1̸ 0		1		2
B 4̸ 0	4			
C 5				
D 8̸ 4̸ 0	4		4	

The 5 units left at depot C are therefore sent to farm I, 1 unit, and farm II, 4 units.

The complete plan is now shown in Table 3.14.

Table 3.14

	I	II	III	IV
A	8	5 1	2	1 2
B	5 4	8	6	2
C	6 1	9 4	5	3
D	2 4	4	1 4	5

The unit costs of transporting over each route have been shown with the number of units transported. Hence we may obtain the cost of this plan:

$$\text{cost} = 1 \times 5 + 2 \times 1 + 4 \times 5 + 1 \times 6 + 4 \times 9 + 4 \times 2 + 4 \times 1 = 81.$$

TEST PROCEDURE

The test procedure is to ascertain whether a particular plan is optimal. There are two stages in the test. In the first stage, we decompose the costs of all the used routes into a set of costs for sending a unit from each origin and a set of costs for receiving a unit at each destination. In the second stage we consider all the routes which are not used and decide whether any of these routes could be used with a cost saving. This is achieved by combining the sending and receiving costs and then comparing the result with the actual cost of the route concerned.

STAGE ONE – FIRST ITERATION

In this stage we have to determine the four costs of sending a unit from A, B, C and D indicated at the end of each row as S_A, S_B, S_C, S_D, respectively and the four costs of receiving a unit at I, II, III and IV indicated at the bottom of each column as R_I, R_{II}, R_{III} and R_{IV} respectively.

Table 3.15 shows the eight values required outside the square. Inside the grid the cost of transporting a unit is indicated *only* for routes which are *used* in the plan.

Table 3.15

	I	II	III	IV	
A		5		1	S_A
B	5				S_B
C	6	9			S_C
D	2		1		S_D
	R_I	R_{II}	R_{III}	R_{IV}	

These seven costs are now used to determine the sending and receiving costs. The method requires that the sending cost added to the receiving cost over each route used must equal the cost of the route used. The process is started by arbitrarily assigning to the first origin the sending cost of zero, i.e. $S_A = 0$. It continues until all seven sending and receiving costs have been determined. Incidentally, this will require that all the used routes must be 'independent' — which will be considered later. A scan of the first row reveals two used routes, AII costing 5 and AIV costing 1. Hence, $R_{II} + S_A = 5$ and $R_{IV} + S_A = 1$. As $S_A = 0$ we have $R_{II} = 5$ and $R_{IV} = 1$.

The situation is shown in Table 3.16.

Table 3.16

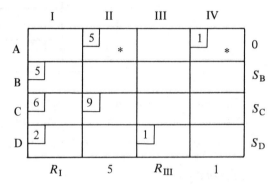

We have used the two costs in row A(*) and we now use the remaining five costs to determine the remaining five outstanding sending/receiving costs. R_{IV} can be used no further so we continue with R_{II}. Route CII is now chosen as $R_{II} + S_C = 9$, and as $R_{II} = 5$ we obtain $S_C = 4$. We now use S_C. Route CI is next considered as $R_I + S_C = 6$. As $S_C = 4$, then $R_I = 2$. Four costs (starred) have now been used — three remain (Table 3.17).

Table 3.17

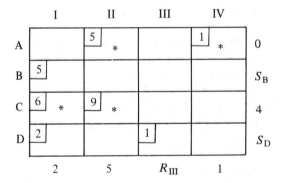

From column I, $R_I + S_B = 5$ and $R_I + S_D = 2$; hence, as $R_I = 2$, we have $S_B = 3$ and $S_D = 0$. Finally we complete this stage with $R_{III} = 1$ ($R_{III} + 0 = 1$), route DIII.

It should be noted all the costs are positive in this example — negative values may arise and they are treated similarly.

STAGE TWO – FIRST ITERATION

In this stage we are concerned with testing each unused route to find whether total costs could be reduced by using each particular route. All *used* routes are shown starred and all *unused* routes contain the unit transporting cost. So we ignore starred routes and just consider the routes with the costs shown in Table 3.18.

Table 3.18

	I	II	III	IV	
A	8	*	2	*	0
B	*	8	6	2	3
C	*	*	5	3	4
D	*	4	*	5	0
	2	5	1	1	

To test each route we compare the combined cost of sending and receiving with the actual cost. Only where the actual cost is 'less than' the combined cost can a saving be achieved. If this does not occur for any unused route, then an optimal plan has been obtained. We now compare actual costs with combined costs for each route and tabulate the result (Table 3.19).

Table 3.19

Unused route	Actual	Sending	Unit costs		Saving Comparison
			Receiving	Combined	
AI	8	0	2	2	NONE $(8 \geqslant 2)$
AIII	2	0	1	1	NONE $(2 \geqslant 1)$
BII	8	3	5	8	NONE $(8 \geqslant 8)$
BIII	6	3	1	4	NONE $(6 \geqslant 4)$
BIV	2	3	1	4	YES $(2 < 4)$
CIII	5	4	1	5	NONE $(5 \geqslant 5)$
CIV	3	4	1	5	YES $(3 < 5)$
DII	4	0	5	5	YES $(4 < 5)$
DIV	5	0	1	1	NONE $(5 \geqslant 1)$

Routinely, the tabulation shown may be omitted and a tick placed in a cell where there is no saving. However, we note that three routes present us with the opportunity of a saving. The extent of the saving achievable per unit is the value that the actual cost is 'less than' the combined cost. In routes BIV, CIV and DII the savings are therefore 2 (4 − 2), 2 (5 − 3) and 1 (5 − 4) respectively. The savings are indicated in the grid by enclosing each saving in a small circle (Table 3.20).

Table 3.20

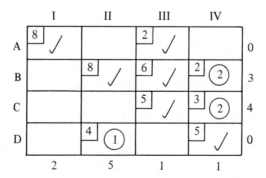

As we have three routes indicating a possible saving we do *not* have an optimal plan.

We proceed now to an improvement phase.

In order to carry out an improvement in the plan, a transfer of units will be attempted so that as many units as possible will be transferred into a route where a saving is possible. Note that in this phase *only one* route will be considered for transfer, and when the transfer is complete the test procedure will be used before any further attempt at transfer is made. Of the three routes considered, BIV and CIV both have a saving of two, while DII has a saving of only one. We favour the highest-saving routes, BIV and CIV, and work with CIV for simplicity. BIV will be considered later in this section when the adjustment procedure is more familiar. See Example 3.3.2, Table 3.3.4.

Table 3.21

	I (9)	II (5)	III (4)	IV (2)
A (3)		1		2
B (4)	4			
C (5)	1	4		$+\theta$
D (8)	4		4	

The symbol $(+\theta)$ is now shown (Table 3.21) in route CIV to indicate that an extra quantity θ is to be transported through this route. However, any adjustments to the plan must satisfy the initial availabilities and requirements. So any row or column adjusted must include both a $(+\theta)$ and a $(-\theta)$. A further point concerning the improvement is that apart from the selected route, CIV, no θ value can be placed in an unused route. Hence we now consider obtaining a set of θ values with $+\theta$ in the route chosen for maximum saving, and all rows and columns requiring both a $+\theta$ and a $-\theta$ appearing only in the routes which are used (Table 3.22).

Table 3.22

	1		2	$-\theta$
4				
1	4			$+\theta$
4		4		

First, consider column IV where 2 units have to be supplied. This column now requires a $-\theta$, and as it must be in a route which is used, we show $-\theta$ in AIV. Second, consider row A. This row has only $-\theta$ so $+\theta$ is required in cell AII. Third, consider column II. This column has only $+\theta$, so $-\theta$ is required. As CII is the only other route used in this column, $-\theta$ is shown in CII. Fourth, by considering row C, we find both $-\theta$ and $+\theta$, hence the row is balanced. The complete arrangement is as shown in Table 3.23, forming a square of θs.

Next, a value of θ has to be found. Recalling that each unit transferred into CIV reduces the cost of the plan by 2, we prefer a large θ value, but by reference to cells AIV and CII, where θ is removed, only 2 units and 4 units respectively may be removed. As removing any higher value than 2 from AIV is not possible, we conclude that the maximum θ value is 2.

Table 3.23

	$+\theta$ 1		$-\theta$ 2
4			
1	$-\theta$ 4		$+\theta$
4		4	

The improvement is completed by specifying the new plan by carrying out the θ modifications to the old plan as shown in Table 3.24. The row totals and column totals should be checked to ensure the plan satisfies the requirements.

Table 3.24

	9	5	4	2
3		5 3		
4	5 4			
5	6 1	9 2		3 2
8	2 4		1 4	

The saving achieved is 4, as two θ units are transferred, each saving 2. As a check we may evaluate the complete plan:

$$\text{new cost} = 3 \times 5 + 4 \times 5 + 1 \times 6 + 2 \times 9 + 2 \times 3 + 4 \times 2 + 4 \times 1 = 77.$$

This is less than the old plan which cost 81.

STAGE ONE – SECOND ITERATION

This will show that it is possible for negative values to arise among the receiving costs (Table 3.25). This should not be considered to be of particular significance.

Table 3.25

		5 3			0
	5 4				3
	6 1	9 2		3 2	4
	2 4		1 4		0
	2	5	1	-1	

Initially S_A is set at 0, hence as cost of AII = 5, then $R_{II} = 5$.

As the cost of route CII = 9 = $R_{II} + S_C$ we obtain $S_C = 4$.

As the cost of route CI = 6 = $S_C + R_I$ we obtain $R_I = 2$.

As the cost of route BI = 5 = $S_B + R_I$ we obtain $S_B = 3$.

As the cost of route DI = 2 = $S_D + R_I$ we obtain $S_D = 0$.

As the cost of route DIII = 1 = $S_D + R_{III}$ we obtain $R_{III} = 1$.

This leaves R_{IV} to be found.

Now, as the cost of route CIV = 3 = $S_C + R_{IV}$ and $S_C = 4$, then $R_{IV} = 3 - 4 = -1$.

As the eight sending and receiving costs have been found we continue with the second stage.

STAGE TWO – SECOND ITERATION

Table 3.26 shows the comparison of the actual cost and the combined cost for each unused route. We conclude that no optimum has yet been found, as route DII can be brought into use with a saving of 1 (5 − 4) for each unit transferred to this route.

Table 3.26	Unused route	Actual	Sending	Receiving	Combined	Saving	Comparison
	AI	8	0	2	2	NONE	(8 ⩾ 2)
	AIII	2	0	1	1	NONE	(2 ⩾ 1)
	AIV	1	0	−1	−1	NONE	(1 ⩾ −1)
	BII	8	3	5	8	NONE	(8 ⩾ 8)
	BIII	6	3	1	4	NONE	(6 ⩾ 4)
	BIV	2	3	−1	2	NONE	(2 ⩾ 2)
	CIII	5	4	1	5	NONE	(5 ⩾ 5)
	DII	4	0	5	5	YES	(4 < 5)
	DIV	5	0	−1	−1	NONE	(5 ⩾ −1)

Table 3.26 is summarised in the grid (Table 3.27), again showing the saving of (1) for each unit transferred into route DII.

Table 3.27

[8] ✓	3	[2] ✓	[1] ✓	0
4	[8] ✓	[6] ✓	[2] ✓	3
1	2	[5] ✓	2	4
4	[4] (1)	4	[5] ✓	0

IMPROVEMENT PHASE – SECOND ITERATION

To commence the improvement, $+\theta$ is shown in route DII (Table 3.28). We now seek to balance out the $+\theta$.

First we consider row D. Routes DI and DIII appear possibles for $-\theta$. However, by inspection, column III has only one route in use, hence no $-\theta$ in DIII is possible as it has to be balanced by a $+\theta$ in another used route in this column. We are then left with the only possibility of $-\theta$ in route DI.

Table 3.28

	3		
4			
1	2		2
4 $-\theta$	$+\theta$ 4		

Second we consider column I. Route BI and route CI appear possibilities for $+\theta$. Again, inspection of row B leads to a cul-de-sac (only one used route, so no scope for $+\theta$ and $-\theta$); this leaves us with $+\theta$ in CI.

Third we consider row C, but CIV is the only used route in column IV, so $-\theta$ is shown in CII (Table 3.29).

Table 3.29

	3		
4			
1 $+\theta$	2 $-\theta$		2
4 $-\theta$	$+\theta$ 4		

Fourth, referring to column II we find a balance as both $+\theta$ and $-\theta$ are found.

The maximum value of θ is 2 (found by referring to CII and DI and observing that at most 2 units be taken from CII). This will enable the next plan to be formulated. The saving will be 2 at this iteration (2 units saving 1 unit each). Hence the new cost is now 75 (77 − 2). The revised plan is shown in Table 3.30.

Table 3.30

	3		
4			
3			2
2	2	4	

STAGE ONE – THIRD ITERATION

This is commenced by assigning S_A the value of 0. By considering the following sequence of costs and used routes the respective sending and receiving costs are obtained:

AII costing 5 gives $R_{II} = 5$.

DII costing 4 gives $S_D = -1$.

DIII costing 1 gives $R_{III} = 2$.

DI costing 2 gives $R_I = 3$.

BI costing 5 gives $S_{II} = 2$.

CI costing 6 gives $S_{III} = 3$.

CIV costing 3 gives $R_{IV} = 0$.

This is shown in the completed first-stage table (Table 3.31), in which costs of used routes are included for convenience.

Table 3.31

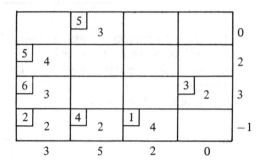

STAGE TWO – THIRD ITERATION

Table 3.32 shows the second stage completed with a tick in each route not used. This shows that in *no* case is the actual cost less than the combined cost of sending and receiving. Hence the test indicates we have an optimal plan of sending the 20 combine harvesters as cheaply as possible to the farms requiring them.

Table 3.32

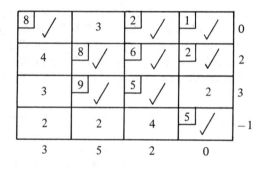

The cost is $3 \times 5 + 4 \times 5 + 3 \times 6 + 2 \times 3 + 2 \times 2 + 2 \times 4 + 4 \times 1 = 75$.

It is helpful to follow the testing and improvement iterations by referring to the appropriate parts of Fig. 3.1.

Exercise 3.3.1

A manufacturing company requires upgrading of automatic machinery at each of plants I, II, III and IV and has the capacity to carry out the changes using resources available at depots A, B, C and D. The costs of the upgrading of the machinery by the various depots are given in Table 3.33. Find a plan to minimise the total cost.

Table 3.33

	I	II	III	IV	Availability
A	16	14	17	12	2
B	18	12	11	18	3
C	14	14	17	15	2
D	16	17	15	16	4
Requirements	1	3	4	3	

Developments of the Algorithm

The algorithm we have followed has worked relatively 'trouble-free'. We must, however, be able to cope with various quirks which may arise. Suppose, for example, one or more of the following situations were to occur.

(a) Cell BIV was chosen in the improvement phase — first iteration for showing the $+\theta$.
(b) It was not possible to follow through a sequence of routes used to obtain the sending costs and the receiving costs.
(c) It was not possible to arrange the $+\theta$ and $-\theta$ in the improvement phase.
(d) The quantities supplied and required did not balance, for instance if a combine harvester developed a fault, or a farm cancelled a request.
(e) The cost matrix indicates profits instead of costs.

We now examine case (a) as a short example. In cases (b) and (c), we find that special rules about the number of routes used are implemented to enable the problems to be overcome. In fact, it is a requirement that the number of routes used must be equal to the number of origins added to the number of destinations minus one. An example is considered in section 3.4. In case (d), we overcome the problem by including either a new 'dummy' origin or destination to ensure a balance of supply with demand; see section 3.5. Case (e) is considered in section 3.6.

Example 3.3.2

Rework the improvement phase of Example 3.3.1, choosing cell BIV for $+\theta$.

ANSWER

Returning to the improvement phase — first iteration, we see in Table 3.34 that cell BIV has $+\theta$ shown. We can consider column IV. As the only routes to be adjusted must now be *used* routes, AIV has $-\theta$ (Table 3.35). Considering row A means AII has $+\theta$. Considering column II, entry CII requires $-\theta$. So far we have used four θs, but we continue.

Table 3.34

	1		2
4			$+\theta$
1	4		
4		4	

Table 3.35

	$+\theta$ 1		$-\theta$ 2
4			$+\theta$
1	$-\theta$ 4		
4		4	

43

Considering row C, CI must have $+\theta$ (Table 3.36). Now an important choice is made: BI or DI for $-\theta$?

DI is eliminated as it leads to DIII and no further, so we put $-\theta$ into BI.

Table 3.36

	1 $+\theta$		2 $-\theta$
4 $-\theta$			$+\theta$
1 $+\theta$	4 $-\theta$		
4		4	

Last we consider row B and find a balance with BI and BIV. Consequently $\theta = 2$ because 2 is the minimum quantity in a route containing $-\theta$.

Note: The sequence of routes considered for a θ adjustment may be more complex than a simple square or rectangle.

Exercise 3.3.2

Complete example 3.3.2 to obtain an optimal plan.

3.4 Degeneracy

This is the term we use to describe a plan for transportation which arises when the number of routes used does not satisfy the rule

number of routes used = number of rows + number of columns − 1.

This is sometimes known as the $m + n - 1$ rule for the number of routes used. Applying the rule to example 3.3.1, we find 4 rows and 4 columns give 7 $(4 + 4 - 1)$ as the number of routes used. As an initial exercise it is helpful to verify that the rule is satisfied at each iteration of example 3.3.1. However, a situation may arise as shown in Table 3.37 in which we observe the units supplied and required balance, but only 6 routes are used in the plan. Hence this plan is degenerate. We will modify the plan to become non-degenerate, but first we will observe why it causes a difficulty.

Table 3.37

	9	5	4	2
3		1		2
4	4			
5	5			
8		4	4	

To test this plan we first apply stage one.

$S_A = 0$ gives $R_{II} = 5$ and $R_{IV} = 1$ by considering AII and AIV (Table 3.38). From DII then DIII we obtain $S_D = -1$ then $R_{III} = 2$ respectively.

Table 3.38

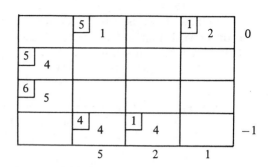

But what happens now? We have no route in use to connect to row B, row C nor column I.

The impasse is resolved by 'pretending' to use a route. This is known as creating a dummy route. However, we must take care. Such a step should be taken only when all other used routes have been examined to see if the process can continue. Having completed the check, we pretend to use a route which must consequently be in row B, row C or column 1, as *that is where it is needed* to enable the process to continue. So we now select a route from AI, BII, BIII, BIV, CII, CIII, CIV and DI for which the unit costs are 8, 8, 6, 2, 9, 5, 3 and 2 respectively. For convenience we select a 'low-cost' route to use as a dummy route. So we choose BIV. (As an exercise you may wish to choose DI.) To indicate that BIV is to change status from 'unused' route to 'used' route we show 0 in the cell (Table 3.39). For convenience we may assume that a small quantity is transported over a dummy route — a quantity that is actually infinitesimal so that its cost of transportation may be neglected.

Table 3.39

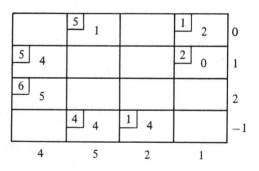

We immediately find that the process of determining sending cost and receiving costs may continue. We use route BIV to find $S_B = 1$ from R_{IV}. We complete this stage by considering cost of BI then CI to obtain $R_I = 4$ then $S_{III} = 2$.

We now invoke stage two.

Referring to Table 3.40, we find route DI has a saving of 1, so the test is negative and we proceed with the improvement.

Table 3.40

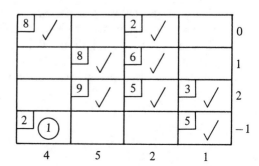

45

The new route used is DI, shown by $+\theta$ (Table 3.41). A column scan of used routes reveals that BI has $-\theta$, as CI leads to a 'cul-de-sac'. Now we are led to route BIV as it is the only 'used' route in row B to compensate the $-\theta$ of BI, hence we show $+\theta$ in cell BIV (Table 3.42).

Table 3.41

	1		2
4 $^{-\theta}$			0
5			
$^{+\theta}$	4	4	

Table 3.42

	1 $^{+\theta}$		2 $^{-\theta}$
4 $^{-\theta}$			0 $^{+\theta}$
5			
$^{+\theta}$	4 $^{-\theta}$	4	

The sequence continues with AIV, AII and DII and back to DI. The maximum θ value we may choose is 2 (comparisons of the quantities in cells AIV, BI and DII).

This gives the new plan shown in Table 3.43, which may be tested for optimality as an exercise.

Table 3.43

	9	5	4	2
3		3		
4	2			2
5	5			
8	2	2	4	

Notes

(a) This example shows the use of one dummy route. It may be necessary on occasions to assign two or more routes as dummy routes.

(b) We found that we required $+\theta$ in the dummy route BIV. On occasions $-\theta$ may arise in a dummy route. In this case take $\theta = 0$ and then adjust the plan, which results in a change of location for the dummy route.

3.5 Inequality of Supply and Demand

We have so far considered balanced problems. We now examine the situation arising when supply and demand are unequal. You are referred to Fig. 3.1 to see the linking of the adjustment for inequality into the transportation algorithm.

Example 3.5.1

Start the application of the transportation algorithm towards the determination of an optimal plan for transporting combine harvesters to farms as in example 3.3.1, with the modifications that

(a) Due to mechanical failure, only 7 units are available at depot D.
(b) Owing to slower growth farm IV will make a new arrangement for combine harvesters.

ANSWER

We now have supplies at A, B, C and D of 3, 4, 5 and 7 and requirements at I, II and III of 9, 5 and 4, respectively. We note that supply = 3 + 4 + 5 + 7 = 19 units, while demand = 9 + 5 + 4 = 18. This presents us with an unbalanced problem. We overcome this problem by a modification which will give us a balanced problem. The difference between supply and demand is found to be 1 (19 − 18) extra unit in the supply. The trick here is to invent a dummy destination, or in our example a fictitious farm which requires the spare combine harvester. Having decided to have the extra farm we need to decide on the costs of transporting units to the farm. Now, providing we are indifferent as to which unit remains at the depot we assign the same cost of transporting a unit from each depot to the fictitious farm.

Normally, this cost is chosen to be 0 for simplicity. However, if there is a cost disadvantage if a unit remains at a depot, this can be reflected by choosing suitable costs.

The modified cost matrix is now shown. When the modification has been completed the problem is then solved using the basic transportation algorithm (Table 3.44).

Table 3.44

	9	5	4	1
3	8	5	2	0
4	5	8	6	0
5	6	9	5	0
7	2	4	1	0

The first feasible solution is shown in Table 3.45.

Table 3.45

	9	5	4	1
3		2		1
4	4			
5	2	3		
7	3		4	

Table 3.46 shows the first and second stages of the test and you are referred to Table 3.44 to check the costs of unused routes for potential savings. In the succeeding exercise you may wish to extend this practice in order to reduce your own 'iteration time'.

Table 3.46

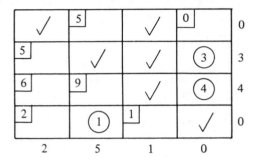

Exercise 3.5.1

Complete the solution of example 3.5.1.

Notes
(a) When you complete example 3.5.1, you will find the optimal plan includes an entry in column IV. This means that the combine harvester it refers to remains at the depot.
(b) In the case of demand exceeding supply then a dummy supplier is invented, or in the case of example 3.3.1 a fictitious depot is added. Providing there is an indifference as to the penalty of not supplying a particular farm then it is convenient to assign a cost of 0 from this new depot to each farm. The procedure then proceeds as in the case of exercise 3.3.5.

3.6 Maximisation — Transportation and Allocation

We consider the case in which the problem posed in example 3.3.1 is modified so that the cost matrix now represents the profit to the combine harvester supplier when a unit is supplied to a particular farm. You are referred to Fig. 3.1 to see the linking of maximisation into the allocation algorithm and the transportation algorithm.

Example 3.6.1

Obtain an optimal plan for example 3.3.1 by using the profit here (Table 3.47).

Table 3.47

	I	II	III	IV
A	8	5	2	1
B	5	8	6	2
C	6	9	5	3
D	2	4	1	5

ANSWER

Two choices are open to us here. Either we have to modify the previous algorithm we used or we can modify the question and use the previous algorithm. The policy adopted here is the latter. It has two advantages. First, each maximisation problem gives the opportunity to practise and reinforce the minimisation method, also it avoids the complication of confusing the procedure covered — if ever that were possible! The modification required is the conversion of a set of profits to a set of costs.

This is achieved by scanning the profit matrix for the route with the maximum profit — which is cell CII with a profit of 9 for each unit — and then each route has a new value calculated. The new value is the maximum value minus the old value. This can be expressed as a matrix operation as shown below:

$$\text{maximum profit} \quad\quad \text{actual profit} \quad\quad \text{new cost}$$

$$\begin{bmatrix} 9 & 9 & 9 & 9 \\ 9 & 9 & 9 & 9 \\ 9 & 9 & 9 & 9 \\ 9 & 9 & 9 & 9 \end{bmatrix} - \begin{bmatrix} 8 & 5 & 2 & 1 \\ 5 & 8 & 6 & 2 \\ 6 & 9 & 5 & 3 \\ 2 & 4 & 1 & 5 \end{bmatrix} = \begin{bmatrix} 1 & 4 & 7 & 8 \\ 4 & 1 & 3 & 7 \\ 3 & 0 & 4 & 6 \\ 7 & 5 & 8 & 4 \end{bmatrix}.$$

We may consider the cost matrix to indicate a penalty in terms of the amount by which the profit falls below a 'target' value of 9.

We continue by finding a first feasible solution as shown in Table 3.48. It may be observed that the solution is degenerate as only five routes are needed.

Table 3.48

	9	5	4	2
3	3			
4			4	
5		5		
8	6			2

The test procedure is now used in stage one; by considering the cost of routes AI, DI and DIV we may determine $R_I = 1$, $S_D = 6$ and $R_{IV} = -2$ before we reach an impasse (Table 3.49).

Table 3.49

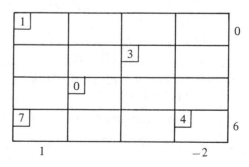

We continue by bringing into use an unused route in the rows and columns requiring sending costs, namely rows B and C and columns II and III; we initially exclude BII and CIII as they are not of immediate help. As we find the lowest cost is 3 in cell CI, we let CI become a dummy route shown by a zero. This enables S_C and R_{II} to be found to be 2 and -2 respectively (Table 3.50).

A further impasse arises, which is again resolved by a dummy route. This time we select route BII. We now complete the set of costs as $S_B = 3$ and finally $R_{III} = 0$ (Table 3.51).

Table 3.50

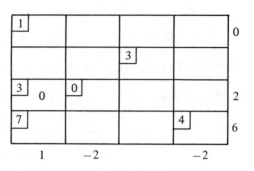

Table 3.51

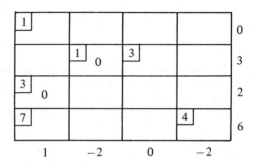

We are now in a position to start stage two. By reference to Table 3.52 we find, however, that the plan is optimal.

Table 3.52

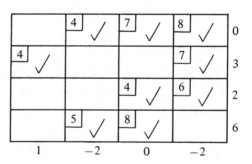

In order to complete the example, we need to determine the optimal profit so we refer back to the original profit figures.

Hence (Table 3.53):

$$\text{optimal profit} = 3 \times 8 + 4 \times 6 + 5 \times 9 + 6 \times 2 + 2 \times 5 = 115.$$

Table 3.53

Exercise 3.6.1

A firm has four categories of salesmen A, B, C, D and four sales areas, I, II, III, IV. Table 3.54 indicates the expected sales generated by each salesman in each area. Obtain a plan to maximise the expected sales for the firm.

Table 3.54

	I	II	III	IV	Availability
A	16	14	17	12	2
B	18	12	11	18	3
C	14	14	17	15	3
D	16	17	15	16	4
Requirement	1	3	4	3	

We next consider a further modification to cope with the case where each origin supplies one unit and each destination requires one unit and the requirement is for maximisation.

Example 3.6.2

Obtain an optimal plan for example 3.3.1 where one combine harvester is available from each depot and one is required at each farm. Use the profit figures shown in Table 3.47.

ANSWER

We proceed as for answer 3.6.1 up to the stage where we obtain the cost matrix shown. However, we now apply the allocation algorithm as indicated in Fig. 3.1.

We now follow the normal procedure cost matrix:

$$\begin{array}{cccc} 1 & 4 & 7 & 8 \\ 4 & 1 & 3 & 7 \\ 3 & 0 & 4 & 6 \\ 7 & 5 & 8 & 4 \end{array}$$

Row reduction:

$$\begin{array}{cccc} 0 & 3 & 6 & 7 \\ 3 & 0 & 2 & 6 \\ 3 & 0 & 4 & 6 \\ 3 & 1 & 4 & 0 \end{array}$$

Column reduction:

$$\begin{array}{cccc} 0 & 3 & 4 & 7 \\ 3 & 0 & 0 & 6 \\ 3 & 0 & 2 & 6 \\ 3 & 1 & 2 & 0 \end{array}$$

Optimal situation as four lines are required:

$$\begin{array}{cccc} -0^*\!-3 & -4 & -7 \\ -3 & -0 & -0^*\!-6 \\ 3 & 0^* & 2 & 6 \\ 3 & 1 & 2 & 0^* \end{array}$$

Here we allocate according to where the asterisks are shown with the optimal unique plan AI, BIII, CII and DIV, with the respective profits of 8, 6, 9 and 5 by reference back to the actual profit table values. The total optimal profit is 8 + 6 + 9 + 5 = 28. It may be noted that this solution is unique.

Use the table given in exercise 3.6.1 to obtain an optimal plan when only one salesman is available in each category and each area requires one salesman in order to maximise total expected sales.

3.7 Uniqueness

In seeking optimal plans, reference has usually been made to 'an' optimal plan, implying that there is only one. The question naturally arises as to whether alternative solutions exist. A quick check is possible by referring to the grid used in the final iteration relating to an optimal plan. See the lower part of Fig. 3.1.

Example 3.7.1

By reference to an optimal solution to example 3.3.1,

(a) determine whether the solution is unique, and
(b) if it is not then suggest an alternative.

ANSWER

Table 3.55

8 ✓	3	2 ✓=	1 ✓	0
4	8 ✓	6 ✓	2 ✓=	2
3	9 ✓	5 ✓=	2	3
2	2	4	5 ✓	−1
3	5	2	0	

(a) Table 3.55 is taken from the final iteration of example 3.3.1. An alternative solution will be obtained if we are able to find an unused route which will allow units to be transferred into that route at no extra cost. Whether or not it will cost more for units to be transferred into a particular unused route is decided by comparing the actual cost of that route with its combined cost. As we have a final iteration shown, we know that for each unused route for which we satisfy the requirement, the actual cost must exceed or equal the combined cost. Each unused route is now examined and we identify any route where 'actual cost equals combined cost' (=). The unused routes are, respectively, AI, AIII, AIV, BII, BIII, BIV, CII, CIII and DIV, and the excesses of actual cost over combined cost are, respectively, 5, 0, 1, 1, 2, 0, 1, 0 and 6. Hence the routes where 'actual cost equals combined cost' are AIII, BIV and CIII. So the answer to this part is No; the optimal solution is not unique as three unused routes have been formed where 'actual cost equals combined cost'. In fact the difference between these two costs indicates the extra cost of each unit transferred into a particular route and in three cases the value is 0.

(b) If we arbitrarily select the first route AIII then we may obtain the θ adjustment in the improvement phase. This is shown in Table 3.56 and θ may take the value of 1, or 2, to generate two further solutions.

Table 3.56

	9	5	4	2
3		3 $-\theta$	$+\theta$	
4	4			
5	3			2
8	2	2 $+\theta$	4 $-\theta$	

As an example, Table 3.57 shows the case where $\theta = 1$.

Table 3.57

	9	5	4	2
3		2	1	
4	4			
5	3			2
8	2	3	3	

Note

When we are considering different optimal solutions we do not need to satisfy the 'number of rows plus number of columns minus one' rule.

Exercise 3.7.1

Test the solutions you have found to exercises 3.3.1, 3.5.1 and 3.6.1 to find whether your plan is unique. Where the plan is not unique find an alternative solution.

Further Exercises

Hints

You should now be equipped to solve the following exercises, but there may be particular cases where you may find it easier to carry out a simplifying process to the cost matrix in the transportation problem.

First, you may apply the row reductions and column reductions, used routinely in allocation, to the transportation cost matrix.

Second, you may multiply the whole matrix by any positive constant.

Third, you may add or subtract a convenient constant from the entire matrix, or just a row, or just a column.

In all cases, remember that when you have found an optimal plan you must refer back to the original matrix to obtain the cost of each route. Additionally, it may be helpful to refer to Fig. 3.1 to structure your approach. Good luck!

Exercises

3.1 The transport manager of a company which has three factories, A, B and C, and four warehouses, 1, 2, 3 and 4, is faced with the problem of determining the way in which factories should supply warehouses so as to minimise total transportation costs.

In a given month, the supply requirements of each warehouse, the production capacities of the factories and the cost of shipping one unit of product from each factory to each warehouse in pounds sterling are shown in Table 3.58.

Table 3.58

			Warehouse				Production available units
		1	2	3	4		
Factory	A	12	23	43	3	6	
	B	63	23	33	53	8	
	C	33	1	63	13	17	
Required units		4	7	6	14	31	

You are required to determine the minimum-cost transportation plan.

(ICMA Part IV)

3.2 A steel company is concerned with the problem of distributing imported ore from three ports to four steel mills situated throughout the country.

The supplies of ore arriving at ports are:

Port	Tons per week
a	20 000
b	38 000
c	16 000

Demands at the steel mills are·

Steel mill	Tons per week
A	10 000
B	18 000
C	22 000
D	24 000

Transportation costs are £0.05 per ton mile. The distances between the ports and the steel mills are given in Table 3.59.

Table 3.59

	A	B	C	D
a	50	60	100	50
b	80	40	70	50
c	90	70	30	50

You are required to calculate the transportation plan which will minimise ore distribution costs for the steel company. State the cost of this distribution plan.

(ICMA Part IV)

4 The Theory of Games

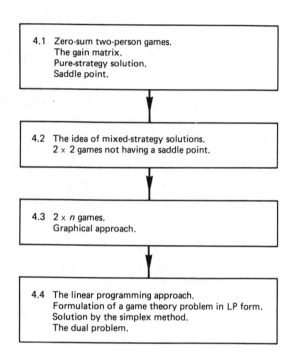

4.1 Zero-sum two-person games.
The gain matrix.
Pure-strategy solution.
Saddle point.

4.2 The idea of mixed-strategy solutions.
2 × 2 games not having a saddle point.

4.3 2 × n games.
Graphical approach.

4.4 The linear programming approach.
Formulation of a game theory problem in LP form.
Solution by the simplex method.
The dual problem.

4.1 Introduction

Game theory is concerned with deciding on a course of action in situations where the decision maker has open to him a number of possible actions or 'strategies'. The basis of game theory is the *two-person* game where two decision makers are considered operating in competition with each other, each seeking to use his strategies so as to optimise his overall return at the expense of the other person.

Game theory can be applied to competitive situations in business, economics, politics and sociology as well as to military problems. It can be used in situations involving just one decision maker by regarding the other player as nature or the rest of the world.

There are a number of definitions and pieces of notation which are fundamental to any discussion of game theory and we seek to introduce and explain these in this section.

First we look at the idea of a gain matrix. We consider two players, A and B, each having to choose between a number of strategies available to him. Each choice is made independently and unknown to the opponent. When the choice is played we assume a payment is made from B to A. Hence a negative figure would denote a gain for B. These payments are shown in what is called the gain matrix for player A:

$$
\begin{array}{c}
\text{B}\\
\begin{array}{cccccc}
 & \text{I} & \text{II} & \text{III} & & n
\end{array}\\
\begin{array}{c}
\text{I}\\
\text{II}\\
\text{A} \quad \text{III}\\
\cdot\\
\cdot\\
\cdot\\
m
\end{array}
\left(
\begin{array}{ccccc}
a_{11} & a_{12} & a_{13} & \cdots & a_{1n}\\
a_{21} & a_{22} & a_{23} & \cdots & a_{2n}\\
a_{31} & a_{32} & a_{33} & \cdots & a_{3n}\\
\cdot & & & & \cdot\\
\cdot & & & & \cdot\\
\cdot & & & & \cdot\\
a_{m1} & \cdots\cdots\cdots\cdots & & & a_{mn}
\end{array}
\right)
\end{array}
$$

For example, when A plays I and B plays II then the amount a_{12} is paid by B to A.

A zero-sum game is one where there are no penalties borne by either player so that the total resources owned by A and B combined remain constant. Thus if the gain matrix for B were written down as well as the gain matrix for A then the sum of all entries in both matrices would be zero. It would be possible for all the entries in A's gain matrix to be positive in a zero-sum game. This would imply that all the entries in B's gain matrix were negative.

A commonly used criterion employed in game theory to enable a player to determine his best strategy is the so-called maximin criterion. Here the player looks at the minimum gain he stands to make from each of his different possible strategies. This is based on the pessimistic view that whatever he does his opponent will behave in such a way that success will be minimised. Once these minima are established, the criterion then says that the best strategy is the one corresponding to the maximum of these minima. This is illustrated by means of an example as follows.

Consider the two-person zero-sum game where A has the following gain matrix:

$$
\begin{array}{c}
\text{B}\\
\begin{array}{cc}
\text{I} & \text{II}
\end{array}\\
\begin{array}{c}
\text{A} \quad \begin{array}{c}\text{I}\\\text{II}\end{array}
\end{array}
\left(
\begin{array}{cc}
3 & 4\\
1 & 2
\end{array}
\right)
\end{array}
$$

If A plays strategy I then the minimum gain he stands to make is 3. If A plays strategy II then the minimum gain he stands to make is 1. Let us write these beside the matrix at the ends of the appropriate rows:

$$
\left(
\begin{array}{cc}
3 & 4\\
1 & 2
\end{array}
\right)
\begin{array}{c}
3\\
1
\end{array}
$$

The larger of these two minima is 3, so the maximin criterion tells A that he should use strategy I in the expectation that B will use his strategy I and give A a gain of 3. We show the relevant element of the game matrix circled:

$$
\left(
\begin{array}{cc}
③ & 4\\
1 & 2
\end{array}
\right)
$$

Next let us consider the game from the point of view of player B. The elements in his gain matrix are the negatives of those in the gain matrix for A so when he looks at the 'minimum gain' from each of his possible strategies it is the largest number in each column of A's gain matrix which represents the worst that can happen to him. If B plays strategy I, then the minimum gain he stands to make is -3. If B plays strategy II, then the minimum gain he stands to make is -4. The larger of these two gains is -3, so the maximin criterion tells B that he should use strategy I in the expectation that A will use his strategy I, giving B a loss of 3 units. In setting out the solution to the problem from B's point of view it is usual to employ A's gain matrix and look at B's *worst losses* under his various strategies.

Then choose the strategy for which the largest loss is smallest. Thus the criterion becomes a *minimax* criterion on B's losses.

Writing B's worst losses at the bottoms of the appropriate columns of A's gain matrix:

$$\begin{pmatrix} 3 & 4 \\ 1 & 2 \end{pmatrix}$$
$$\quad 3 \quad 4$$

The smaller of these is 3, which we show circled in the gain matrix:

$$\begin{pmatrix} ③ & 4 \\ 1 & 2 \end{pmatrix}$$

In this case we see that having analysed the game from the point of view of each player in turn we have arrived at the same circled element in the gain matrix. The value 3 shown is both the maximum of A's minimum gains and the minimum of B's maximum losses. An element which represents both of these is called the saddle point of the game. By no means all games possess a saddle point, as we shall see in subsequent sections. Where a saddle point does exist, as here, the game is said to have a pure-strategy solution. In this case, for example, A should use always strategy I and never anything else. The saddle-point figure is called the *value* of the game. Each time the game is played with both players using their best strategy there will be a gain of 3 for A.

Exercise 4.1.1

Find the best strategy for each player and the value of the game for the following two-person zero-sum game:

$$\begin{array}{c} & & & B & \\ & & I & II & III & IV & V \\ & I & \begin{pmatrix} -2 & 0 & 0 & 5 & 3 \\ 3 & 2 & 1 & 2 & 2 \\ -4 & -3 & 0 & -2 & 6 \\ 5 & 3 & -4 & 2 & -6 \end{pmatrix} \\ A & \begin{array}{c} II \\ III \\ IV \end{array} \end{array}$$

4.2 Mixed-strategy Solutions — 2 × 2 Games

Consider the 3 x 3 gain matrix for player A shown below for a zero-sum two-person game:

$$\begin{array}{c} & & B & \\ & I & II & III \\ I & \begin{pmatrix} 5 & 4 & 7 \\ 3 & 6 & 8 \\ 2 & 1 & 5 \end{pmatrix} \\ A \quad \begin{array}{c} I \\ II \\ III \end{array} \end{array}$$

Let us try to approach this game by the maximin criterion explained in section 4.1. We write by each row the minimum gain for A under the strategy concerned and by each column the maximum loss for B under the strategy:

$$\begin{array}{ccccc} & I & II & III & \\ I & \begin{pmatrix} 5 & 4 & 7 \\ 3 & 6 & 8 \\ 2 & 1 & 5 \end{pmatrix} & 4 \\ II & & & & 3 \\ III & & & & 1 \\ & 5 & 6 & 8 & \end{array}$$

The best strategy for A is seen to be I because 4 is the largest of the minimum gains, while the best strategy for B is seen to be I because 5 is the smallest of the maximum losses. We show the relevant gain matrix elements circled:

$$
\begin{array}{c} & \begin{array}{ccc} \text{I} & \text{II} & \text{III} \end{array} \\ \begin{array}{c} \text{I} \\ \text{II} \\ \text{III} \end{array} & \begin{pmatrix} ⑤ & ④ & 7 \\ 3 & 6 & 8 \\ 2 & 1 & 5 \end{pmatrix} \end{array}
$$

Thus, looking at the game from the two different points of view has not led to the circling of the same figure. Therefore the game does not have a saddle point and there is not a pure-strategy solution. The maximin rule suggests that A should use strategy I, but this is in the expectation of B's using his strategy II. In fact, B will not always want to use strategy II because the same criterion suggests to him that I is his best strategy.

So we have to look for a mixed strategy for each player. By this is meant a set of proportions associated with the respective strategies such that the player's return is optimised (in the maximin sense) by playing the strategies in those proportions over many repetitions of the game.

The next point to note about the game being considered here is that player A should never use strategy III because, whatever B plays, he will do better with either I or II. Thus strategy III is *dominated* by the other two and is redundant. It is also the case for player B in this example that his strategy III is dominated.

Thus the 3 x 3 game can in this case be reduced to the following 2 x 2 game:

$$
\begin{array}{c} & \text{B} \\ & \begin{array}{cc} \text{I} & \text{II} \end{array} \\ \text{A} \begin{array}{c} \text{I} \\ \text{II} \end{array} & \begin{pmatrix} 5 & 4 \\ 3 & 6 \end{pmatrix} \end{array}
$$

In seeking a mixed strategy we are looking for the value q which is the proportion of times A should play I. It follows that the proportion of times A should then play II is $1 - q$.

The expected gain for A if B plays I is $5q + 3(1 - q) = 2q + 3$; and

the expected gain for A if B plays II is $4q + 6(1 - q) = -2q + 6$.

Let V be the value of the game to A (that is, the amount A will win per game if he plays his best strategy consistently and B plays the best possible counter-strategy against him) and then our problem is to find q so as to maximise V where

$$V \leqslant 2q + 3$$

and

$$V \leqslant -2q + 6.$$

These inequalities hold because the right-hand sides are what A will win per game against B's pure strategies I and II respectively. It follows that what he will win per game against B's best mixed strategy cannot exceed either of these.

Thus we want to consider for each value of q the smaller of the two functions $2q + 3$ and $-2q + 6$ and then choose the value of q for which the smaller function is as large as possible. How this can be done is seen by considering the graph in Fig. 4.1 showing the functions $V = 2p + 3$ and $V = -2q + 6$. Examining this graph, we see that the lower line has its highest point where the two lines intersect. This must be the case in every such problem. So in this case we see that the optimum value of q is where

$$2q + 3 = - 2q + 6,$$

i.e. where $4q = 3$ and hence $q = 0.75$.

Player A should use strategy I 75 per cent of the time and strategy II 25 per cent of the time.

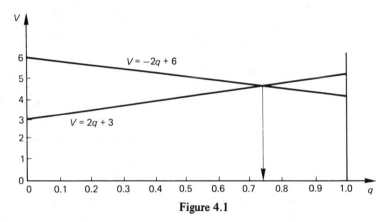

Figure 4.1

The same argument can be used to show that player B should use each of his strategies I and II 50 per cent of the time. You should check this. The value of the game for A is

$$V = 2 \times 0.75 + 3 = 1.5 + 3 = 4.5.$$

At this point we turn to the *general* 2 x 2 game and use the reasoning above to arrive at formulae for the best mixed strategies for A and B and for the value of the game in cases where there is no saddle point.

$$
\begin{array}{cc}
 & \text{B} \\
 & \begin{array}{cc} \text{I} & \text{II} \end{array} \\
\text{A} \ \begin{array}{c} \text{I} \\ \text{II} \end{array} & \begin{pmatrix} a & b \\ c & d \end{pmatrix}
\end{array}
$$

Suppose player A uses strategy I proportion q of the time. Then his expected gain if player B uses his strategy I is $aq + c(1 - q)$ and his expected gain if player B uses his strategy II is $bq + d(1 - q)$. As we saw in the example, the best value of q is the one for which these are equal.

Hence $aq + c - cq = bq + d - dq.$

So $q(a + d - b - c) = d - c.$

and $q = \dfrac{d - c}{a + d - b - c} .$

The value of the game to A is therefore

$$
a\left(\frac{d - c}{a + d - b - c}\right) + c\left(1 - \frac{d - c}{a + d - b - c}\right)
$$

$$
= \frac{ad - ac + c(a + \cancel{d} - b - \cancel{c} - \cancel{d} + \cancel{c})}{a + d - b - c} = \frac{ad - \cancel{ac} + \cancel{ac} - bc}{a + d - b - c} .
$$

The value of the game to A is $V = \dfrac{ad - bc}{a + d - b - c} .$

Suppose player B uses strategy I proportion r of the time.

Then his expected gain if A uses his strategy I is $-ar - b(1 - r)$; and

his expected gain if A uses his strategy II is $-cr - d(1 - r).$

59

The best value of r makes these equal so $-ar - b + br = -cr - d + dr$

Hence
$$r(a + d - b - c) = d - b$$

and
$$r = \frac{d - b}{a + d - b - c} \, .$$

The foregoing has considered the best strategies for both players in a two-person game played against a rational opponent whose objective is to maximise his own gain. If player A observes that B is not using his best strategy then he can modify his own behaviour so as to increase his expected gain. For instance, in the numerical example considered earlier, if A had observed that B employed strategy II more than the 50 per cent of the time he should employ it then A could have responded and increased his own gain by more frequent use of his own strategy II.

Exercise 4.2.1

Reduce as far as possible the gain matrix for A given below for a two-person zero-sum game.

Then find the best combination of strategies for each player and the value of the game.

$$
\begin{array}{c}
 & & \text{B} \\
 & & \begin{array}{ccc} \text{I} & \text{II} & \text{III} \end{array} \\
\text{A} \quad
\begin{array}{c} \text{I} \\ \text{II} \\ \text{III} \end{array}
&
\left(
\begin{array}{ccc}
-4 & 6 & 8 \\
-8 & -3 & 6 \\
2 & -3 & 4
\end{array}
\right)
\end{array}
$$

4.3 $2 \times n$ Games

Games without saddle points where one player has only two possible strategies can be solved by an extension of tne graphical approach explained in section 4.2.

Consider the following example where A has two strategies and B has three:

$$
\begin{array}{c}
 & & \text{B} \\
 & & \begin{array}{ccc} \text{I} & \text{II} & \text{III} \end{array} \\
\text{A} \quad
\begin{array}{c} \text{I} \\ \text{II} \end{array}
&
\left(
\begin{array}{ccc}
2 & 6 & 22 \\
16 & 10 & 4
\end{array}
\right)
\end{array}
$$

This game does not have a saddle point and no strategies are dominated. Since A has only two strategies, we can, from his point of view, approach this problem in exactly the same way as we tackled the 2×2 game in section 4.2. Suppose A plays strategy I proportion q of the time and strategy II proportion $1 - q$ of the time. Then:

his expected gain if B plays I is $2q + 16(1 - q) = 16 - 14q$;

his expected gain if B plays II is $6q + 10(1 - q) = 10 - 4q$;

his expected gain if B plays III is $22q + 4(1 - q) = 4 + 18q$;

So A's problem is to maximise his game value V subject to

$$V \leqslant 16 - 14q, \qquad V \leqslant 10 - 4q, \qquad V \leqslant 4 + 18q$$

by appropriate choice of q.

We can find the value of q which achieves this by plotting the functions
$$V = 16 - 14q, \qquad V = 10 - 4q, \qquad V = 4 + 18q$$
on a graph. See Fig. 4.2.

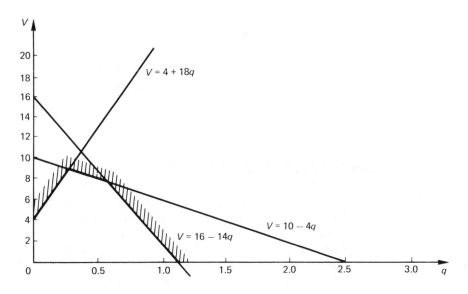

Figure 4.2

Hence A can maximise the value of the game by choosing the value of q corresponding to the highest point of the unshaded area. From Fig. 4.2 we can see that this highest point is at the intersection of the lines $V = 10 - 4q$ and $V = 4 + 18q$. The value of q for which this occurs is given by

$$10 - 4q = 4 + 18q.$$

Hence
$$22q = 6$$
$$q = \tfrac{3}{11}.$$

Thus A should use strategy I for $\tfrac{3}{11}$ of the time and strategy II for $\tfrac{8}{11}$.

The value of the game is then $10 - 4 \times \tfrac{3}{11} = 10 - \tfrac{12}{11} = \tfrac{98}{11}$.

We see also from Fig. 4.2 that B must use only strategies II and III and never strategy I if he is to minimise A's gain when the latter plays his best combination of strategies. This illustrates a feature of $2 \times n$ games, which is that the player with n strategies at his disposal will, in fact, be able to use only two of them in his best mix. This follows from the fact that the combination his opponent will use is at the intersection of lines corresponding to two strategies. Introducing any strategies other than these two will give the opponent a greater gain than necessary.

Having discovered that B must use strategies II and III, we can use the formula obtained in section 4.2 to find the proportion of the time he must use II. It is

$$r = \frac{4 - 22}{6 + 4 - 22 - 10} = \frac{-18}{-22} = \frac{9}{11}.$$

B should use strategy II for $\tfrac{9}{11}$ of the time and strategy III for $\tfrac{2}{11}$.

The method of this section can be applied equally well to games where B has the two strategies and A has n strategies.

Find for the game having the gain matrix for A shown below the best combination of strategies to be adopted by each player and the value of the game.

$$
\begin{array}{cc}
 & \text{B} \\
 & \begin{array}{cc} \text{I} & \text{II} \end{array} \\
\text{A}\quad\begin{array}{c} \text{I} \\ \text{II} \\ \text{III} \\ \text{IV} \\ \text{V} \end{array} &
\left(\begin{array}{cc}
9 & -5 \\
5 & 0 \\
4 & 4 \\
1 & 6 \\
0 & 10
\end{array}\right)
\end{array}
$$

4.4   A General Method of Solution

So far we have considered pure strategy games, games which can be reduced to 2×2 form and games which can be reduced to $2 \times n$ form. We turn now to the general form of game-theory problem where there is no saddle point and where neither player can be reduced by dominance to just two strategies. We shall explain the method for this problem in terms of the smallest of its kind, which is a 3×3 game. However, the principles carry over in their entirety to larger games with no additional theory being needed.

Basically, the general game-theory problem can be solved as a linear programming problem by the methods explained in Chapter 2. The only additional matters we have to concern ourselves with here are the method for formulating the linear programming problem and the interpretation of its solution. As was emphasised in Chapter 2, these are the most important aspects of any linear programming problem, as the mechanics of the simplex method can be readily carried out on a computer. (For any problem larger than 3×3, a computer would almost always be used.) The application of linear programming to game-theory problems also provides an interesting example of the use of the dual method, as the problem seen from the point of view of player A is the dual of the problem seen from the point of view of player B.

To illustrate the method consider the game having the following gain matrix for player A:

$$
\begin{array}{cc}
 & \text{B} \\
 & \begin{array}{ccc} \text{I} & \text{II} & \text{III} \end{array} \\
\text{A}\quad\begin{array}{c} \text{I} \\ \text{II} \\ \text{III} \end{array} &
\left(\begin{array}{ccc}
0 & -3 & -1 \\
-2 & 0 & 1 \\
-0.5 & 0.5 & -1
\end{array}\right)
\end{array}
$$

This game has no saddle point and no strategies are dominated. Let the value of the game to A be V. Suppose B's optimum result is obtained by using strategies I, II and III in proportions r_1, r_2 and r_3 respectively.

For the sake of convenience we can make all the elements in the gain matrix positive by adding any constant to all of them. If in this case we add 5 to each element we obtain the gain matrix shown below and the value of this new game is v where $v = V + 5$:

$$
\begin{array}{cc}
 & \text{B} \\
 & \begin{array}{ccc} \text{I} & \text{II} & \text{III} \end{array} \\
\text{A}\quad\begin{array}{c} \text{I} \\ \text{II} \\ \text{III} \end{array} &
\left(\begin{array}{ccc}
5 & 2 & 4 \\
3 & 5 & 6 \\
4.5 & 5.5 & 4
\end{array}\right)
\end{array}
$$

B is seeking to minimise v. If A plays his strategy I, then the expected loss sustained by B is

$$5r_1 + 2r_2 + 4r_3.$$

Since the value of the game is v, the choice of r_1, r_2 and r_3 must be such as to ensure that B does not lose more than v when A plays his strategy I.

Thus $\qquad\qquad\qquad\qquad 5r_1 + 2r_2 + 4r_3 \leqslant v.$

Similarly for the other A strategies:

$$3r_1 + 5r_2 + 6r_3 \leqslant v$$
$$4.5r_1 + 5.5r_2 + 4r_3 \leqslant v,$$

where $\qquad\qquad\qquad r_1 \geqslant 0, \qquad r_2 \geqslant 0, \qquad r_3 \geqslant 0$

and $\qquad\qquad\qquad\qquad r_1 + r_2 + r_3 = 1,$

since r_1, r_2 and r_3 are proportions.

Dividing everywhere by v and writing $R_1 = \dfrac{r_1}{v}$, $R_2 = \dfrac{r_2}{v}$ and $R_3 = \dfrac{r_3}{v}$, this problem can be restated as follows:

$$5R_1 + 2R_2 + 4R_3 \leqslant 1$$
$$3R_1 + 5R_2 + 6R_3 \leqslant 1$$
$$4.5R_1 + 5.5R_2 + 4R_3 \leqslant 1,$$
$$R_1 \geqslant 0, \qquad R_2 \geqslant 0, \qquad R_3 \geqslant 0,$$
$$R_1 + R_2 + R_3 = \frac{1}{v}.$$

The objective is to minimise v, which means maximising $\dfrac{1}{v}$. This is a routine linear programming problem which can be solved by the simplex method. Introducing slacks and writing the problem in standard form we have:

$$5R_1 + 2R_2 + 4R_3 + S_1 = 1$$
$$3R_1 + 5R_2 + 6R_3 + S_2 = 1$$
$$4.5R_1 + 5.5R_2 + 4R_3 + S_3 = 1,$$
$$R_1 \geqslant 0, \qquad R_2 \geqslant 0, \qquad R_3 \geqslant 0, \qquad S_1 \geqslant 0, \qquad S_2 \geqslant 0, \qquad S_3 \geqslant 0,$$
$$\frac{1}{v} - R_1 - R_2 - R_3 = 0.$$

The simplex tableaux for solving this problem are shown in Table 4.1 overleaf.

We obtain $R_1 = \frac{14}{118}$, $R_2 = \frac{2}{118}$, $R_3 = \frac{11}{118}$, giving $\dfrac{1}{v} = \frac{27}{118}$.

Hence $v = \frac{118}{27}$ while $r_1 = R_1 v = \frac{14}{27}$, $r_2 = R_2 v = \frac{2}{27}$, $r_3 = R_3 v = \frac{11}{27}$.

So the value of the original game is $V = v - 5 = \frac{118}{27} - 5 = -\frac{17}{27}$.

The optimum policy for B is to play strategy I on $\frac{14}{27}$ of occasions, strategy II on $\frac{2}{27}$ of occasions and strategy III on $\frac{11}{27}$ of occasions.

Next, let us consider the formulation of the problem from the point of view of player A.

Let the proportions of times when A uses strategies I, II and III be q_1, q_2 and q_3 respectively. Now v, the value of the game to A, cannot be greater than his expected gain under each of B's three strategies.

Table 4.1

Basic	R_1	R_2	R_3	S_1	S_2	S_3	Values
S_1	5*	2	4	1	0	0	1
S_2	3	5	6	0	1	0	1
S_3	4.5	5.5	4	0	0	1	1
$\dfrac{1}{v}$	-1	-1	-1	0	0	0	0
R_1	1	0.4	0.8	0.2	0	0	0.2
S_2	0	3.8	3.6	-0.6	1	0	0.4
S_3	0	3.7*	0.4	-0.9	0	1	0.1
$\dfrac{1}{v}$	0	-0.6	-0.2	0.2	0	0	0.2
R_1	1	0	$\frac{28}{37}$	$\frac{11}{37}$	0	$-\frac{4}{37}$	$\frac{7}{37}$
S_2	0	0	$\frac{118}{37}$*	$\frac{12}{37}$	1	$-\frac{38}{37}$	$\frac{11}{37}$
R_2	0	1	$\frac{4}{37}$	$-\frac{9}{37}$	0	$\frac{10}{37}$	$\frac{1}{37}$
$\dfrac{1}{v}$	0	0	$-\frac{5}{37}$	$\frac{2}{37}$	0	$\frac{6}{37}$	$\frac{8}{37}$
R_1	1	0	0	$\frac{26}{118}$	$-\frac{28}{118}$	$\frac{16}{118}$	$\frac{14}{118}$
R_3	0	0	1	$\frac{12}{118}$	$\frac{37}{118}$	$-\frac{38}{118}$	$\frac{11}{118}$
R_2	0	1	0	$-\frac{30}{118}$	$-\frac{4}{118}$	$\frac{36}{118}$	$\frac{2}{118}$
$\dfrac{1}{v}$	0	0	0	$\frac{8}{118}$	$\frac{5}{118}$	$\frac{14}{118}$	$\frac{27}{118}$

Hence we have
$$5q_1 + 3q_2 + 4.5q_3 \geqslant v$$
$$2q_1 + 5q_2 + 5.5q_3 \geqslant v$$
$$4q_1 + 6q_2 + 4q_3 \geqslant v$$

where
$$q_1 \geqslant 0, \qquad q_2 \geqslant 0, \qquad q_3 \geqslant 0$$
$$q_1 + q_2 + q_3 = 1$$

and v is to be maximised.

Dividing everywhere by v and writing $Q_1 = \dfrac{q_1}{v}$, $Q_2 = \dfrac{q_2}{v}$ and $Q_3 = \dfrac{q_3}{v}$,

we have
$$5Q_1 + 3Q_2 + 4.5Q_3 \geqslant 1$$
$$2Q_1 + 5Q_2 + 5.5Q_3 \geqslant 1$$
$$4Q_1 + 6Q_2 + 4Q_3 \geqslant 1$$
$$Q_1 \geqslant 0, \qquad Q_2 \geqslant 0, \qquad Q_3 \geqslant 0$$
$$Q_1 + Q_2 + Q_3 = \frac{1}{v}$$

The objective is to maximise v, which means minimising $\dfrac{1}{v}$. This is the dual of the linear programming problem which we had above when the problem was looked at from B's point of view.

Inserting slacks and writing the problem in standard form, we have the following:

$$5Q_1 + 3Q_2 + 4.5Q_3 - t_1 = 1$$
$$2Q_1 + 5Q_2 + 5.5Q_3 - t_2 = 1$$
$$4Q_1 + 6Q_2 + 4Q_3 \quad - t_3 = 1,$$

$$Q_1 \geqslant 0, \qquad Q_2 \geqslant 0, \qquad Q_3 \geqslant 0, \qquad t_1 \geqslant 0, \qquad t_2 \geqslant 0, \qquad t_3 \geqslant 0,$$

$$\frac{1}{v} = Q_1 - Q_2 - Q_3 = 0.$$

The correspondence between variables in the two problems is:

$$R_1 \quad R_2 \quad R_3 \quad S_1 \quad S_2 \quad S_3$$
$$t_1 \quad t_2 \quad t_3 \quad Q_1 \quad Q_2 \quad Q_3.$$

Since this linear programming problem is the dual of the one already considered, we can find the proportions of times that A should use strategies I, II and III by reading off the objective-row coefficients for the corresponding variables in the solution tableau for the earlier problem.

We find $Q_1 = \frac{8}{118}, Q_2 = \frac{5}{118}, Q_3 = \frac{14}{118}$, giving $\frac{1}{v} = \frac{27}{118}$.

Hence $v = \frac{118}{27}$ and we have $q_1 = Q_1 v = \frac{8}{27}, q_2 = Q_2 v = \frac{5}{27}, q_3 = Q_3 v = \frac{14}{27}$.

Player A should use strategy I on $\frac{8}{27}$ of occasions, strategy II on $\frac{5}{27}$ of occasions and strategy III on $\frac{14}{27}$ of occasions.

Exercise 4.4.1

In a two-person, zero-sum game the gain matrix for player A is as follows:

$$
\begin{array}{c}
 & & \text{B} \\
 & & \begin{array}{ccc} \text{I} & \text{II} & \text{III} \end{array} \\
\text{A} \begin{array}{c} \text{I} \\ \text{II} \\ \text{III} \end{array} & & \left(\begin{array}{ccc} -1 & -2 & 2 \\ 5 & 4 & -3 \\ -4 & 6 & -2 \end{array} \right)
\end{array}
$$

Use linear programming to find the optimal proportions for A and B respectively to use their strategies, and find also the value of the game.

Further Exercises

4.1 For the two-person zero-sum game represented by the following gain matrix for player A, find the best strategy for each player and the value of the game:

$$
\begin{array}{c}
 & & \text{B} \\
 & & \begin{array}{ccc} \text{I} & \text{II} & \text{III} \end{array} \\
\text{A} \begin{array}{c} \text{I} \\ \text{II} \end{array} & & \left(\begin{array}{ccc} -10 & -3 & 0.5 \\ -2 & 1 & 0 \end{array} \right)
\end{array}
$$

4.2 The Scote and Sawfaye supermarkets face each other across the high street of Sloymee and competition between them for customers is considerable. The main methods used by both stores are price cutting and intensive local advertising. Each uses one or other of these on a weekly basis decided in advance. In weeks when both stores use the same method it has been found that Sawfaye net profit for the week increases by £1000 while Scote net profit decreases by this amount.

However, if Sawfaye decide on price cutting when Scote have a major advertising campaign then Scote profits increase by £3000 at the expense of Sawfaye, while if the reverse combination of policies arises then Scote profits increase by £2000 at the expense of Sawfaye. Find the best strategy for each store to adopt and the average weekly gain in profit for Scote if each store uses its best strategy consistently.

4.3   Road and rail operators on a particular major passenger route are operating Sunday press campaigns to attract passengers. Each week's advertising by each operator emphasises one particular advantage of that mode of travel. The rail operator uses speed and comfort while the road operator also uses these but in addition uses some advertisements emphasising the cost advantage of road travel.

Experience so far in the campaign suggests that in weeks when the rail advertisement emphasises speed then rail gains 2000 passengers from road if road concentrates on speed and gains 4000 from road if road concentrates on comfort, but loses 5000 to road if road concentrates on cost. On the other hand, if the rail advertisement concentrates on comfort, then rail will gain 1000 passengers from road if road concentrates on speed, lose 6000 to road if road concentrates on comfort and lose 1000 to road if road concentrates on cost.

Find the best mixture of advertisements which should be used by each operator and the average number of passengers gained per week by road if each operator uses his best strategy.

4.4   An oil company negotiating drilling rights with a developing country has three possible strategies. The country also has three strategies and the payoff matrix showing gains for the company in millions of pounds is as follows:

$$\begin{array}{c}\text{Country}\\\begin{array}{ccc}\text{I} & \text{II} & \text{III}\end{array}\\\text{Company}\quad\begin{array}{c}\text{I}\\\text{II}\\\text{III}\end{array}\begin{pmatrix}8 & 4 & 2\\2 & 8 & 4\\2 & 1 & 8\end{pmatrix}\end{array}$$

Find   (a) the best combination of strategies for the country;
       (b) the best combination of strategies for the company;
       (c) the value of the game.

5 Network Analysis

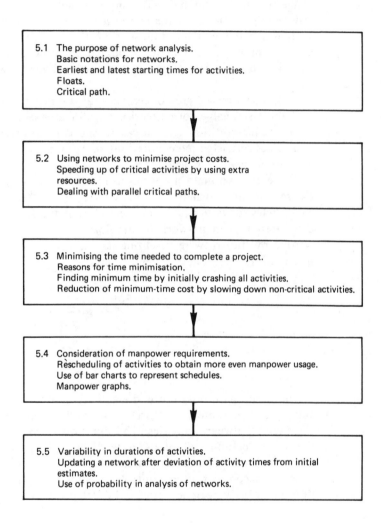

5.1 The purpose of network analysis.
Basic notations for networks.
Earliest and latest starting times for activities.
Floats.
Critical path.

5.2 Using networks to minimise project costs.
Speeding up of critical activities by using extra resources.
Dealing with parallel critical paths.

5.3 Minimising the time needed to complete a project.
Reasons for time minimisation.
Finding minimum time by initially crashing all activities.
Reduction of minimum-time cost by slowing down non-critical activities.

5.4 Consideration of manpower requirements.
Rescheduling of activities to obtain more even manpower usage.
Use of bar charts to represent schedules.
Manpower graphs.

5.5 Variability in durations of activities.
Updating a network after deviation of activity times from initial estimates.
Use of probability in analysis of networks.

5.1 Introduction and Notations

Network analysis is a powerful tool in the management of projects, particularly those consisting of large numbers of activities related in complex ways. Drawing a network provides a visual display of the relationships concerned and a way of answering various questions about the project. The method has application in a very wide variety of fields including construction, engineering, manufacturing and the management of administrative systems. Examples of the kinds of questions for which it facilitates answers are:

(a) Which are the activities in the project which determine the time needed for its completion?

(b) Is it financially desirable to allocate additional resources to some activities in order to complete the project more quickly?

(c) Where are the peaks of manpower usage in the project, and can they be levelled out by delaying the start of some activities?

There exist a number of computer systems for handling network analysis and recent computing developments such as expanded on-line terminal access to main-frame computers and the microcomputer explosion have been particularly relevant. It is now possible to have a computer terminal or a microcomputer in a location such as a building site so that data on the current state of a project can be input and the network immediately updated to show such things as which activities have become critical and where the new peak-manpower requirements are likely to be.

In this section we are concerned with the notations for network diagrams and with the basic analysis of networks. Then in later sections we will look at questions of allocating additional resources to speed up projects, manpower implications and situations where the durations of activities are uncertain and probabilities need to be taken into account.

There are two main notations used in network diagrams. The first is the *arrow diagram* notation where each activity is represented by a line (or *arrow*) joining two circles (or *nodes*). The nodes represent transitions between activities, which are referred to in network terminology as *events*. The duration of an activity is written by the arrow representing it. Fig. 5.1 shows an event x in arrow diagram notation, the duration of x being 5 days.

Figure 5.1

The other main notation is the activity-on-node (or AON) diagram. Here each activity is represented by a circle and the lines represent the events which are the transitions between activities. The duration of an activity is written by each of the arrows coming out of its node. Figure 5.2 shows event x in AON diagram notation, assuming it to have three successors.

We next consider an example which illustrates the use of both the above notations in the drawing of networks and which involves the basic analysis of a network.

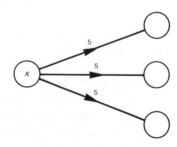

Figure 5.2

Example 5.1.1

There are at least two different diagrammatic representations of networks, one in which the activity is represented by the line joining two nodes (arrow diagram) and the other in which the activity is represented by the node itself (AON).

The information shown in Table 5.1 on the project upon which you have been asked to advise has been collected.

Table 5.1

Activity	Immediate predecessors	Estimated duration (days)	Normal cost per day	Days that could be 'saved'	Cost per day of saving 1 day
a	b	2	£50	1	£20
b	—	3	60	1	60
c	b	4	70	2	30
r	c, a	2	40	—	—
p	r	3	30	1	40
n	p	1	75	—	—
q	b	15	20	6	70
m	q, n	3	50	1	90

You are required to:

(a) draw the arrow diagram clearly, indicating the meaning of any notation you have used and including the duration of each activity, the earliest and latest starting times;

(b) draw the activity-on-node (AON) diagram clearly, explaining any symbols you have used and including the duration of each activity, plus the earliest and latest starting times;

(c) state the critical activities;

(d) calculate and state the duration at normal cost and the total cost of the project on the normal cost-basis;

(e) calculate the minimum cost of completing the project in 16 days.

(ICMA Part IV)

ANSWER

(a) The arrow diagram is shown in Fig. 5.3. Note the broken line joining the nodes at the ends of activities *a* and *c*. This is called a dummy activity and has

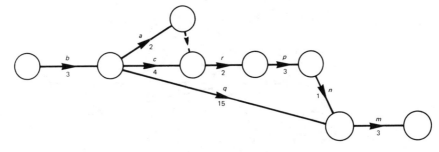

Figure 5.3

zero duration. It is needed here because activities *a* and *c* have a common predecessor in *b* and a common successor in *r*. Hence they need to start at the same node and to end at the same node. This is not geometrically possible, so they are given different end-nodes which are then linked by the dummy activity which indicates that *r* cannot begin until *c* and the dummy (and hence *a*) are completed.

As well as being asked to draw the diagram here we are required to find the earliest and latest starting times for the activities. The first step towards doing this is to number the nodes if, as here, they do not have any numbers. (In some situations, as we shall see in later examples, activities in an arrow diagram are *defined* in terms of the numbers of the nodes at their ends. In such cases the node-numbering step would not be required.) The numbering begins by giving the start node number 1 and then goes from left to right. At each step no node can be given a number if it has an arrow coming into it from an unnumbered node. For this example the procedure leads to the unique numbering shown in Fig. 5.4, but in general the numbering need not be unique.

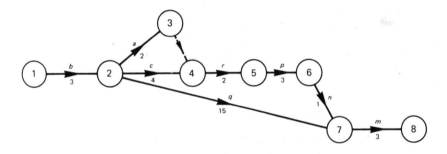

Figure 5.4

Having numbered the nodes, we can find the earliest starting times by performing a *forward pass* through the system, that is to say a working through the nodes in numerical order, writing by each node the earliest time that activities beginning there can start. A variety of ways exists for writing down this time. We shall adopt the notation which puts the earliest start time in a box □ by the node concerned. Figure 5.5 shows the arrow diagram with the earliest starting times inserted. Note that where there is more than one arrow coming into a node it is the *largest* accumulated value which goes in the box on that node as *all* activities ending on that node must be completed before those beginning there can start. This applies at nodes 4 and 7 in the example. We note that the total time needed to complete the project here is 21 days.

Next, in order to find the latest starting times we perform a *backward pass* through the system, that is to say a working through the nodes in reverse

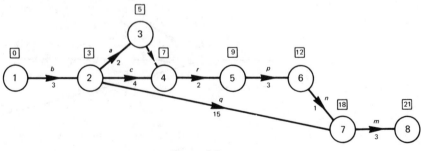

Figure 5.5

numerical order, writing by each node the latest time that the activities beginning there can start if completion of the project is to be achieved in the time found on the forward pass. In the case of the example this means that we start with 21 on node 8 and work backward through the nodes, subtracting the durations of the activities. Again there are various notations for writing down the latest starting times. We shall use the notation which puts the latest starting time in a triangle △ by the node concerned.

Figure 5.6 shows the arrow diagram with the latest starting times inserted.

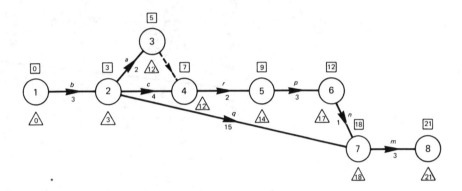

Figure 5.6

Note that where there is more than one arrow emerging from a node, as at node 2 in the example, it is the *smallest* value which goes in a triangle. Thus what is recorded is the latest starting time of the most urgent activity beginning at that node. It may be possible for some of the other activities beginning there to start later. For instance at node 2 in the example it is q which must start no later than time 3. The start of c could be delayed until time 8 and the start of a until time 10.

(b) The AON diagram is shown as Fig. 5.7. No dummy activities are needed in an AON diagram. However, something which is necessary that we did not see in the arrow diagram is a finish node in order to show the duration of the last activity or activities.

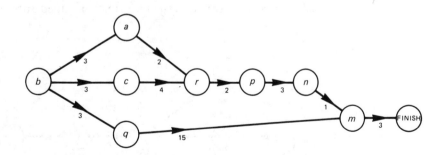

Figure 5.7

To find the earliest and latest starting times we go through exactly the same procedure as for the arrow diagram. We number the nodes according to the rule described earlier, and we carry out a forward pass entering the earliest starting times in boxes and then a backward pass entering the latest starting times in triangles. The result of doing all this for the AON diagram in this example is shown in Fig. 5.8.

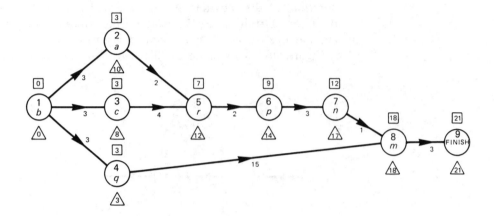

Figure 5.8

In this diagram the latest starting time for every individual activity is shown by the figure in the triangle on its node.

(c) Having found the earliest and latest starting times for the activities we can find how much time there is to spare on each by looking at the difference between the two. This time that can be lost without completion of the project being delayed is called the *float* of the activity concerned. In the AON diagram where we have the earliest and latest starting times explicity on each node the calculation is very simple:

---

float of an activity in AON diagram = figure on its $\triangle$ node — figure on its $\square$ node.

Activities which have float zero are called critical activities. If one of these is delayed at all, then completion of the whole project will be held up. Figure 5.9 shows the AON diagram with floats included at the bottoms of the nodes.

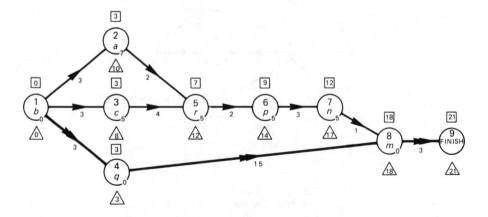

Figure 5.9

Also, in accordance with standard practice, the arrows joining the nodes for the critical activities are shown in heavy print with double arrow heads. These arrows form what is called the critical path through the network. The critical activities here are b, q and m.

In the arrow diagram we do not have a latest starting time for every activity. More strictly, we see that the numbers in the triangles can be interpreted as latest finishing times for the activities ending on the node. Hence the latest starting time for an activity can be found by taking the number in the triangle on its termination node and subtracting its duration. Thus we can say that:

$$\text{float of an activity in arrow diagram} = \overset{\triangle}{\underset{\text{end node}}{\text{figure on its}}} - \underset{\text{the activity}}{\text{duration of}} - \overset{\square}{\underset{\text{start node}}{\text{figure on its}}}.$$

Figure 5.10 shows the arrow diagram with the floats included on the arrows. Again, the critical path is shown in heavy print with double arrow heads and we see that the critical activities are b, q and m.

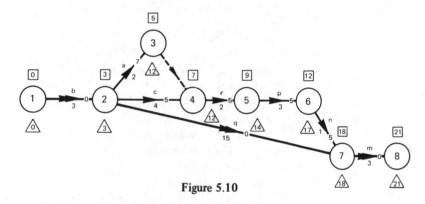

Figure 5.10

(d) We see from our various diagrams that the duration of the project at normal cost is 21 days.

The total cost is

$$2 \times £50 + 3 \times £60 + 4 \times £70 + 2 \times £40 + 3 \times £30 + 1 \times £75 + 15 \times £20 + 3 \times £50$$
$$= £(100 + 180 + 280 + 80 + 90 + 75 + 300 + 150)$$
$$= £1255.$$

(e) In this last part of the question we approach the topic which will concern us in the next two sections, namely speeding up a project by providing additional resources for some of the activities. The costs of such resources are described here as a cost of saving one day. This expression always means cost *additional to total normal cost*. The normal cost must not be reduced by the days saved.

In this particular case we are asked to reduce to 16 days at the least possible additional cost. The first and essential thing to note is that only critical activities need be considered for speeding up. The others have time to spare already and there is no point in trying to do them faster. So we must consider b, q and m.

As we want to speed up as cheaply as possible we should choose first the one cheapest to speed up. This is b at £60 per day. So first save the one available day on b. This cuts total project time to 20 days and does not affect any floats as b is completed before any other activities begin.

The next cheapest critical activity to speed up is q at £70 per day. This has 6 days available for saving so reduce it by 4 to achieve the required 16 days for the project. An effect of speeding up q by 4 days in this way is to reduce the floats on a, c, r, p and n by 4 days because there are now 4 days less available to complete the work between nodes 2 and 7 in the arrow diagram.

The required minimum cost of completing in 16 days is thus seen to be

$$£1255 + £60 + 4 \times £70 = £1255 + £60 + £280 = £1255 + £340$$
$$= £1595.$$

Exercise 5.1.1

The major jobs to be completed in building a particular type of house, with their necessary predecessors and estimated duration times, are listed below:

Job	Description	Immediate predecessors	Duration in days
1	Start: clear site and level	–	2
2	Pour slab	1	1
3	Erect wooden wall frame	2	2
4	Erect roof	3	3
5	Fasten wall sheeting	4	2
6	Plaster inside walls	5	2
7	Install and timber window and door frames	3	2
8	Finish carpentry	6, 7	6
9	Sand, stain and varnish wood panelling	8	3
10	Install baths and fittings	9	1
11	Lay bathroom tiles	10	2
12	Install remaining plumbing	11	1
13	Lay general flooring (wood and vinyl)	12	2
14	Install hot water heater	5	1
15	Lay brickwork of exterior walls	4	3
16	Tile roof	3	2
17	Attach roof guttering and downspouts	15, 16	2
18	Paint exterior fittings	17	2
19	Insulate attic	6, 15	1
20	Make paths and driveway	15	1
21	Landscape garden	20	1
22	Install electrical outlets, switches, lighting fixtures	14	1
23	Final test of electrical system	22	1
24	Clean up inside	13, 18, 19, 23	1
25	Clean up outside: finish	21, 24	1

You are required to:

(a) *Either:* draw an activity-on-node diagram, labelling each node;
    Or: draw an arrow diagram, including necessary dummy activities;
(b) calculate, using the diagram drawn in answer to (a) the earliest starting and latest starting times;
(c) identify the critical path and state the minimum duration of the project.

(ICMA Part IV)

5.2 Completion of Projects at Minimum Cost

In part (e) of example 5.1.1 we approached the problem of how to use network analysis to speed up the completion of a project. Usually the purpose of speeding up is to save money on project overheads, to avoid penalty clauses in contracts or, sometimes, to earn bonuses for early completion. In this section we shall consider the process of speeding up in more detail. The complication which arises, which did not emerge in example 5.1.1, is that as critical activities are speeded up more and more, then other activities also become critical and further speeding up of the project requires time to be saved on *all* critical paths. We explain the procedure using the following example.

Example 5.2.1

A local authority intends to carry out a capital project using direct labour. Table 5.2 shows for each activity needed to complete the project the normal time, the shortest time in which the activity can be completed and the cost per day for reducing the time of each activity. The cost of reduction remains the same per day irrespective of the number of days involved.

Table 5.2

Activity	Normal time (days)	Shortest time (days)	Cost of reduction per day
1–2	6	4	£80
1–3	8	4	90
1–4	5	3	30
2–4	3	3	–
2–5	5	3	40
3–6	12	8	200
4–6	8	5	50
5–6	6	6	–

The cost of completing the eight activities in normal time is £5800, excluding site overhead. The overhead cost of general site activities is £160 per day.

You are required to:

calculate the normal duration of the project, its cost and the critical path;
calculate and plot on a graph the cost/time function for the project and state:

(a) the lowest cost and associated time;
(b) the shortest time and the associated cost.

(*ICMA Prof 1*)

ANSWER

The way the activities are described in this question suggests that we use an arrow diagram. The arrow diagram for normal completion, including earliest and latest starting times, floats and critical path, is shown in Fig. 5.11.

The normal duration of the project is seen to be 20 days and the critical activities are 1–3 and 3–6. The cost of completing the project at normal speed is £5800 + 20 × £160 = £9000. Of the two critical activities the cheaper to speed up is 1–3 at £90 per day. Saving 3 days on 1–3 reduces the total project time to 17 days.

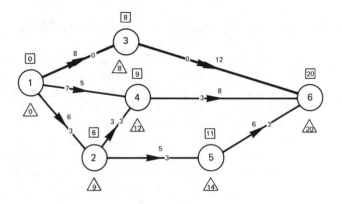

Figure 5.11

New total cost = original cost − overhead for 3 days + 3 days' saving on 1–3
$$= £(9000 − 3 × 160 + 3 × 90) = £(9000 − 480 + 270) = £8790.$$

All activities are now critical except 1–4 on which the float has been reduced to 4 days. This has happened because the total time available to get from node 1 to node 6 on all paths has been reduced by 3 days.

For purposes of explanation we have redrawn the network after this 3-day reduction in 1–3 as Fig. 5.12. However, for dealing with network problems it is important that you should develop by practice the facility to keep track of what is happening to the floats as speeding up takes place without the need to go through the time-consuming procedure of redrawing the network any more than is absolutely necessary.

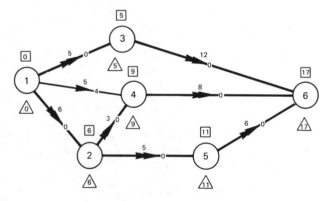

Figure 5.12

By considering Fig. 5.12 we see that there is no point in just saving the one remaining day available on 1–3. This will not reduce the total project time below 17 days, and thereby save any money, because paths 1–2–4–6 and 1–2–5–6 will both still require 17 days. In order to achieve any further saving it is necessary to reduce the time along *all critical paths simultaneously*.

The cheapest way this can be done in the example is to save one day on 1–3 and 1–2 simultaneously. This is adequate because 1–2 is part of two critical paths and so saving on these two activities reduces all three critical paths. The total time for the project is reduced to 16 days. The cost of this saving is £90 + £80 = £170.

Since this is the cheapest saving that can be made and it costs more than the £160 overhead saved, we see that 17 days at £8790 is the minimum cost completion. All further time savings made in this case will increase total cost. New total cost = £8790 − £160 + £170 = £8800.

All activities are critical except 1-4, on which the float has been reduced to 3 days. Activity 1-3 is now reduced to its minimum duration of 4 days so any further time reductions must involve reducing 3-6 in order to shorten the time on the critical path 1-3-6. Activity 1-2 still has one day that can be saved, so the cheapest reduction is using 3-6 and 1-2, which reduces total time to 15 days.

The cost of this saving is £200 + £80 = £280.

So new total cost = £8800 − £160 + £280 = £8920.

All activities are critical except 1-4, on which the float has been reduced to 2 days. Activity 1-2 is now reduced to its minimum time and no reductions at all are possible on 2-4 and 5-6. Hence the only remaining combination of activities which can be reduced is 3-6 with 4-6 and 2-5. It is possible to save 2 days on this combination before 2-5 is reduced to its minimum time of 3 days. This reduces the total time to 13 days.

The cost of this saving is

$$2 \times (£200 + £50 + £40) = 2 \times £290 = £580.$$

So the new total cost is

$$£8920 − 2 \times £160 + £580 = £8920 − £320 + £580 = £9180.$$

All activities are now critical.

This time of 13 days, with associated cost of £9180, is the minimum-time completion of the project because no further time reduction is possible on the critical path 1-2-5-6.

For the purpose of plotting the required cost/time graph we summarise in Table 5.3 the costs and durations of the project normally and after the various time reductions described.

Table 5.3

Cost (£)	Duration (days)
9000	20
8790	17
8800	16
8920	15
9180	13

The cost/time graph is shown as Fig. 5.13.

The lowest point of the graph indicates the minimum-cost completion at £8790 in 17 days.

The leftmost point of the graph indicates the minimum-time completion in 13 days with an associated cost of £9180.

Finally in this section, we give a further cost-minimisation example which uses the AON notation and introduces another consideration we must bear in mind when we are speeding up a project to reduce costs.

Example 5.2.2

The information given in Table 5.4 relates to a construction project for which your company is about to sign a contract.

Seven activities are necessary and the normal duration, cost, crash duration and crash cost have been derived from the best available sources.

Each activity may be reduced to the crash duration in weekly stages at a pro-rata cost. There is a fixed cost of £500 per week.

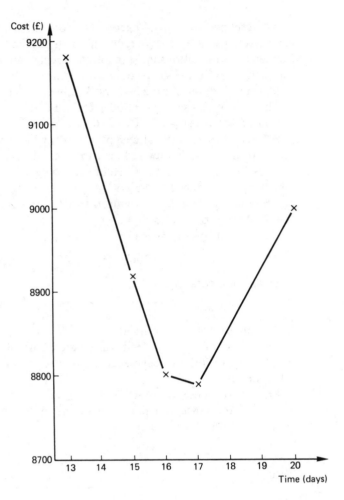

Figure 5.13

Table 5.4

Activity	Preceding activity	Duration in weeks		Direct cost (£)	
		Normal	Crash	Normal	Crash
a	—	15	12	4500	5250
b	—	19	14	4000	4500
c	—	9	5	2500	4500
d	a	6	5	1700	1940
e	a	14	9	4300	5350
f	b, d	9	6	2600	3440
g	c	8	3	1800	3400

You are required to:

(a) draw, clearly labelled, a network and indicate the notation pattern used;
(b) indicate the critical path and state the normal duration and cost;
(c) calculate the minimum total cost, showing clearly your workings, and the revised duration and cost for each activity.

(ICMA Part IV)

(a) Figure 5.14 shows the AON diagram for this project with earliest and latest starting times, floats and critical path indicated. Note that it is normal practice to have a unique starting mode for a network so where, as here, several activities have no predecessors we include a start node as shown.

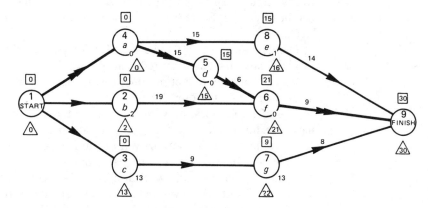

Figure 5.14

(b) The critical path is the one involving activities a, d and f. Normal duration is 30 weeks.

The normal cost is:

$$£(4500 + 4000 + 2500 + 1700 + 4300 + 2600 + 1800 + 30 \times 500) = £36\,400.$$

(c) In order to see which activities it is best to speed up at any point it is sensible, with the data given here, to draw up a table (see Table 5.5).

Table 5.5

Activity	Normal duration (weeks)	Crash duration (weeks)	Possible saving (weeks)	Normal cost (£)	Crash cost (£)	Cost of crashing (£)	Cost per week saved (£)
a	15	12	3	4500	5250	750	250
b	19	14	5	4000	4500	500	100
c	9	5	4	2500	4500	2000	500
d	6	5	1	1700	1940	240	240
e	14	9	5	4300	5350	1050	210
f	9	6	3	2600	3440	840	280
g	8	3	5	1800	3400	1600	320

The cheapest of the three critical activities to speed up is d, by its one available week at £240. This reduces total time to 29 weeks.

The new total cost is £$(36\,400 - 500 + 240) = £36140$.

Activity e is now critical. The float on b is reduced to one week. The floats on c and g are reduced to 12 weeks. The next-cheapest saving that can be made is 1 week on a at £250. This reduces total time to 28 weeks.

The new total cost is £$(36\,140 - 500 + 250) = £35\,890$.

Activity b is now critical. The floats on c and g are reduced to 11 weeks. There are now three critical paths through the network and the cheapest saving that can be made is to cut 2 weeks from a (which reduces two of the critical paths) and from *b*. The total cost of this is 2 × (£250 + £100) = £700. This reduces total time to 26 weeks.

The new total cost is £(35 890 − 1000 + 700) = £35 590.

The floats on *c* and *g* are reduced to 9 weeks.

Activities *a* and *d* are now at crash duration so the only combination still available that will reduce all three critical paths is *e* and *f*. The weekly cost of this is £210 + £280 = £490 so it is worthwhile as this is still less than the £500 overhead charge. So reduce *e* and *f* by 3 weeks. This reduces total time to 23 weeks.

The new total cost is £(35 590 − 1500 + 1470) = £35 560.

The floats on *c* and *g* are reduced to 6 weeks.

No further time-reductions are possible because activities *a*, *d* and *f* are now all at their minimum durations.

This example does, however, raise an interesting issue because although we have steadily made cost reductions, always speeding up the cheapest activities first, we have *not*, in fact, arrived at the least-cost completion of the project.

Note that if we allow activities *b*, *d* and *e* all to slow down by 1 week then the project will take one week longer at 24 weeks and our overhead will increase by £500. However, what we are spending to speed up these three activities by a week is £100 + £240 + £210 = £550.

So this slowing down will actually save a further £50.

The true answer is that the minimum cost at which this project can be completed is £35 510 in 24 weeks.

The moral is that when you think you have arrived at the minimum cost by successively speeding up activities you should check that there is no combination which if *slowed down* could reduce your total cost further.

The duration and cost of each activity at minimum-cost completion, as requested, is given in Table 5.6.

Table 5.6	Activity	a	b	c	d	e	f	g
	Duration (weeks)	12	18	9	6	12	6	8
	Cost (£)	5250	4100	2500	1700	4720	3440	1800

Exercise 5.2.1

The activities in a certain project had relationships, durations and costs as shown in Table 5.7.

Table 5.7

Activity	a	b	c	d	e	f	g	h	i	j
Predecessors	−	−	−	a	a	b, e	c	d	f, g	h, i
Normal duration (days)	5	7	9	8	8	6	9	7	4	5
Normal total cost (£)	550	450	300	700	800	200	800	200	300	350
Extra cost per day saved (£)	120	70	40	100	110	40	110	15	75	80
Minimum duration (days)	2	3	7	4	4	2	5	4	2	3

Draw the network.

Find the normal duration and cost.

What are the critical activities?

If every day saved on the project as a whole can be reckoned to have a monetary value of £100, what is the optimum time in which to complete the project?

State the duration and cost of each activity when the project is completed at minimum total cost. State also the total cost of the project in this situation.

5.3 Completion of Projects in Minimum Time

In some circumstances the primary interest when completing a project is to get it done in the least possible time even if this does not mean the least possible cost. This could be the case, for instance, if the equipment being used for the project were urgently needed for profitable work elsewhere. The gain from having the equipment available for this other work could more than outweigh the loss from not completing the current project at minimum cost. Given that minimum time is the target, it is, of course, essential that it is achieved at the least possible associated cost.

One way of finding minimum time for completion of a project is to start with the normal completion network and gradually make reductions in critical activities until the minimum duration is reached. We did actually see this done in both example 5.2.1 and example 5.2.2. In 5.2.1 we were asked to draw the cost/time graph and so had to find the point corresponding to shortest time. In 5.2.2 we happened to see the minimum duration of 23 weeks on our way to finding the least-cost completion in 24 weeks.

However, if it is minimum time which is of interest then there is another and more efficient way of proceeding. This is to first crash every activity and look at the resulting network. Doing this will certainly give us the minimum duration of the project immediately. However, it will probably be a highly wasteful way of achieving the minimum duration. So to complete the solution what we need to do is to consider the activities which are *not* critical and allow the most expensive of these to slow down as much as possible without the duration of the project being increased above the desired minimum. This approach is illustrated in the following example.

Example 5.3.1

The data shown in Table 5.8 relate to a contract being undertaken. There are also site costs of £500 per day.

You are required to:

(a) calculate and state the time for completion on a normal basis;
(b) calculate and state the critical path on this basis, and the cost;
(c) calculate and state the cost of completion in the shortest possible time.

(ICMA Prof. 1)

ANSWER

(a) The specification of the activities in this question again suggests that an arrow diagram would be appropriate. The network for normal completion is shown with the earliest and latest starting times, floats and critical path in Fig. 5.15. We see immediately from this diagram that normal completion time is 39 days.

Table 5.8

Activity	Time for completion, normal basis (days)	Cost for total activity, normal basis (£)	Possible reduction in time (days)	Extra cost for reduction of one day (£)
1–2	5	6 000	1	300
1–3	8	10 000	2	200
1–4	15	17 000	4	700
2–3	4	5 000	1	400
2–5	12	15 000	3	200
3–4	6	8 000	2	200
4–5	7	9 000	1	400
4–6	11	13 000	3	300
4–7	10	12 000	2	600
5–6	8	14 000	2	300
6–8	9	25 000	3	100
7–8	10	13 000	2	500

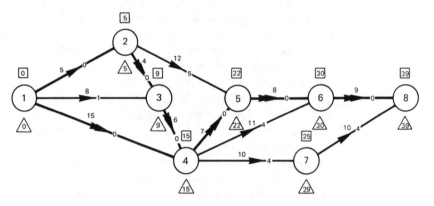

Figure 5.15

(b) On the normal basis there are two critical paths:

$$1–2–3–4–5–6–8 \quad \text{and} \quad 1–4–5–6–8.$$

The cost on the normal basis is:

$$£(6000 + 10\,000 + 17\,000 + 5000 + 15\,000 + 8000 + 9000 + 13\,000 + 1200 \\ + 14\,000 + 25\,000 + 13\,000 + 39 \times 500) = £166\,500.$$

(c) This question should be understood to imply that the least achievable cost of completing in minimum time is required.

To find this we consider the network shown in Fig. 5.16, which is obtained by crashing all the activities.

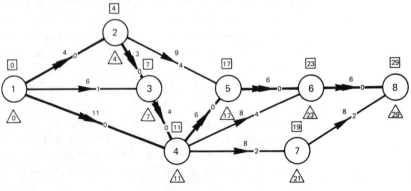

Figure 5.16

The minimum time for completing the contract is seen to be 29 days. Money can be saved by allowing the slowing down of those non-critical activities most expensive to speed up.

First let 4–7 take its full 10 days. Then 4–7 and 7–8 are critical. Other floats are unchanged. Next let 4–6 take its full 11 days. The float on 4–6 is then reduced to 1. Next let 2–5 take its full 12 days. The float on 2–5 is then reduced to 1. Finally let 1–3 take 7 days. Activity 1–3 is then critical.

No further savings are possible as the three non-critical activities are all now at normal duration. Hence the least possible cost of completing in 29 days is:

$$£(166\,500 - 10 \times 500 + 1 \times 300 + 1 \times 200 + 4 \times 700 + 1 \times 400 + 2 \times 200 + 1 \times 400 + 2 \times 300 + 3 \times 100 + 2 \times 500)$$

$$= £(166\,500 - 5000 + 300 + 200 + 2800 + 400 + 400 + 400 + 600 + 300 + 1000) = £167\,900.$$

The least possible cost of completion in minimum time is £167 900.

Exercise 5.3.1

Consider the activities shown in Table 5.8 in a construction project with associated times, costs and preceding activities.

Table 5.9

Activity	Preceding activities	Normal		Crash	
		Time (days)	Cost (£)	Time (days)	Cost (£)
A	–	7	6 500	4	8 000
B	–	10	8 000	7	10 000
C	–	5	7 000	5	7 000
D	A, B	8	12 000	5	15 000
E	B, C	9	14 000	6	18 000
F	C, D	12	13 500	9	16 500
G	D, E	14	12 750	10	17 750
H	F, G	6	4 000	3	5 000

The crash information represents the minimum time in which the activity could be completed and the associated cost is the best estimate of the total cost of completing the activity within the shorter time. The choice is between normal time and cost, or crash time and cost, i.e. it is not possible to save one day on a particular activity for a proportionate increase in cost. In addition to the costs for each activity there is a site cost of £750 per day.

You are required to:

(a) calculate and state the normal time and associated minimum cost;
(b) calculate and state the minimum time and associated minimum cost;
(c) calculate and state the minimum cost and associated minimum time;
(d) state and explain two practical problems which may arise when attempting to use this planning tool.

(*ICMA Prof. 1*)

5.4 Bar Charts and Manpower Requirements

In this section we look at the manpower requirements of projects, and consider the use of bar charts to indicate which combinations of activities are in progress at various stages. This is a useful thing to do as it allows us to look at the possibility of delaying the start of some activities in order to vary the distribution of man-power utilisation over the project. The following example illustrates the use of bar charts and the inclusion of manpower considerations.

Example 5.4.1

Table 5.10 shows the durations of the various activities involved in a certain project, and the logical relationships between those activities.

Table 5.10	Activity	A	B	C	D	E	F	G	H	I	J
	Duration (days)	9	10	4	10	5	9	7	8	7	8
	Preceding activity	–	–	B	A	A	A	E	D	C,F	G,H,I

(a) Draw an AON diagram for the project and determine the activities on the critical path.
     What is the length (in days) of the critical path?
(b) If the number of men used each day on each activity is as follows:

A	B	C	D	E	F	G	H	I	J
7	3	6	5	7	6	6	5	7	8

and assuming that each activity begins as soon as possible, draw:
 (i) a bar chart showing the combinations of activities in progress at each stage of the project,
(ii) a graph showing the number of men used each day over the life of the project. State what is the maximum manpower requirement during the project and indicate a way of reducing this peak by rescheduling the starts of some of the activities. What is the total number of man-days used in the project?

ANSWER

(a) The network diagram for this project is shown as Fig. 5.17.

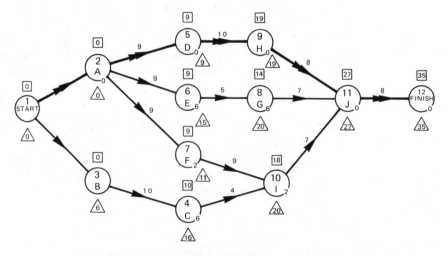

Figure 5.17

The critical path activities are A, D, H and J.
The length of the critical path is 35 days.

(b) (i) Figure 5.18 is the required bar chart showing the combinations of activities in progress throughout the life of the project.

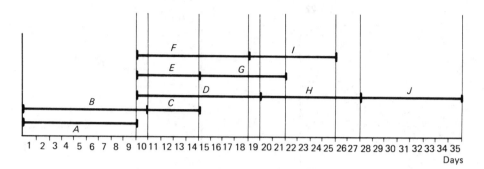

Figure 5.18

(ii) Using the bar chart and the information given on manpower needs of each activity, we can draw up a table (Table 5.11) of total manpower needs on each of the 35 days of the project.

Table 5.11

Days	Activities in progress	Number of men needed
1-9	A, B	10
10	B, D, E, F	21
11-14	C, D, E, F	24
15-18	D, F, G	17
19	D, I, G	18
20-21	G, H, I	18
22-25	H, I	12
26-27	H	5
28-35	J	8

The graph showing manpower requirements appears in Fig. 5.18. We see that the maximum requirement is for 24 men on days 11–14. By examination of the bar chart in Fig. 5.18 we see that this peak could be reduced if the requirement that every activity starts as early as possible is relaxed.

If, for example, the starts for E and F are postponed until day 11, the start of C until day 16, the start of I until day 20 and the start of G until day 20 then the new table of manpower requirements is as shown in Table 5.12.

Table 5.12

Days	Activities in progress	Number of men needed
1-9	A, B	10
10	B, D	8
11-15	D, E, F	18
16-19	C, D, F	17
20-26	G, H, I	18
27	H	5
28-35	J	8

The total number of man-days used in the project, represented by the area under the graph in Fig. 5.19, can be calculated using either Table 5.11 or Table 5.12 showing possible schedules of activities or Table 5.10 showing the manpower

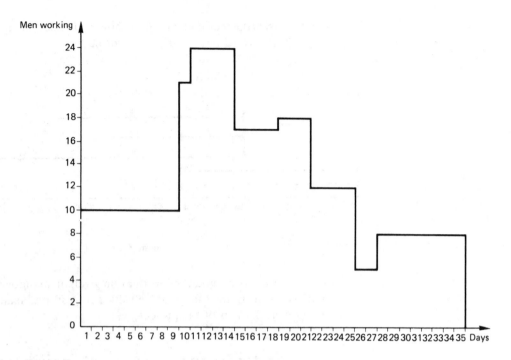

Figure 5.19

requirements of the individual activities. Using Table 5.12 we find the number of man days needed to be:

$$9 \times 10 + 1 \times 8 + 5 \times 18 + 4 \times 17 + 7 \times 18 + 1 \times 5 + 8 \times 8$$
$$= 90 + 8 + 90 + 68 + 126 + 5 + 64 = 451.$$

Exercise 5.4.1

Consider the project which requires the activities shown in Table 5.13.

Table 5.13

Activity		Activity time (days)		Total cost (normal) (£)	Resources (normal number of men per day)
Initial node	Terminal node	Normal	Crash		
0	9	6	3	480	4
0	10	10	5	900	5
10	7	7	4	490	5
7	8	9	2	540	4
9	2	8	4	560	6
3	4	5	2	300	4
7	3	6	3	500	4
6	11	6	3	520	6
1	6	7	4	510	5
8	4	10	5	920	6
4	5	8	4	580	6
2	8	10	5	940	5
0	1	9	6	560	4
11	4	8	4	480	4

The activities that can be 'crashed' must take either the normal time or the crash time. There is no opportunity to reduce the time of an activity by one or two days. The cost of crashing any activity is £100 per day.

You are required to:

(a) calculate the normal duration of the project, its normal cost and the critical path;
(b) state the number of different paths from start to finish;
(c) calculate the minimum time in which the project can be completed and state the critical activities;
(d) state the maximum number of men required to complete the project if all activities commence at the earliest start date.

(*ICMA Prof. 1*)

5.5 Updating Networks and Variable Activity Durations

So far we have assumed that all activity durations in project networks are given. In reality, the values used as durations when setting up a network diagram are almost always estimates likely to need later revision and subject to variable influences. In this section we consider first the updating of a network after some activities have been carried out and found to take times different from those initially estimated. Then we go on to problems where probability is taken into account in the initial specification and used in the network construction and calculations. We can inevitably consider only relatively simple examples here; these areas of updating and incorporating probabilities, which can require involved and repetitive calculations, are ones in which the many computer packages available for network analysis become indispensible for problems of any magnitude.

Example 5.5.1

Table 5.14 shows the activities involved in a project, their relationships and durations. It also shows the costs of the activities when carried out at normal speed, their crash durations and their respective costs per day saved.

Table 5.14

Activity	Normal duration (days)	Normal total cost (£)	Minimum crash duration (days)	Cost per day saved (£)
1–2	3	140	1	110
2–3	2	200	1	175
2–4	3	160	1	125
2–5	2	300	1	200
3–6	2	250	1	175
4–6	6	400	1	70
5–6	5	230	1	70
6–7	5	220	1	90

There is a bonus of £100 per day for every day saved below the contract period of 15 days and a penalty of £200 for each day after the 15 days.

You are required to:

(a) calculate the normal duration and the normal cost;

(b) calculate the cost of completing the project in 15 days;
(c) state the optimum plan for the company to attempt;
(d) revert to the normal programme and normal costs and state what action you would recommend to ensure completion by the contract date if, after the tenth day, the actual situation was as follows:

activities completed at normal cost: 1–2; 2–3; 3–6; 2–4; 2–5;

activities not yet started: 4–6; 5–6; 6–7.

You are also required to calculate the revised cost of the project under these circumstances.

(ICMA Part IV)

ANSWER

(a) The arrow diagram for normal completion of the project is shown as Fig. 5.20. From this diagram we see that the normal duration of the project is 17 days. The normal cost is the sum of the costs for the individual activities plus two penalties of £200 for the two days over the contract period.

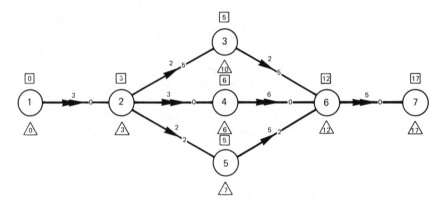

Figure 5.20

Thus the normal cost is:

$$£(140 + 200 + 160 + 300 + 250 + 400 + 230 + 220 + 400) = £(1900 + 400)$$
$$= £2300.$$

(b) The most cost-effective way to complete the project in 15 days is to save 2 days on activity 4–6. This costs £140 and saves the £400 in penalties. Thus the required cost of completing the project in 15 days is £(2300 − 400 + 140) = £2040. The effect of speeding up 4–6 in this way is to make 2–5 and 5–6 critical and to reduce the floats on both 2–3 and 3–6 to 3 days.

(c) Further financial savings can be made by reducing the time spent on activity 6–7 from 5 days to 1 day. The cost of this is 4 × £90 = £360. It gains bonuses of 4 × £100 = £400. Hence the net saving is £400 − £360 = £40.

No other financial savings can be made. Activities 1–2, 2–4 and 2–5 all cost individually more per day to speed up than the £100 per day bonus. The only other way to obtain a bonus is to speed up 4–6 and 5–6 together, but the total cost per day of doing this is £70 + £70 = £140. This also exceeds the £100 per day bonus figure. Hence the optimum plan is to complete the project in 11 days by reducing the time spent on 4-6 to 4 days and the time spent on 6-7 to 1 day, while all other activities are carried out at normal speed.

The total cost of this optimum plan is £2040 − £40 = £2000.

(d) This is the part which brings in the idea of updating a network. The method is basically quite simple. We set up a new network for the not-yet-completed activities taking the current time (day 10 in this example) as the starting-point. This enables us to find the critical activities and the final completion time for the project and hence to work out penalties or bonus and possible savings to be made. The arrow diagram for the situation specified here is shown as Fig. 5.21.

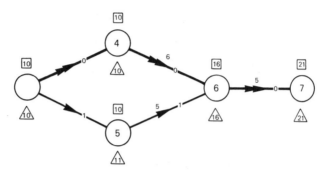

Figure 5.21

From this diagram we see that activities 4-6 and 6-7 are now critical, while 5-6 has a float of 1 day and total time for completion is 21 days. To ensure completion by the contract date first reduce 4-6 by 1 day. This costs £70 and saves a £200 penalty so the net saving is £130. All these activities are now critical and the total time is 20 days. Next save all the 4 days available for saving on 6-7. This costs £360 and saves £800 in penalties, so the net saving is £440. The total time is reduced to 16 days.

Finally, to achieve the contract time of 15 days it is necessary to reduce 4-6 and 5-6 simultaneously by 1 day. This costs 2 × £70 = £140 and saves £200 so the net saving is £60.

Thus the overall recommendation to ensure completion by the contract date is to complete 4-6 in 4 days, 5-6 in 4 days and 6-7 in 1 day. This is also the optimum completion under the revised circumstances, as any further saving would cost £140 per day to reduce 4-6 and 5-6 together and earn only £100 per day.

The revised cost is the sum of the normal costs for all the activities plus the costs of speeding up 4-6, 5-6 and 6-7 as specified.

Hence the cost is:

£(1900 + 2 × 70 + 1 × 70 + 1 × 70 + 4 × 90) = £(1900 + 140 + 70 + 360) = £2470.

We turn now from the matter of updating a network after finding activity durations to have deviated from what was anticipated to considering how variations in durations can be taken into account in an initial network specification by means of probabilities. There are many different ways in which the probabilities can arise. We give an example where probabilities follow normal distributions and then an exercise involving discrete probabilities.

Example 5.5.2

Consider the schedule of activities and related information for the construction of a new plant shown in Table 5.15.

Table 5.15

Activity	Expected time		Expected cost (£000)
	Months	*Variance*	
1, 2	4	1	5
2, 3	2	1	3
3, 5	3	1	4
2, 4	6	2	9
1, 6	2	1	2
6, 5	5	1	12
4, 5	9	5	20
6, 7	7	8	7
7, 8	10	16	14
5, 8	1	1	4

You should assume that the cost and time required for one activity are not dependent upon the cost and time of any other activity and variations are expected to follow a normal distribution.

You are required to calculate:

(a) the critical path;
(b) the expected cost of constructing the plant;
(c) the expected time required to build the plant;
(d) the standard deviation of the expected time;
(e) the probability of completing the plant in 24 months or less.

(*ICMA Prof. 1*)

ANSWER

The arrow diagram for this project is shown as Fig. 5.22. The answers to parts (a), (b) and (c) of the question are immediately apparent from the diagram and the given set of costs.

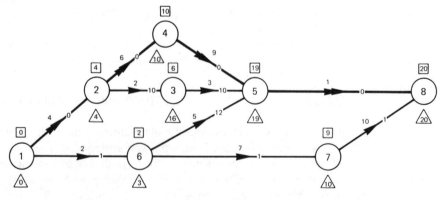

Figure 5.22

(a) The critical path involves activities (1, 2), (2, 4), (4, 5) and (5, 8).
(b) The expected cost is £80 000.
(c) The expected time required to build the plant is 20 months.

90

(d) To find the standard deviation of the expected time we need to look at the variances for the activities on the critical path.

Since the times required for the activities are independent, the variance of the time needed to complete the critical path will be the sum of the variances of the times of the individual activities on that path.

Hence the standard deviation is $\sqrt{1 + 2 + 5 + 1}$ months $= \sqrt{9}$ months
$$= 3 \text{ months}.$$

(e) The time needed to complete the critical path follows a normal distribution with mean 20 months and standard deviation 3 months. Hence we can find the probability of completing the critical path in 24 months or less by finding the number of standard deviations by which 24 exceeds 20. This is $\frac{24 - 20}{3} = \frac{4}{3} = 1.33$.

Using normal-distribution tables, we find that the total area below a value which is 1.33 standard deviations above the mean is 0.908. However, the path (1, 6), (6, 7), (7, 8) has expected time 19 months, so if this path exceeded its expectation by more than 5 months we should again fail to complete the construction of the plant in 24 months or less.

The standard deviation for this path is $\sqrt{1 + 8 + 16}$ months $= \sqrt{25}$ months $= 5$ months. $\frac{24 - 19}{5} = \frac{5}{5} = 1$, so the probability of completing the activities on this path in 24 months or less is the area under a normal curve below a value which is 1 standard deviation above the mean. This is 0.8413.

Activities (2, 3), (3, 5) and (6, 5) are irrelevant here as their floats are very large compared with their standard deviations.

So in order to complete the construction of the plant in 24 months or less we must achieve this target on both the critical path and the path with float 1. As the paths have no activities in common and the completion times for individual activities are independent, it follows that this probability is the product of the two individual probabilities.

The probability of completion in 24 months or less is $0.908 \times 0.8413 = 0.7639$.

Exercise 5.5.1

Consider the activities listed in Table 5.16 which are required to complete the processing of a customer's order. The times for activities 1, 3 and 5 are fixed; for activity 2 there is a 0.5 probability that it will require 2 days and a 0.5 probability that it will require 6 days; for activity 4 a 0.7 probability of taking 4 days, 0.2 of taking 6 days, and 0.1 of taking 10 days.

Table 5.16

Activity	Preceding activities	Average time in days	Normal variable cost per day (£)
1 Receipt of order, checking credit rating etc.	—	2	5
2 Preparation of material specification, availability of material etc.	1	4	10
3 Inspection, packing etc.	2	1	7
4 Arrangement of transport facilities etc.	1	5	5
5 Delivery	3, 4	3	2

You are required to:

(a) draw the network (it is very simple) twice, first using an arrow diagram and secondly an activity-on-node presentation, clearly indicating the meaning of any symbols that you use;
(b) indicate the critical path, calculate average duration and variable cost under normal conditions;
(c) calculate the minimum and maximum times and the probabilities associated with them.

(ICMA Prof. 1)

Further Exercises

5.1 You are given information concerning a project which consists of eight activities, A to H (Table 5.17).

Table 5.17

Activity	Preceding activity	Duration (days)
A	–	4
B	–	5
C	A	2
D	A	3
E	B, C	3
F	B, C	4
G	D, E	5
H	F	2

Required:

(a) Draw a network for the project and determine the activities that lie on the critical path, and also its length.
(b) If activity F has also to precede activity G, will the critical path change?
   If it does change, draw your new network and compute the length of the new critical path.
(c) Assume that it has been found that certain activities in the original network can be shortened by hiring extra resources at the following costs:

Activity	B	D	E	F	G	H
Shortened duration (days)	3	2	2	3	3	1
Extra cost (£)	200	150	50	200	250	300

On the assumption that the extra costs are linear, determine the possible expedited times and their associated costs.

(ACCA Prof. 2)

5.2 The project leader of an operational research group has analysed a project to be tackled into eleven activities as shown in Table 5.18.
   Required:

(a) Draw a network for the project and hence determine the critical path and its duration.
(b) Activities B, E, F, H, I are all to be carried out by the computing staff but there is only sufficient staff to carry out one activity at a time. What is the latest time that activity B, investigation of computer requirements, can be carried out such that the project can be completed at the earliest possible time?

Table 5.18	Activity	Preceding activity	Duration (weeks)
	A Pilot survey	–	2
	B Investigation of computer requirements	–	1
	C Preliminary data analysis	A	1
	D Write initial report	B, C	1
	E Program design	B	1
	F Program testing and debugging	E	2
	G Main data collection	C	4
	H Data collation	G	1
	I Run program on collated data	F, D, H	1
	J Discussion and analysis of results	I	1
	K Final report	J	2

(c) If the number of staff required for each activity is as follows, what is the minimum size of the project team required to complete the project on time?

Activity	A	B	C	D	E	F	G	H	I	J	K
Staff required	3	2	1	1	2	2	4	2	2	4	2

(ACCA Prof. 2)

5.3 Each autumn the Quantitative Accountants Association prepares and distributes an annual programme. The programme gives dates of meetings and a list of speakers with summaries of their talks. Also included is an up-to-date list of paid-up members. The activities to be carried out to complete the preparation of the programme are given in Table 5.19.

Table 5.19		Immediate predecessor	Estimated time (days)
	A Select dates for programme	–	4
	B Secure agreement from speakers and prepare summaries of their talks	A	12
	C Obtain advertising material for programme	A	11
	D Mail membership renewal notices	–	20
	E Prepare list of paid-up members	D	6
	F Send membership list to printer and read proofs	B, C, E	7
	G Print and assemble programme	F	10
	H Obtain computer printed address labels of members	E	5
	I Send out programmes	G, H	4

Required:

(a) Draw a network for the scheme of activities set out above. Include full information on earliest and latest event times and indicate the critical path.
(b) Draw a bar chart for the scheme and state the total float for each activity.
(c) If each activity requires one member of the office staff of the association, so that the activities may be completed in the estimated times, what is the minimum number of staff that should be allocated to the scheme?
(d) What would be the effect on the total time if one of the allocated staff was taken ill for the duration of the scheme and not replaced?

(ACCA Prof. 2)

6 Stock Control

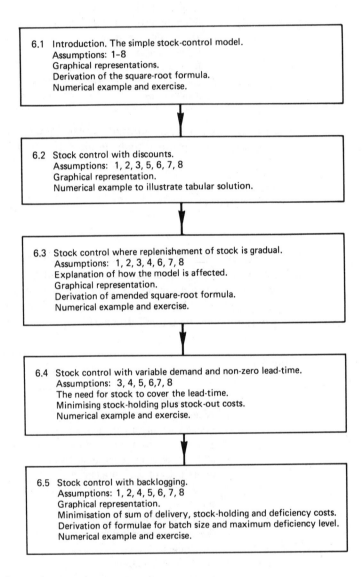

6.1 Introduction. The simple stock-control model.
Assumptions: 1–8
Graphical representations.
Derivation of the square-root formula.
Numerical example and exercise.

6.2 Stock control with discounts.
Assumptions: 1, 2, 3, 5, 6, 7, 8
Graphical representation.
Numerical example to illustrate tabular solution.

6.3 Stock control where replenishement of stock is gradual.
Assumptions: 1, 2, 3, 4, 6, 7, 8
Explanation of how the model is affected.
Graphical representation.
Derivation of amended square-root formula.
Numerical example and exercise.

6.4 Stock control with variable demand and non-zero lead-time.
Assumptions: 3, 4, 5, 6,7, 8
The need for stock to cover the lead-time.
Minimising stock-holding plus stock-out costs.
Numerical example and exercise.

6.5 Stock control with backlogging.
Assumptions: 1, 2, 4, 5, 6, 7, 8
Graphical representation.
Minimisation of sum of delivery, stock-holding and deficiency costs.
Derivation of formulae for batch size and maximum deficiency level.
Numerical example and exercise.

6.1 Introduction — the Simple Stock–control Model

Stock is a major element of the working capital of many organisations. Hence its proper control is crucial to the health of the business. Stock can be of raw materials, of work-in-progress or of finished goods awaiting despatch. Which of these is most important will vary from business to business and in some cases two or even all these will be of major importance.

In this section we begin by looking at some specific functions of a stock-control system and at some of the considerations which must be borne in mind in devising a system. We conclude the section by considering a system suitable for a very simple situation where a number of simplifying assumptions apply. We then in the subsequent sections consider the extension of this system to situations where various subsets of the assumptions do not apply and we are closer to conditions likely to be actually met in practice. We see that the simple model, despite its large number of assumptions, is a sensible starting-point because it gives results which are the basis of those appropriate to more realistic situations.

Stock-control systems, applied to the different types of stock mentioned in the first paragraph, are important for the following purposes:

(a) Ensuring that raw material is available for production processes.
(b) Ensuring that finished goods are available for dispatch to customers.
(c) Enabling work in progress to be valued.
(d) Controlling the amount of cash tied up in stock.
(e) Helping to control wastage and pilferage of material.

Which of the above functions is most important will depend on the type of business.

In deciding on a stock-control system the fundamental choice is between having large orders delivered infrequently or having small orders at frequent intervals. The factors in favour of these respective possibilities are set out below. Of these factors it is cash tied up in stock which is usually the most potent deterrent to having excessively high stock levels and purchasing costs which militate against having too many small orders.

Factors in favour of large orders made infrequently	Factors in favour of small orders made frequently
Economy of purchasing	Less cash tied up in stock
Security of supply in cases of delivery difficulty	Less space needed
Flexibility of production	Lower insurance costs
Immediate availability of goods for sale	Less chance of deterioration of material
Ability to gain from price increases	Less risk of obsolescence

It will be clear from the foregoing discussion that controlling stock is a complex matter and we will not be able to take into account all the possible factors. What we will do is begin here with a consideration of the simple stock-control model and then extend this in later sections.

The simple stock-control model is based on the following eight assumptions:

1. Demand rate is constant.
2. There is zero lead-time on orders.
3. The stockist does not choose to spend any non-zero time out of stock.
4. No discounts are available for large orders.
5. Orders arrive instantaneously and not gradually.
6. The variable overhead cost for each delivery is the same.
7. The cost of holding stock is constant (either in monetary terms or as a proportion of item value).
8. No DCF considerations are applied to any costs.

These assumptions are simplistic and unlikely to be met in practice but the model is none the less useful because the order-size formula to which it leads can be used as a first approximation in cases where they do not apply and will result in a sensible order size. Furthermore, as we see in later sections, some of the assumptions can be relaxed to give more realistic situations and the results of the simple model can be extended. In section 6.2 we consider the relaxation of assumption 4 to allow discounts and in section 6.3 we see assumption 5 relaxed so that arriving orders are built up gradually. In section 6.4 we see assumptions 1 and 2 relaxed together. This causes us to have to consider holding safety stocks to carry us through the time while an order is outstanding, with the amount to be demanded in that time being uncertain. Finally in section 6.5 we see assumption 3 of the simple model relaxed, allowing periods when there is no stock. This leads to the idea of backlogging, that is accumulating orders to be met when the next order has arrived.

Under the assumptions of the simple stock-control model, maximum levels of stock occur immediately after receipt of orders. The only question that requires to be answered in the simple model is that of how many items should be ordered in each batch.

If two few items are ordered in each batch, a large number of batches will be needed each year and we shall have high annual ordering and delivery costs. (Stock-holding costs, on the other hand, will be low.)

If too many items are ordered in each batch, average stock-levels held will be high and we shall have high annual stock-holding costs. (Ordering and delivery costs in this situation will be low.)

The appropriate quantity to order each time is that which minimises the *sum* of delivery costs and stock-holding costs. This is the economic batch quantity (EBQ). In some contexts this may be referred to as the economic order quantity (EOQ). See, for example, Exercise 6.3.1.

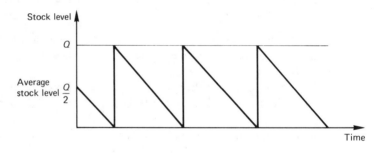

Figure 6.1

Figure 6.1 shows the graph of stock level against time under the simple-model assumptions.

Derivation of the EBQ Formula

Let the delivery cost for each order be c.
Let the (constant) demand rate be d items per year.
Let the cost of holding stock for a year be proportion i of stock value.
Let the value of each item be p.

Note: The cost of holding one item for one year is ip. Hence if we know stock-holding cost as a percentage or proportion of stock value we know i, but if we know stock-holding cost as an actual *money* figure we know ip.

We need altogether d items per year. Let there be Q in each delivery.

Then the number of deliveries needed is $\dfrac{d}{Q}$.

Each delivery costs c so the total delivery-cost per year is $\dfrac{cd}{Q}$.

Average stock level through the year is $\dfrac{Q}{2}$.

Each item is worth p so the average value of stock through the year is $\dfrac{pQ}{2}$.

Hence the annual stock-holding cost is $\dfrac{ipQ}{2}$.

The relationship between these costs and the batch size, Q, is shown graphically in Fig. 6.2. Note that inclusion of any fixed costs (not depending on Q) would merely move the whole cost curve upwards and would not affect the Q value at the minimum point.

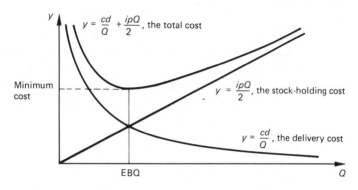

Figure 6.2

We can carry out the minimisation as follows using calculus:

$$\frac{dy}{dQ} = -\frac{cd}{Q^2} + \frac{ip}{2}.$$

Then $\qquad \dfrac{dy}{dQ} = 0 \qquad$ gives $\qquad \dfrac{ip}{2} = \dfrac{cd}{Q^2}.$

So $\qquad Q^2 = \dfrac{2cd}{ip} \qquad$ and we have $\qquad \boxed{Q = \sqrt{\dfrac{2cd}{ip}}.}$

$\dfrac{d^2y}{dQ^2} = \dfrac{2cd}{Q^3}$ which is positive for any positive Q.

Hence $Q = \sqrt{\dfrac{2cd}{ip}}$ does indeed give a *minimum* value of X.

$$\boxed{Q = \sqrt{\frac{2cd}{ip}} \text{ is the economic batch quantity.}}$$

(Writing the formula in this particular way can be helpful as an aid to memory as all the letters appear in their alphabet order.)

Notice that when $Q = \sqrt{\dfrac{2cd}{ip}}$ we have

$$\text{stock-holding cost} = \frac{ip}{2}\sqrt{\frac{2cd}{ip}} = \sqrt{\frac{cdip}{2}}$$

and
$$\text{delivery cost} = \frac{cd}{Q} = \frac{cd}{\sqrt{\dfrac{2cd}{ip}}} = \sqrt{\frac{cdip}{2}}.$$

That is, $\text{stock-holding cost} = \text{delivery cost at EBQ.}$

It follows that minimum total variable cost $= \sqrt{\dfrac{cdip}{2}} + \sqrt{\dfrac{cdip}{2}}$

$$= 2\sqrt{\frac{cdip}{2}} = \sqrt{2cdip}.$$

This is represented in Fig. 6.2 by the fact that the stock-holding line and the delivery cost curve intersect at the same value of Q as that at which the total cost curve has its minimum point.

Example 6.1.1

A manufacturer needs 10 000 components per year of a particular type. Each one is worth £40 and stock-holding costs are 10 per cent of stock value per year. If the cost of placing an order is £32 and the assumptions of the simple stock control model can be believed to hold, calculate the economic batch quantity.

ANSWER

$c = 32$,
$d = 10\,000$,
$i = 0.10$,
$p = 40$.

Hence the EBQ is $Q = \sqrt{\dfrac{2 \times 32 \times 10\,000}{0.1 \times 40}} = \sqrt{\dfrac{640\,000}{4}} = \sqrt{160\,000} = 400$,

i.e. the manufacturer should order 400 items at a time.

Exercise 6.1.1

A company works 50 weeks in a year. For a certain part, included in the asembly of several products, there is an annual demand of 10 000 units. The part may be obtained from either an outside supplier or a subsidiary company.

The data set out in Table 6.1 relating to the part are given.

Table 6.1

	From outside supplier	From subsidiary company
Purchase price, per unit	£12	£13
Storage and all carrying costs, including capital costs per unit per annum	£2	£2
Cost of placing an order	£10	£10
Cost of receiving an order	£20	£15
Delivery time, certain	10 weeks	5 weeks

You are required to:

(a) calculate the minimum cost for a year using the outside supplier;
(b) calculate the minimum cost for a year using the subsidiary company.

(*ICMA Prof. 1*)

6.2 Stock Control with Discounts

In the remaining sections of this chapter, as explained in the introduction, we consider the situations which result when certain of the assumptions of the simple stock-control model, listed in section 6.1, are relaxed.

In the present section we consider the relaxation of assumption 4 and look at a situation where all the assumptions of the simple model hold except that there are now discounts available for large orders. This is a situation which will commonly occur in practice.

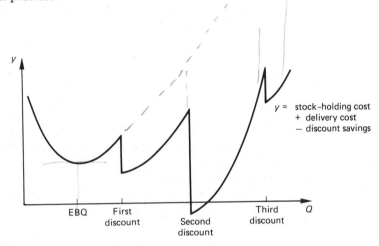

Figure 6.3

If we consider the graph, shown in Fig. 6.3, of

delivery cost + stock-holding cost − discount saving

we see that it looks like the simple-model total-cost curve shown in Fig. 6.2, but has 'kinks' at those values of Q for which discounts are just obtained.

As in the simple model, we need to know the value of Q for which this graph has its lowest point.

The procedure in such a case is to first find the EBQ, and then evaluate

> stock-holding cost + delivery cost − discount savings

at the EBQ and also at those values of Q for which each discount is just obtained. This gives us the values on the curve at the EBQ minimum point and at the bottom of each of the kinks.

The quantity to order each time is that which gives us the lowest figure. For the case shown in Fig. 6.3 the best quantity to buy each time is that which just takes advantage of the second discount.

An efficient way to set out the solution to a problem of this type is in the form of a table, as illustrated in the following example.

Example 6.2.1

A firm is able to obtain quantity discounts on its orders of material as shown in Table 6.2.

The annual demand for the material is 4000 tons. Stock-holding costs are 20

Table 6.2

Price per ton (£)	Tons bought
6.0	less than 250
5.9	250 and less than 800
5.8	800 and less than 2000
5.7	2000 and less than 4000
5.6	4000 and over

per cent per year of material cost. The delivery cost per order is £6. Calculate the best quantity to order.

(ICMA Part IV)

ANSWER

The EBQ is $\quad Q = \sqrt{\dfrac{2cd}{ip}} = \sqrt{\dfrac{2 \times 6 \times 4000}{0.2 \times 6}} = \sqrt{40\,000} = 200.$

(This is calculated on the assumption that $p = £6$. If the value obtained for Q had exceeded 250 tons, it would have been necessary to recalculate Q using the appropriate smaller value of p.)

Now we calculate stock-holding cost + delivery cost − discount savings for all the appropriate values of Q in Table 6.3.

Table 6.3

Q	Delivery cost = $\dfrac{6 \times 4000}{Q} = \dfrac{24\,000}{Q}$	Stock-holding cost = $0.2 \times p \times \dfrac{Q}{2} = \dfrac{pQ}{10}$	Discount saving = $4000 \times (6 - p)$	Delivery + stock-holding − discount saving
200	120	120	0	240
250	96	147.50	400	−156.50
800	30	464	800	−306
2000	12	1140	1200	−48
4000	6	2240	1600	646

The smallest value in the final column is −306, corresponding to $Q = 800$. Thus the best policy in this case is to just take advantage of the second discount.

Thus <u>buy in batches of 800 tons.</u>

Exercise 6.2.1

The raw material needed by a company for its operation costs £200 per ton and has associated with it a cost of £200 for each delivery made. Variable costs of storage are 5 per cent per year of value of stock held. A further storage cost arises in that special containers have to be hired in which to store the material. These must be hired for at least a year at a time and the hire cost per year is £1000. Each container is capable of holding 320 tons of material.

If the total demand per year is 100 000 tons, determine the optimum reorder quantity.

6.3 Stock Control with Gradual Replenishment

In this section we consider the situation where all the assumptions of the simple stock-control model (as listed in section 6.1) hold except for number 5. That is to say, a batch is not now assumed to arrive all at once but is built up at a uniform rate.

The position under consideration here arises when, for example, the stockist is also the producer of the item stocked. As soon as stock runs out he can immediately embark on production of a new batch.

While production of this batch is still going on, items made earlier can be sold. The effect of this is that stock levels are lower in the instantaneous delivery case.

The EBQ formula is, as we shall see, very similar to that for the ordinary simple model.

Derivation of the EBQ Formula

Let the set-up cost per batch be c.
Let the demand rate be d items per year.
Let the production rate be r items per year of production time.
Let the annual proportional stock-holding cost be i.
Let the value of each item be p.
Suppose we have Q items in each order.

In terms of a diagram similar to Fig. 6.1 for the simple model we have Fig. 6.4.

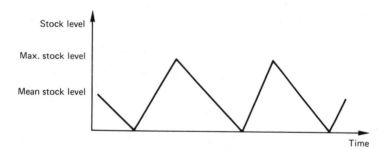

Figure 6.4

We need altogether d items per year and Q are made in each batch so the number of batches needed is $\dfrac{d}{Q}$.

Each batch costs c to set up so the total annual set-up cost is $\dfrac{cd}{Q}$.

Maximum stock-level = Q − number of items sold in time taken to produce a batch

$$= Q - \text{number sold in time } \frac{Q}{r}$$

$$= Q - d \cdot \frac{Q}{r} = Q\left(1 - \frac{d}{r}\right).$$

Hence average stock-level during the year is $\dfrac{Q}{2}\left(1 - \dfrac{d}{2}\right)$.

Hence the annual stock-holding cost is $\dfrac{ipQ}{2}\left(1 - \dfrac{d}{r}\right)$.

Thus we must choose Q so as to minimise

$$X = \frac{cd}{Q} + \frac{ipQ}{2}\left(1 - \frac{d}{r}\right).$$

This is just the same as for the simple model except for the factor of $1 - \frac{d}{r}$ in the stock-holding term resulting from the lower stock-levels. Hence the same differentiation steps will lead to the following formula for economic batch quantity:

$$EBQ = \sqrt{\frac{2cd}{ip\left(1 - \dfrac{d}{r}\right)}}.$$

Example 6.3.1

A company sells items at the rate of 500 per day throughout a year of 250 days. It can produce at a rate of 800 per day with a set-up cost per batch of £600 and a cost per item of £4. If the proportionate stock-holding cost is 25 per cent per year, find the economic batch quantity.   (*ICMA Part IV*)

ANSWER

$c = 600$, $d = 500 \times 250 = 125\,000$, $r = 800 \times 250 = 200\,000$,

$i = 0.25$, $p = 4$.

The EBQ is

$$Q = \sqrt{\frac{2 \times 600 \times 125\,000}{0.25 \times 4 \times \left(1 - \dfrac{125\,000}{200\,000}\right)}} = \sqrt{\frac{150\,000\,000}{\left(1 - \dfrac{5}{8}\right)}} = \sqrt{\frac{150\,000\,000}{\dfrac{3}{8}}}$$

$$= \sqrt{400\,000\,000} = 20\,000,$$

i.e. produce in batches of 20 000 items.

Exercise 6.3.1

The demand for a particular product is 12 000 units per year. The costs associated with ordering include fixed salaries and costs of £4000 per annum and variable costs of £30 per order. Storage costs consist of rent of £2000 per annum and interest and variable costs at the rate of £25 per unit of product.

Calculate the economic order quantity with replenishment taking place:

(a) of the whole order at the same time;
(b) at the rate of 50 000 per annum.   (*ICMA Prof. 1*)

6.4 Stock Control When Demand Rate is Variable and Lead-time is Non-zero

In this section we consider the situation where assumptions 1 and 2 of the simple model (see section 6.1) are no longer taken to hold. Thus demand is no longer assumed constant and we are recognising that there will be a time-lag between placing and receiving an order.

Dropping either assumption 1 or assumption 2 alone makes no serious difference to the simple model. If demand is variable but there is zero lead-time on orders then there is no problem because we can still get a new order delivered the instant stock runs out, whenever that might be. If there is a known order lead-time but demand is constant then there is again no problem because we are in a position to place the order sufficiently far in advance of stock running out for what we have left to exactly cover the lead-time period.

A problem worthy of consideration arises when, as is usual in practical stock-control situations, assumptions 1 and 2 break down together. Then we have to order before stock has run out completely in order to cover the lead-time, but because demand is variable we do not know exactly how much will be demanded during the lead-time.

Hence there is a danger of stock-outs occurring as a result of there being insufficient stock to cover the time between placing an order and receiving delivery of it.

Note carefully the definition of a stock-out. A stock-out occurs every time a request for an item cannot be met from stock. Hence there could be several stock-outs during one period of zero stock. On the other hand, if no requests are received, there might be no stock-outs during such a period.

In the situation now being considered there are two matters that have to be decided: how much to order at a time and when to place the order.

The first question can be answered by looking at the average demand-rate and using this as d in the square-root formula

$$\sqrt{\frac{2cd}{ip}}.$$

So answering this question requires no more than in the simple cases considered earlier where demand was constant.

To answer the second question we have to set a *reorder level*. That is a level such that when stock falls to it we have to put in a new order immediately.

This level must not be too high, as that would inflate our stock-holding costs. On the other hand, it must not be too low as this would lead to excessive stock-outs which can also be expensive in a direct financial way through the need to obtain emergency supplies, or in terms of customer goodwill if requests have to be turned down.

To arrive at a reorder level these conflicting requirements must be balanced one against the other. To do this we need to know the distribution of demand in probability terms. Knowing this, we can calculate the *expected* cost of stock-outs per lead-time for various possible reorder levels, add this to the stock-holding cost and then choose the reorder level for which this sum is smallest. The following example illustrates this method.

Example 6.4.1

The demands per week for items from a warehouse are distributed as shown in Table 6.4, with a mean of 6 items per week. The value of an item is £40 and there is an ordering cost of £4 per batch. Replenishment lead-time is one week.

An item can be produced instantly from supplier in the case of a stock-out at a cost of £8.

If the annual cost of stock-holding is 15 per cent of stock value, to what level should stock be allowed to fall before a replenishment order is placed, and how much should be ordered at a time? (Assume 50 weeks in a year.)

103

Table 6.4

No. of items	Probability of this number being demanded	No. of items	Probability of this number being demanded
14	0.00	7	0.14
13	0.01	6	0.16
12	0.01	5	0.16
11	0.02	4	0.15
10	0.04	3	0.09
9	0.07	2	0.04
8	0.10	1	0.01
		0	0.00

ANSWER

Let the stock-holding cost associated with the reorder level zero be Y per year. Each additional item carried will incur annual cost ip.

So if the reorder level is x, the annual stock-holding cost is $Y + ipx$.

For this example where $i = 0.15$ and $p = 40$, the annual stock-holding cost is thus
$\underline{Y + 6x}$.

The annual cost of stock-outs is

(expected number of stock-outs per year) $\times$ (stock-out cost)

= (expected number of stock-outs per lead time) $\times$ (number of lead times per year)
$\times$ (stock-out cost)

= (expected number of stock-outs per lead time) $\times \dfrac{d}{Q} \times$ (stock-out cost)

where Q is the number of items in each order.

The value of Q is given by the EBQ formula:

$$Q = \sqrt{\frac{2cd}{ip}} = \sqrt{\frac{2 \times 4 \times 6 \times 50}{0.15 \times 40}} = \sqrt{400} = 20,$$

$$d = 6 \times 50 = 300 \qquad \text{and} \qquad \text{stock-out cost} = £8.$$

Thus the annual stock-out cost is

$$\text{(expected number of stock-outs per lead time)} \times \frac{300}{20} \times 8$$
$$= \underline{\text{(expected number of stock-outs per lead time)} \times 120}.$$

The expected number of stock-outs per lead time can be found for different reorder levels by accumulating the probabilities twice.

Having done this, we can find the expected annual stock-out cost as above and then add on the annual stock-holding cost for each reorder level. The reorder level for which this sum is smallest is the one to use.

Reorder level	13	12	11	10	9	8	7
First accumulation = P(1 or more stock-outs)	0.00	0.01	0.02	0.04	0.08	0.15	0.25
Second accumulation = expected number per lead-time	0.00	0.01	0.03	0.07	0.15	0.30	0.55

Stock-out cost
= 120 × expected number   0   1.2   3.6   8.4   18   36   66

Stock-holding cost
= Y + 6 × reorder level Y+78 Y+72 Y+66 Y+60 Y+54 Y+48 Y+42

Stock-holding +
stock-out costs Y+78 Y+73.2 Y+69.6 Y+68.4 Y+72 Y+84 Y+108

The smallest total cost, Y + 68.4, is achieved using a reorder level of 10. Thus an order should be placed when the stock level falls to 10. The amount to order each time is 20 items.

Exercise 6.4.1

A company has an annual demand for material X of 250 tons per annum. Order lead-time is 4 days and usage during lead-time as shown by past records is shown in Table 6.5.

Table 6.5

Usage (tons)	Frequency	Usage (tons)	Frequency
0	0	5	0.30
1	0.01	6	0.10
2	0.05	7	0.09
3	0.15	8	0.05
4	0.25		

The cost price per ton is £20 and stock-holding cost is 25 per cent per annum of the stock value. Delivery cost per batch is £4. The cost of a stock-out is also estimated to be £4.

You are required to:

(a) calculate the economic batch quantity;
(b) ascertain the reorder level taking the information given above into consideration.

(ICMA Part IV)

6.5   Stock Control with Backlogging

In this section we consider the situation where number 3 of the simple stock-control model assumptions given in section 6.1 no longer holds. We assume here that the stockist is allowed to choose to spend time out of stock. During this time he builds up a backlog of orders to be satisfied later after the next delivery has been received.

This could be a sensible choice in cases where it proved possible to associate a cost with the backlogged orders and where incurring some of that cost was worth while in order to reduce stock-holding costs.

Thus we are considering a stock-control situation where constant demand-rate and zero lead-time are assumed but where the stockist is allowed to spend time out of stock. We have in this case two parameters at our disposal: the batch size, Q, and the level, y, to which accumulated orders are allowed to rise before a new batch is received. Suppose a cost c_s can be arrived at as the average annual cost per accumulated order in the same way as ip is the average annual cost per unit of stock carried. Let all other notation be exactly as for the simple model.

The diagram for this case will be like that for the simple model but will be displaced downwards by distance y (see Fig. 6.5).

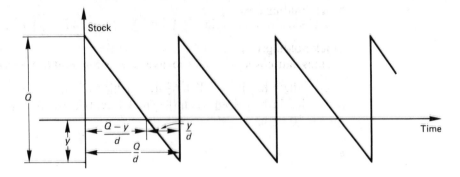

Figure 6.5

The number of orders placed per year is $\dfrac{d}{Q}$ so the total annual ordering cost is $\dfrac{cd}{Q}$.

Average number of items held in stock through the year is

$$\frac{\frac{1}{2} \times (Q-y) \times \dfrac{(Q-y)}{d}}{\dfrac{Q}{d}} = \frac{\text{area of } \triangle \text{ above axis}}{\text{total time represented}} = \frac{(Q-y)^2}{2Q}.$$

So the annual holding cost is $\dfrac{ip(Q-y)^2}{2Q}$.

Average number of accumulated orders carried through the year is

$$\frac{\frac{1}{2} \times y \times \dfrac{y}{d}}{\dfrac{Q}{d}} = \frac{\text{area of } \triangle \text{ below axis}}{\text{total time represented}} = \frac{y^2}{2Q}.$$ So annual deficiency cost $= \dfrac{c_s y^2}{2Q}$.

Thus we have to find Q and y so as to minimise total annual stock-cost, which is

$$X = \frac{cd}{Q} + \frac{ip(Q-y)^2}{2Q} + \frac{c_s y^2}{2Q},$$

i.e. minimise
$$X = \frac{cd}{Q} + \frac{ipQ}{2} - ipy + \frac{(ip + c_s)y^2}{2Q}. \tag{1}$$

We can minimise this function of two variables by finding the partial derivatives and equating to zero:

$$\frac{\partial X}{\partial Q} = -\frac{cd}{Q^2} + \frac{ip}{2} - \frac{(ip + c_s)y^2}{2Q^2} = 0, \tag{2}$$

$$\frac{\partial X}{\partial y} = -\frac{ip}{2} + \frac{(ip + c_s)y}{Q} = 0. \tag{3}$$

From (3) we have
$$y = \frac{ipQ}{ip + c_s}. \tag{4}$$

Substituting this in (2) gives $\quad -\dfrac{cd}{Q^2} + \dfrac{ip}{2} - \dfrac{(ip)^2}{2(ip + c_s)} = 0.$

So $\qquad\qquad\qquad\qquad \dfrac{cd}{Q^2} = \dfrac{ipc_s}{2(ip + c_s)}.$

Hence $\qquad\qquad\qquad\quad Q^2 = \dfrac{2cd(ip + c_s)}{ipc_s}.$

So we can write $\qquad\boxed{Q = \sqrt{\dfrac{2cd}{ip}} \cdot \sqrt{\dfrac{ip + c_s}{c_s}} = \sqrt{\dfrac{2cd}{ip}} \cdot \sqrt{1 + \dfrac{ip}{c_s}}.}$

The best batch-size emerges as just the usual square-root formula multiplied by an adjustment factor whose magnitude depends on the relative sizes of ip and c_s.

If c_s is large relative to ip (making deficiencies unattractive) then the adjustment factor will be close to one, giving a batch size very similar to the usual square-root formula.

If ip is large relative to c_s then there will be larger batch-sizes in this case.

Substituting the Q result in (4) we have.

$$y = \dfrac{ip}{ip + c_s} \sqrt{\dfrac{2cd}{ip}} \cdot \sqrt{\dfrac{ip + c_s}{c_s}}.$$

Thus $\qquad\boxed{y = \sqrt{\dfrac{2cdip}{c_s(ip + c_s)}} = \sqrt{\dfrac{2cd}{c_s\left(1 + \dfrac{c_s}{ip}\right)}}}$

This emphasises that if c_s is large then y should be small, while if c_s is small then y will be large.

Example 6.5.1

The simple stock-control model leads to the formula $Q = \sqrt{\dfrac{2cd}{ip}}$ for the optimum batch-size. This model includes among its assumptions that no stock-outs are permitted. In many situations it is possible to accumulate orders received, when there is no inventory to satisfy them, and deliver the accumulated orders immediately the product is received from the supplier. There may be a variety of costs associated with this situation and in the following calculations you should assume that these costs are equal to £2.

Other data, from which you should select those which are relevant includes: annual uniform demand 24 000 units per annum; the cost of placing an order is £20, of receiving, inspecting and checking a delivery is £70, the cost of carrying stock is £3 per unit per annum; lead-time is 1/24th of a year, interest paid by the company, on average, for funds employed is 12 per cent per annum, and the cost of extra storage facilities would be £500 per annum.

You are required to:

(a) Calculate the EBQ and reorder point if no stock-outs are permitted.
(b) Calculate the EBQ and reorder point when stock-outs are permitted.

(ICMA Prof. 1)

ANSWER

(a) If no stock-outs are allowed we have

$$Q = \sqrt{\frac{2cd}{ip}} = \sqrt{\frac{2 \times 90 \times 24\,000}{3}} = 1200.$$

Since the lead-time is $\frac{1}{24}$ of a year, a batch needs to be ordered when supplies for $\frac{1}{24}$ of a year remain. $\frac{1}{24} \times 24\,000 = 1000$.

The EBQ is 120 units and the reorder level is 1000 units.

(b) If stock-outs are allowed we have

$$Q = \sqrt{\frac{2cd}{ip}} \cdot \sqrt{1 + \left(\frac{ip}{c_s}\right)} = 1200 \sqrt{1 + \frac{3}{2}} = 1200\sqrt{2.5} = 1897.$$

$$y = \frac{ipQ}{ip + c_s} = \frac{3 \times 1897}{3 + 2} = \frac{5691}{5} = 1138.$$

The number of orders which is to be allowed to accumulate is 1138.

Since 1000 units are demanded in the lead time, it follows that the order level should be placed when 138 orders have been accumulated.

The EBQ is 1897 units and the reorder level is when 138 orders have been accumulated.

Exercise 6.5.1

The demand rate for items of a particular type can be regarded as constant with a value of 3000 per year. The set-up cost of a batch is £20 and the items can be produced at a rate of 5000 per year. The cost of holding an item for a year is 40p and stock-outs incur a penalty which amounts to 50p for each item by which stock is on average deficient through the year. Find the EBQ and the reorder level.

Further Exercises

6.1 Data relevant to component K used by Engineering Plc in 22 different assemblies and to the company include:

purchase price £15 per 100,
annual usage 100 000 units,
cost of buying office: fixed £15 575 per annum, variable £12 per order,
rent of components store £3000 per annum,
heating £700 per annum,
interest 25 per cent per annum, insurance 0.05 per cent per annum based on total purchases,
deterioration has been expressed as 1 per cent per annum of all items purchased.
You are required to:

(a) calculate the EOQ for component K;
(b) calculate the percentage change in total annual variable costs relating to component K if the annual usage was:
(i) 125 000 units, and (ii) 75 000 units;
(c) use these figures to comment on the sensitivity of the EOQ to changes in the annual usage.

(ICMA Prof. 1)

6.2 The simple basic economic batch quantity (EBQ) ordering model may be presented as:

$$Q = \sqrt{\frac{2cd}{ip}} \, ,$$

where Q = economic batch quantity,
d = annual cost,
c = costs associated with an order,
ip = the cost of holding one unit in stock for one year.

For part Z the annual demand is stable throughout the year and amounts to 250 000 units per annum. The price is £750 per 100 with discount of 20 per cent for orders and deliveries totalling in excess of 4 500 units. The cost of placing an order has been estimated at £20 and the variable costs associated with the receipt of a delivery into stores at £30. The firm requires a return of 20 per cent on any investment. Assume a working year of 50 weeks.

You are required to:

(a) derive from first principles the minimum-total-cost formula;
(b) calculate the EBQ and total cost for part Z for one year;
(c) state, with reasons, four problems that may arise when attempting to implement a stockholding policy based upon the simple EBQ formula.

(ICMA Prof. 1)

6.3 The forecast annual demand for a particular product sold by a retail store is 600 units; the cost is £60 per unit. The cost of ordering and receiving delivery is £15 on each occasion. Stockholding costs are 20 per cent per annum of stock value.

You are required to:

(a) derive the basic economic batch quantity (EBQ) formula defining any symbols used and stating clearly the assumptions you have made;
(b) calculate the optimum order quantity if there is to be instantaneous delivery of an order;
(c) calculate the effect on the EBQ of the supplier offering a quantity discount of 10 per cent when orders equal to, or in excess of, 150 units are placed.

(ICMA Prof. 1)

6.4 The Modernised Manufacturing Company Limited has a choice between establishing standard production for part Z either on a modern high-speed line or on the old, but still productive, plant.

The cost of making one hundred of part Z on the old plant has been estimated as follows: direct materials £50, direct wages £25, and variable production overhead at 100 per cent on direct wages cost. Setting up costs of £40 would be incurred each time a batch was required.

For the modern high-speed line the production cost of making one hundred of part Z has been estimated as follows: direct materials £60, direct wages £10 and variable production overhead at 200 per cent on direct wages cost. Setting up costs of £500 would be incurred each time a batch was required.

Stock-holding costs have been estimated at £20 per 100 of part Z per annum.

You are required to:

(a) derive the simple economic batch quantity (EBQ) formula;
(b) calculate the minimum annual demand which would be necessary to justify the modern line being designated as the standard manufacturing process;
(c) indicate other matters, quantifiable and non-quantifiable, which would influence the decision as to which line should be used when further stock is required.

(ICMA Part IV)

7 Queuing

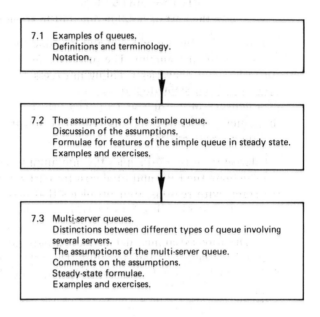

7.1 Examples of queues.
Definitions and terminology.
Notation.

7.2 The assumptions of the simple queue.
Discussion of the assumptions.
Formulae for features of the simple queue in steady state.
Examples and exercises.

7.3 Multi-server queues.
Distinctions between different types of queue involving several servers.
The assumptions of the multi-server queue.
Comments on the assumptions.
Steady-state formulae.
Examples and exercises.

7.1 Introduction

You will be familiar from long experience with the concept of a queue. In this unit we look at some different queuing systems and consider such features as how long it takes on average for a customer to pass through a system from entry to completed service, the average number of customers in the queue at a particular time and the proportion of time that a server is busy.

The kinds of queue with which we are all familiar in supermarkets, post offices, banks, canteens etc. constitute one particular and important application of queuing theory. By analysing these situations to find average waiting-times, average queue-lengths etc. help can be obtained for making decisions on such matters as whether more staff need to be available at particular times of day in order to process customers faster, or whether more queuing space is needed. However, the results of queuing theory have equally if not more important applications in industrial situations such as machines breaking down and needing to join a queuing system to be repaired, or lorries arriving at a factory and needing to queue to be unloaded. In this section we introduce some of the basic terminology and notation of queuing and we then go in later sections to look at some particular types of queuing system.

A queue is said to have reached a *steady-state* situation if it has been running long enough for:

(a) any initial conditions (e.g. a long queue outside a shop on the opening day of the sales) to have been 'forgotten' by the system so that they no longer affect waiting times and queue lengths.

(b) the queuing system not to appear to change significantly if we look at it at any point in the future.

It is only when such steady-state conditions apply that we can meaningfully talk about such things as average waiting-time and average queue-length.

An important distinction in the terminology of this subject which must be noted is that between the 'queue' and the 'system'. The *queue* comprises those customers waiting for service to begin and does not include the one being served. The *system*, on the other hand, comprises all customers, *including* the one being served.

The *traffic intensity* of a queue is defined in general to be

$$\frac{\text{mean arrival-rate}}{\text{mean service-rate}}$$

The usual symbol for traffic intensity is ρ, the Greek letter rho. It is also usual to represent mean arrival-rate by λ, the Greek letter lambda, and mean service-rate for a server by μ, the Greek letter mu.

If there are several servers serving at different average rates then these are represented by using subscripts on mu: μ_1, μ_2, μ_3 etc.

7.2 The Simple Queue

In this section we consider the most basic kind of queuing situation where there is just one server and hence one queue waiting for attention from that server. There are also assumptions about the physical constraints and discipline of the system and about the distributions of the inter-arrival times and service times. The full set of assumptions is as follows:

1. There is no limit to the permissible length of the queue.
2. No customer leaves the queue without being served.
3. There is only one server.
4. The arrivals occur according to a Poisson process.
5. The service times follow a negative exponential distribution.
6. There is a first-in-first-out queue discipline (FIFO).

Assumption 6 normally holds in practice, though there are situations where it does not. In the machine-repair situation, for example, certain machines might be regarded as so important that they must be repaired immediately they break down, regardless of which other machines are waiting. Also, assumption 1 is normally a reasonable assumption in practice.

However, in dealing with queues of human customers assumption 2 is often not valid because people do get tired of waiting and leave. In the language of the subject this is referred to as reneging. A related problem in such queues is that of potential customers deciding not to join the queue at all if it looks too long. This is called baulking and has the effect of distorting the arrival distribution.

It is in fact the distributional assumptions, 4 and 5, which are the most restrictive in the simple model for a single-server queue. The effect of assumption 4 is to say that multiple arrivals are not allowed and that arrivals occur randomly through an interval of time. Thus if the mean arrival-rate is λ then the probability of an arrival during a short interval of length δt is $\lambda \delta t$.

The negative exponential distribution referred to in assumption 5 is a continuous probability distribution having a probability density function (p.d.f.) curve of the shape shown in Fig. 7.1. We see from this that most service times are relatively short but that a certain proportion are long. If the mean service-rate is μ, then the

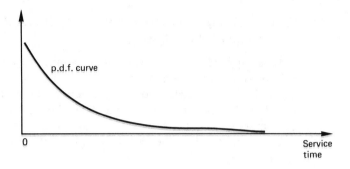

Figure 7.1

equation of the probability density function is $f(t) = \mu e^{-\mu t}$. The Poisson process and the negative exponential distribution are closely related in that the inter-event times in a Poisson process follow a negative exponential distribution. Thus we can think of the probability of a service during a short time-interval of length δt as $\mu \delta t$ and the probability of n services in time t being

$$\frac{(\mu t)^n \, e^{-\mu t}}{n!}.$$

There exist models for the single-server queue using more sophisticated distributional assumptions, but the simple model is commonly used and gives results which are a useful guide for purposes of managing the system.

The simple queue can be represented diagrammatically by the situation shown in Fig. 7.2.

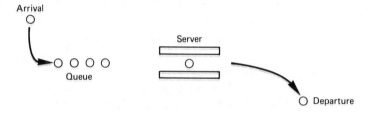

Figure 7.2

If the assumptions of the simple queue can be believed to hold, then we can obtain formulae in terms of the traffic intensity, ρ, and the service rate, μ, for various steady-state features of the queue.

Derivation of these formulae is relatively straight forward for the simple queue, involving operations with Poisson distribution probabilities. However, it is not part of our purpose to work through such derivations; rather, we present the formulae and then demonstrate their use in queuing problems. Note that for the simple queue the traffic intensity is

$$\rho = \frac{\text{mean arrival rate}}{\text{mean service rate}} = \frac{\lambda}{\mu}.$$

We have the following:

(a) Probability of system being empty, i.e. server idle, is $P_0 = 1 - \rho$.

(b) Probability of n customers in the system at any particular time $P_n = (1 - \rho)\rho^n$.

(c) Average number of customers in the system $= \dfrac{\rho}{1 - \rho}$.

(d) Average number of customers in the queue (including times when there is no queue) $= \dfrac{\rho}{1 - \rho}$.

(e) Average number of customers in the queue (averaged only over times when there is a queue) $= \dfrac{1}{1 - \rho}$.

(f) Average time a customer spends in the system $= \dfrac{1}{(1 - \rho)\,\mu}$.

(g) Average time a customer spends in the queue $= \dfrac{\rho}{(1 - \rho)\,\mu}$.

We note that these formulae make sense only if ρ is less than 1, that is to say if the mean service-rate is faster than the mean arrival-rate. Although it would seem fairly obvious that a system where mean service-rate is slower than mean arrival-rate has no chance of coping, you may be a little surprised that systems where the rates are actually equal will degenerate into infinite waiting-times and queue-lengths. The point is that although the mean rates are the same, the distributions are such that the long services more than outweigh the long inter-arrival times and in the long run the system will not cope.

Example 7.2.1

At a tool service-centre the arrival rate is two per hour and the service potential is three per hour. The hourly wage paid to the attendant at the service centre is £1.50 per hour and the hourly cost of a machinist away from his work is £4.00.
  You are required to:

(a) state the assumptions on which simple queuing theory is based;
(b) calculate the average number of machinists being served or waiting to be served at any given time;
(c) calculate the average time a machinist spends waiting for service;
(d) calculate the total cost of operating the system for an 8-hour day;
(e) calculate the cost of the system if there were two attendants working together as a team, each paid £1.50 per hour and each able to service on average two customers per hour.

(ICMA Prof. 1)

ANSWER

(a) This requires a statement of the six simple-queue assumptions given in the text above.

(b) Arrival rate is $\lambda = 2$, service rate is $\mu = 3$ and so $\rho = \dfrac{\lambda}{\mu} = \tfrac{2}{3}$. So average number of machinists in the *system* is

$$\dfrac{\rho}{1 - \rho} = \dfrac{\tfrac{2}{3}}{1 - \tfrac{2}{3}} = \dfrac{\tfrac{2}{3}}{\tfrac{1}{3}} = \underline{2.}$$

(c) Average time spent in the *queue* is $\dfrac{\rho}{(1 - \rho)\,\mu} = \dfrac{\rho}{1 - \rho} \times \tfrac{1}{3} = \tfrac{2}{3}\,\text{h} = \underline{40\ \text{min.}}$

(d) Attendant's wage for an 8-hour day is £$(8 \times 1.50) = £12$. On average there are 2 machinists in the system throughout the day so $2 \times 8 = 16$ man-hours of production are lost. Each of these costs £4 so the total cost of wasted time is $4 \times 16 = £64$. Hence the total cost of operating this system for an 8-hour day is $£12 + £64 = \underline{£76}$.

(e) There is a single-channel system since the attendants work as a team. The effective service rate is 4 per hour.

Thus $\lambda = 2$, $\mu = 4$ $\Rightarrow$ $\rho = \dfrac{\lambda}{\mu} = \dfrac{2}{4} = \tfrac{1}{2}$.

The average number in the system is $\dfrac{\rho}{1-\rho} = \dfrac{\tfrac{1}{2}}{1-\tfrac{1}{2}} = 1$.

Now wages for an 8-hour day are $£(2 \times 8 \times 1.50) = £24$.
Man-hours lost in an 8-hour day are now $1 \times 8 = 8$ h.
Each costs £4 so the value of lost production $= £4 \times 8 = £32$.
So the total cost of operating the system is $£24 + £32 = \underline{£56}$.

Example 7.2.2

Material arrives at the goods-inwards section of a factory at the average rate of five loads per hour. The material is handled by a fork-lift truck which has an average service rate of seven loads per hour. Management requires to know:

(a) the average number of loads at the section waiting to be moved, when there is a queue;
(b) the average length of time an arriving load spends waiting for service;
(c) what the average service-rate must be in order to reduce the expected waiting time to 20 minutes for a load.

(ICMA Part IV)

ANSWER

(a) $\lambda = 5$, $\mu = 7$, so $\rho = \dfrac{\lambda}{\mu} = \dfrac{5}{7}$.

Average number in the queue when there is a queue is $\dfrac{1}{1-\rho} = \dfrac{1}{1-\tfrac{5}{7}} = \dfrac{1}{\tfrac{2}{7}}$

$$= \frac{7}{2} = 3.5.$$

That is, the average number of loads waiting to be moved *when there is a queue* = 3.5.

(b) Average time in queue $= \dfrac{\rho}{(1-\rho)\mu} = \dfrac{\tfrac{5}{7}}{(1-\tfrac{5}{7})\times 7} = \dfrac{\tfrac{5}{7}}{\tfrac{2}{7}\times 7} = \dfrac{5}{14}$ h.

That is, the average time an arriving load spends waiting for service = <u>21.4 min</u>.

(c) Let the average service-rate needed in order to reduce the waiting time to 20 min (i.e. $\tfrac{1}{3}$ h) be x.

Then we have $\dfrac{\rho}{(1-\rho)\mu} = \dfrac{5/x}{(1-5/x)\cdot x} = \dfrac{5}{x(x-5)} = \dfrac{1}{3}$.

Hence $15 = x^2 - 5x$, i.e. $x^2 - 5x - 15 = 0$.

So $x = \dfrac{5 \pm \sqrt{25+60}}{2} = \dfrac{5 \pm \sqrt{85}}{2} = \dfrac{5 \pm 9.2195}{2}$.

The negative value is meaningless in this context so $x = \dfrac{14.2195}{2}$

$$= 7.11.$$

That is, the service rate must be increased to <u>7.11 per hour</u>.

Exercise 7.2.1

A garage has unfortunately been reduced to 1 petrol pump owing to a mechanical breakdown. Normally 40 cars an hour stop for petrol and on average drivers serve themselves in 1 minute. The owner is afraid that people will not wait and is considering employing a temporary attendant who would reduce the average service time to 45 seconds. The garage owner obtains an average profit contribution of £1 per car.

(a) Draw a graph showing the relationship between traffic intensity (x axis) and average number in the system (y axis) for the system described above if there is no attendant.
(b) State the implied value of drivers' time if the cost of employing the attendant is £5 per hour.

(ICMA Prof. 1)

Exercise 7.2.2

A team of 12 men is employed to unload material from lorries delivering agricultural produce from different sources.

The team works for a 4-hour period each day, during which 16 lorries arrive (4 in each hour). It takes 12 minutes to unload a lorry and each lorry is unloaded on a first-in-first-out basis by all 12 men working as a team.

FORMULA:

Average time a customer is in the system $= \dfrac{1}{1-\rho} \times \dfrac{1}{\mu}$.

When lorries are in the system for more than 30 minutes they are compensated at the rate of £3 per hour. The members of the team are each paid £10 for the 4-hour period and it has been proposed that it would be more profitable to increase the size of the team to 16 men, when the unloading time would be reduced to 10 minutes per lorry.

You are required to:

(a) calculate the cost of the present system;
(b) calculate the cost of the proposed system;
(c) discuss the comparative results, commenting on matters of practicality and any policy considerations which appear to be involved.

(ICMA Prof. 1)

7.3 Multi-server Queues

In this section we consider the queuing situation where all the assumptions of the simple queue hold except that our one queue is now being serviced by several servers. Thus we are concerned with the situation shown in Fig. 7.3. This kind of queuing system is now used in many banks and in some building-society offices.

Customers form one queue and go to whichever counter clerk next becomes free. However, in post offices and supermarkets it is more usual for each server to have a separate queue, a situation which can be thought of as more like a series of separate single-server queues, except that simple-queue conditions will generally be violated because if one server becomes idle some customers will leave their queues without being served and go to the server who is free.

In the machine-repair context the situation we have in this section is one where machines as they break down form a single queue waiting for repair. Whichever mechanic next becomes free services the machine at the front of the queue. If, on the other hand, each mechanic were to be given responsibility for a specified subset of the machines we should then have a series of single-server queues where the

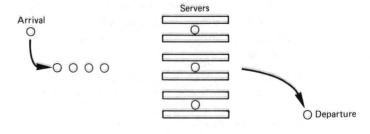

Figure 7.3

conditions and discipline of the simple queue (even if not necessarily the distributional assumptions) could be reckoned to hold because baulking, reneging or swapping between queues would not be possible. A third possibility in the case being considered here would be for all the broken-down machines to form a single queue and for the mechanics to work together as a team on the one at the front of the queue. This would be a single-server queue situation with the service rate being a composite rate based on the rates of the individual mechanics who are working together.

The full set of assumptions for multi-server queues as being considered in this section is as follows:

1. There is no limit to the permissible length of the queue.
2. No customer leaves the queue without being served.
3. Customers form a single queue waiting to be served by whichever of several servers next becomes free.
4. The arrivals occur according to a Poisson process.
5. The service times for each server follow a negative exponential distribution with the same mean.
6. There is a first-in-first-out discipline for the queue.

Comments regarding the validity of these assumptions are similar to those made for the simple queue in section 7.2. Points that should be noted are:

Assumption 5: (that all servers serve at the same average rate): the formulae based on this model all use this average rate and the mathematics and the resulting formulae are vastly more complicated if different rates for different servers are taken into account; the results given, assuming equal rates, are normally an adequate approximation to reality.

Assumption 6: (FIFO): the first-in-first-out discipline for the *queue* will not necessarily mean first-in-first-out for the *system* as not all customers are dealt with by the same server and a later arrival to the system with a short service-time may well leave before a customer who went in earlier to a different server and had a long service-time.

If there are c servers, or service channels in the language of the subject, and the mean service rate in each of those channels is μ, then it follows that the average service-rate for the system as a whole is $c\mu$. Hence, for the multi-server queue we have that

$$\text{traffic intensity } \rho = \frac{\text{mean arrival rate}}{\text{mean service rate}} = \frac{\lambda}{c\mu}.$$

It is standard notation to use μ to mean the service rate *in each channel* and ρ to mean $\dfrac{\lambda}{c\mu}$. We give formulae for certain average features of the queue and then

116

consider examples which make use of some of these formulae. The derivation of the formulae is again based on manipulations involving Poisson and negative exponential distributions.

(a) Probability of system being empty, i.e. all servers idle, is

$$P_0 = \frac{c!\,(1-\rho)}{(\rho c)^c + c!\,(1-\rho)\left[\sum_{r=0}^{c-1} \frac{1}{r!}\,(\rho c)^r\right]}.$$

(b) Probability of n customers in the system is

$$P_n = \frac{(\rho c)^n}{n!}\,P_0 \qquad \text{if } n \leqslant c-1,$$

$$P_n = \frac{\rho^n c^c}{c!}\,P_0 \qquad \text{if } n \geqslant c.$$

(c) Average number of customers in the system is $\dfrac{\rho\,(\rho c)^c}{c!\,(1-\rho)^2}\,P_0 + \rho c.$

(d) Average number of customers in the queue is $\dfrac{\rho(\rho c)^c}{c!\,(1-\rho)^2}\,P_0$

(including times when there is no queue).

(e) Average number of customers in the queue is $\dfrac{1}{1-\rho}$

(averaged only over times when there is a queue).

(f) Average time a customer spends in the system is $\dfrac{(\rho c)^c}{c!\,(1-\rho)^2\,c\mu}\,P_0 + \dfrac{1}{\mu}.$

(g) Average time a customer spends in the queue is $\dfrac{(\rho c)^c}{c!\,(1-\rho)^2\,c\mu}\,P_0.$

Example 7.3.1

Your company is considering changing the present system of serving customers who arrive in person and wait for service. The existing single-service channel can service 10 people an hour at a variable cost of £8 per person. The service facilities have a fixed cost of £50 per hour. The demand for these services has increased from 4 persons per hour when first offered to the current 8 per hour and is expected to increase to 15 per hour next year.

Alternative service patterns have been considered. Either a larger single-service channel that would be able to service 20 people an hour at a variable cost of £7 per person and fixed costs of £120 per hour, or the addition of another single-service channel which would still have a variable cost of £8 per person but additional fixed costs of £60 per hour. Customer time has been estimated to have a value of £25 per hour.

You are required to:

(a) calculate the cost to the company of the optimum service-system, ignoring customers' time, currently and next year;
(b) calculate the cost in each system to the customer next year;
(c) state which system the company should choose next year if it takes into account half the value of customers' time.

(ICMA Prof. 1)

ANSWER

(a) *Cost to company of present system currently:*

$\lambda = 8$, $\mu = 10$ so $\rho = 0.8$.

The cost per hour is £50 + 8 × £8 = £50 + £64 = £114.

Cost to company of present system next year:

$\lambda = 15$, $\mu = 10$ so $\rho = \dfrac{15}{10} = 1.5 > 1$! This system will not work next year. This system will certainly not be the optimum one next year and we disregard it.

Cost to company of enlarged single channel currently:

$\lambda = 8$, $\mu = 20$ so $\rho = 0.4$.

The cost per hour is £120 + 8 × £7 = £120 + £56 = £176.

Cost to company of enlarged single channel next year:

$\lambda = 15$, $\mu = 20$ so $\rho = \dfrac{15}{20} = 0.75$.

The cost per hour is £120 + 15 × £7 = £120 + £105 = £225.

Cost to company of two-channel system currently:

$c = 2$, $\lambda = 8$, $\mu = 10$ so $\rho = \dfrac{\lambda}{c\mu} = \dfrac{8}{2 \times 10} = \dfrac{8}{20} = 0.4$.

The cost per hour is £50 + £60 + 8 × £8 = £110 + £64 = £174.

Cost to company of the two-channel system next year:

$c = 2$, $\lambda = 15$, $\mu = 10$ so $\rho = \dfrac{\lambda}{c\mu} = \dfrac{15}{2 \times 10} = \dfrac{15}{20} = 0.75$.

The cost per hour is £50 + £60 + 15 × £8 = £110 + £120 = £230.

The optimum service system for the company *currently* is the *existing one*. It costs *£114 per hour*. The optimum service system for the company *next year* is the *enlarged single channel*. It costs *£225 per hour*.

(b) If the enlarged single channel is used next year then the average time spent by a customer in the system will be

$$\frac{1}{(1 - \rho)\mu} = \frac{1}{(1 - 0.75) \times 20} = \frac{1}{0.25 \times 20} = \frac{1}{5.0} \text{ h} = \frac{60}{5.0} = 12 \text{ min.}$$

Hence cost per customer next year will be on average $\frac{1}{5}$ × £25 = £5.
15 customers per hour pass through the system so cost per hour of customer time is £75.

For the two-channel system we have

$$P_0 = \frac{2!\,(1 - 0.75)}{(2 \times 0.75)^2 + 2! \times 0.25\,[1 + (2 \times 0.75)^1]} = \frac{0.5}{2.25 + 0.5 \times 2.5}$$

$$= \frac{0.5}{3.50} = \frac{1}{7}.$$

So the average time a customer is in the system is

$$\frac{2.25 \times \frac{1}{7}}{2 \times \frac{1}{16} \times 2 \times 10} + \frac{1}{10} = \frac{9}{70} + \frac{1}{10} = \frac{16}{70} = \frac{8}{35} \text{ h.}$$

So cost per customer next year will be on average $\frac{8}{35}$ × £25 = £5.71.

15 customers per hour pass through the system so cost per hour of customer time is £85.65.

(c) The extra cost per hour for customer time using the 2-channel system is £10.65. Half of this is £5.32$\frac{1}{2}$.

Choose the single-channel system as better for both.

Example 7.3.2

At the present time a servicing department provides answers through one channel, which on average can deal with 24 enquiries per hour at a cost of £3 per enquiry. Increasingly, the customers are complaining that they have to wait for a long time and the department is considering alternative arrangements. These are either a two-service-channel system costing £100 per hour and service rate of 15 per hour in each, or a three-service-channel system costing £125 per hour and a service rate of 10 per hour in each. Customers arrive at the rate of 20 per hour.

You are required to calculate:

(a) the average time a customer is in the system under the present arrangement;
(b) the extra charges per enquiry that would need to be made to recover the extra cost of each of the two arrangements proposed;
(c) the implied value of customers' time per hour if they agreed to pay the extra costs of the two-channel system.

(ICMA Prof. 1)

ANSWER

(a) The average time a customer is in the system under the present arrangement is

$$\frac{1}{(1 - \rho)\,\mu}\,.$$

We have $\mu = 24$ and $\lambda = 20$ so $\rho = \dfrac{\lambda}{\mu} = \dfrac{20}{24} = \frac{5}{6}$.

Hence $\dfrac{1}{(1 - \rho)\,\mu} = \dfrac{1}{\frac{1}{6} \times 24} = \frac{1}{4}$ h.

The average time in the system is 15 minutes.

(b) The average cost per hour of the single-channel system is $20 \times £3 = £60$. The cost per hour of the two-channel system is £100.

So the extra cost to be met per hour is £40. Customers arrive at 20 per hour. Hence the extra charge needed per customer for the two-channel system is $£40 \div 20 = £2$. The cost per hour of the three-channel system is £125.

So the extra cost to be met per hour relative to the present situation is £65. Hence the extra charge needed per customer for the three-channel system is $£65 \div 20 = £3.25$.

(c) For the two-channel system we have $\lambda = 20$, $\mu = 15$ and $c = 2$ so

$$\rho = \frac{\lambda}{c\mu} = \frac{20}{30} = \frac{2}{3}.$$

Hence $P_0 = \dfrac{2\,!\,(1 - \frac{2}{3})}{(\frac{2}{3} \times 2)^2 + 2\,!\,(1 - \frac{2}{3})(1 + \frac{2}{3} \times 2)}$

$$= \frac{2 \times \frac{1}{3}}{\frac{16}{9} + 2 \times \frac{1}{3} \times (1 + \frac{4}{3})} = \frac{\frac{2}{3}}{\frac{16}{9} + \frac{14}{9}} = \frac{\frac{2}{3}}{\frac{30}{9}}\,.$$

Thus $P_0 = \dfrac{2}{3} \times \dfrac{9}{30} = \dfrac{18}{90} = 0.2$.

So the average time a customer would spend in the two-channel system is

$$\frac{(\rho c)^c}{c!\,(1-\rho)^2 c\mu}\,P_0 + \frac{1}{\mu} = \frac{(\tfrac{2}{3}\times 2)^2}{2!\,(1-\tfrac{2}{3})^2 \times 2 \times 15} \times 0.2 + \frac{1}{15}$$

$$= \frac{\tfrac{16}{9}}{2\times \tfrac{1}{9} \times 30} \times 0.2 + \frac{1}{15} = \frac{3.2}{60} + \frac{1}{15} = \frac{7.2}{60}\ \text{h.}$$

Thus the average time spent by a customer in the two-channel system is 7.2 minutes.

It follows from the answer to part (a) that the average time saving per customer is $15 - 7.2 = 7.8$ minutes. The extra cost per customer was found in part (b) to be £2. So if customers are prepared to pay £2 to save on average 7.8 minutes, the implied value of customer time is $200 \div 7.8 = 25.64$ pence per minute. The implied value of customer time is 26 pence per minute, or £15.60 per hour.

Exercise 7.3.1

You have been asked to consider three systems for providing service when customers arrive with a mean arrival-rate of 24 per hour:

(a) a single channel with a mean service-rate of 30 per hour at £5 per customer, and fixed costs of £50 per hour;
(b) 2 channels in parallel each with a mean service rate of 15 per hour at £4 per customer, and fixed costs of £30 per hour per channel;
(c) 3 channels in parallel with a mean service-rate of 10 per hour at £3 per customer, and fixed costs of £25 per hour per channel.

Your tests have confirmed that the system is identical in all other aspects with a simple queue.
You are required to calculate:

(a) the average time a customer is in the system when 1, 2 and 3 channels are in use;
(b) the most economical system to adopt if the value to the firm of customers' time is ignored, and to state the total cost per hour of this system;
(c) the implied value to the firm of customers' time if the firm is indifferent between the 2- and 3-channel systems.

(*ICMA Prof. 1*)

Exercise 7.3.2

Whenever a system is providing a service it may be from a single service channel or several service channels. In the particular system you are asked to consider there is an average arrival rate of 24 per hour. There is a choice of a single channel servicing at a rate of 32 per hour or three channels in parallel each servicing 10 per hour. The total costs to the management asssociated with these two systems are £60 and £48 per hour respectively and the waiting time of a customer is valued at £6 per hour.
You are required to:

(a) calculate the cost of:
    (i) the single-channel system;
    (ii) the multi-channel system; and
(b) advise management which system they should adopt with explanation fror your recommendation.

(*ICMA Part IV*)

Further Exercises

7.1 A repair man is to be hired to repair machines which break down at an average rate of 3 per hour. Non-productive time on a machine is reckoned to cost the company £5 per hour. The company has narrowed down the choice to two repair men, one slow but cheap, the other fast but expensive. The slow, cheap repair man asks £3 per hour; in return he will service broken-down machines at an average rate of 4 per hour. The fast, expensive repair man demands £5 per hour but will repair machines at an average rate of 6 per hour. Taking the simple queue assumptions to hold, decide which repair man should be hired.

7.2 In a supermarket customers arrive in a Poisson process at an average rate of 5 every 30 minutes. The average time it takes to check and calculate the cost of a customer's purchases at the one and only check-out is exponentially distributed with a mean of 4.5 minutes.

(a) What is the average time a customer will have to wait at the check-out before service begins?

(b) What proportion of the time is the cashier working?

7.3 A company is considering installing a tool-grinding machine for use by its operators. The following proposals are under review:

Machine A costs £2000 and has an average grinding time of 10 minutes.
Machine B costs £3000 and has an average grinding time of 5 minutes.
Machine C cost £4000 and has an average grinding time of 2 minutes.

(All machines have to be written-off in 5 years' time.)

If the average arrival rate of operators for grinding is 5 per hour and the cost of an operator waiting (including lost production) is £2 per hour, which machine should be installed by the company? (Assume 50 weeks in each year and 40 hours in each week.)

8 Simulation

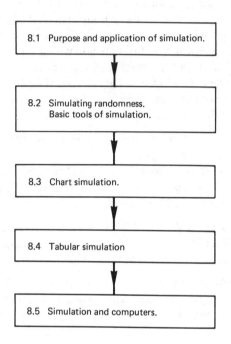

| 8.1 Purpose and application of simulation. |
| 8.2 Simulating randomness. Basic tools of simulation. |
| 8.3 Chart simulation. |
| 8.4 Tabular simulation |
| 8.5 Simulation and computers. |

8.1 Introduction

In this section we consider how simulation is linked into operational research. We then go on in the unit to consider the basic tools of simulation: chart simulation, tabular simulation and computer methods.

Many projects in operational research require the establishment of a model to describe a real-world situation. Such models may be physical models, theoretical deterministic models or some other type of model, for example, the use of a model railway to represent an actual rail network, or the use of the economic-batch-quantity model to predict optimal stock-ordering decisions. The reader may refer to Chapter 1, section 1.4, for further discussion of modelling. However, simulation may be considered to differ from the approaches of both the physical model and the deterministic model. The chart simulation and the tabular simulation we consider here are illustrative simplifications of procedures which may be adopted in practice. In contrast, an industrial simulation may involve a team working for many months.

Simulation has three basic purposes:

(a) to describe a current system,
(b) to explore hypothetical systems,
(c) to design an improved system.

Many OR analysts consider simulation to be a 'method of last resort'. This is because it may be useful when other approaches cannot be used, as for example when a real-world situation is highly complex.

Although simulation is used in a wide variety of contexts, including the training of airline pilots and activities in space, our concern in this unit will be with the construction of simple models applied to business. The cost advantage of simulation arises when the model is used to test alternative policies which may be under consideration by management.

Examples arise in the areas of road systems, maintenance programmes and stock control. It is clearly uneconomic to construct roads which are not essential but merely a hypothetical alternative. However, simulating hypothetical systems using a model is relatively inexpensive.

An important strength of simulation lies in its ability to inter-link various probabilistic strands of a situation. For instance, random arrivals to a queue may be linked to the random availability of service facilities resulting in part from uncertainties about the reliability of service. Such stochastic situations require a simulation of the randomness in the real world. Some examples are considered in the following section.

8.2 Simulating Randomness

The most usual way of simulating randomness is to obtain a set of numbers satisfying a basic criterion. For instance it may be appropriate to use the set of digits

$$\{0, 1, 2, 3, 4, 5, 6, 7, 8, 9\}.$$

The requirement is that each time a selection is made each of the ten digits has an equal chance of being chosen. Repeated selection of this nature will generate a sequence of random numbers. The results of such experiments are given in tables of random numbers such as appear in published books of statistical tables. These published tables of random numbers are normally generated by a computer. In a particular simulation task it may be appropriate to use a published table of random numbers (if the job is not too large) or to work directly with a computer producing random numbers as they are required.

The conventional six-sided fair die may also be used to generate a sequence of random digits in the set

$$\{1, 2, 3, 4, 5, 6\}$$

where each digit has probability $\frac{1}{6}$ of occurrence. Polyhedra with other numbers of faces could be used similarly, but they are less common.

Random procedures also feature in decision making. As an example the reader is referred to the consideration of mixed strategy solutions to game theory problems in section 4.2 onwards of Chapter 4.

We consider now an introductory example involving the simulation of orders obtained by a salesman.

Example 8.2.1

A salesman averages one call each day and his results show that 50 per cent of his calls lead to a sale. Simulate two sequences of results for the salesman covering a period of 10 days. Use the following sequences of random numbers:

8, 4, 3, 7, 9, 0, 6, 1, 5, 6   and   3, 6, 6, 7, 1, 0, 0, 8, 2, 3.

ANSWER

The solution has two parts. The first part specifies the rules and the second part applies them.

The rules must link the random numbers so that success has probability 0.5 and failure has probability 0.5. A simple categorisation of the digits {0, 1, 2, 3, 4, 5, 6, 7, 8, 9} is to have two subsets {0, 1, 2, 3, 4} and {5, 6, 7, 8, 9} where each contains five elements. We associate 'success' with the first group and 'failure' with the second group. (*Note:* This categorisation is far from unique. Any division of the ten digits into two groups of five would be just as good. One that might well have been used is {0, 2, 4, 6, 8} for success and {1, 3, 5, 7, 9} for failure.) It is convenient to summarise the rule in what is referred to as a look-up table:

Result of call	Probability	Random numbers
Successful (+)	0.5	0, 1, 2, 3, 4
Failure (−)	0.5	5, 6, 7, 8, 9

The applications of the rules for the two 10-day periods are shown below with + being used to indicate a successful call and − to indicate a failure to sell:

First 10-day period

Day	1	2	3	4	5	6	7	8	9	10
Random number	8	4	3	7	9	0	6	1	5	6
Result of call	−	+	+	−	−	+	−	+	−	−

Second 10-day period

Day	1	2	3	4	5	6	7	8	9	10
Random number	3	6	6	7	1	0	0	8	2	3
Result of call	+	−	−	−	+	+	+	−	+	+

Exercise 8.2.1

(a) Carry out the simulations requested in example 8.2.1 using the random numbers given in that question but using the subset {0, 2, 4, 6, 8} to indicate success and the subset {1, 3, 5, 7, 9} to indicate failure.

(b) Carry out the simulations requested in example 8.2.1 using a six-sided die to generate the two sets of random numbers required. Use the subset {1, 2, 3} to mean success and the subset {4, 5, 6} to mean failure for the first 10-day period. Use the subset {1, 3, 5} to mean success and the subset {2, 4, 6} to mean failure for the second 10-day period.

Having carried out a simulation it is necessary to calculate appropriate statistics to summarise the situation being studied. From the answer to example 8.2.1 we see that for the first 10-day period there was a 40 per cent success rate and for the second 10-day period there was a 60 per cent success rate. In a more complex simulation many more statistics could usefully be calculated. (The simple problem in example 8.2.1 can, in fact, be modelled by a binomial probability distribution, and if a large number of 10-day simulations were carried out the proportion of these leading to each possible success-rate would be found to agree with the binomial probability calculations.)

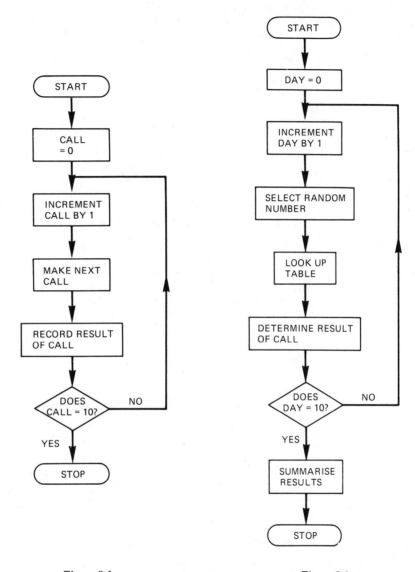

Figure 8.1   Figure 8.2

Flowcharts can be a useful aid to simulation. Figure 8.1 is a flowchart showing the activities of the salesman in example 8.2.1. Then Fig. 8.2 shows the process of simulation which was employed to solve example 8.2.1. It would not normally be necessary for both these flowcharts to be produced for every simulation. However, they show the relationship between the 'real-world' activity and the method used to simulate it.

8.3   Chart Simulation

In this section we extend the ideas introduced in section 8.2 and illustrate how a simulation may be recorded in 'chart' form.

Example 8.3.1

A salesman arranged to make a call each day for the next 10 working days. Previous experience showed that each call arranged had a 10 per cent chance of cancellation. When a call was made he expected the following chances of success in making sales:

Result	Percentage chance
No sale	50
1 unit sold	10
2 units sold	30
3 units sold	10

At the start of the 10-day period he assumed that 5 units were in stock and that a further 5 would be available for dispatch from day 6. It was the policy of his firm to dispatch orders on the same day they were placed with the salesman. However, if no stock was available orders would be held over for dispatch until the next delivery of stock.

Use a chart simulation to cover the 10 days. Show whether each call was made and its result. Show also the level of stock held at the end of each day.

Use the following random-number sequence:

5, 4, 5, 6, 2, 6, 9, 3, 0, 3, 9, 3, 9, 4, 8, 4, 9, 8, 4.

ANSWER

Figure 8.3 is a flowchart representing this simulation. Two look-up tables are required to answer this question. First we need to determine whether the call took place or was cancelled.

State of call	Chance	Random numbers
Took place	90%	0, 1, 2, 3, 4, 5, 6, 7, 8
Cancelled	10%	9

Then if a call took place we need to know the result.

Number of units sold	Chance	Random numbers
0	50%	0, 1, 2, 3, 4
1	10%	5
2	30%	6, 7, 8
3	10%	9

The allocations of random numbers in these tables are based on the fact that each random digit is assumed to have a 10 per cent chance of occurring. Therefore chances of 10 per cent, 30 per cent, 50 per cent and 90 per cent require 1, 3, 5, and 9 digits respectively.

The chart which results, when the simulation is carried out by applying the given sequence of random numbers to these tables, is shown as Fig. 8.4.

Note that the first set of random numbers contains a 9 for day 7 so no call was made that day. This is indicated in the first section of the chart.

Hence for determining the results of calls only 9 random numbers are needed. The corresponding results of calls are shown in the second section of the chart.

126

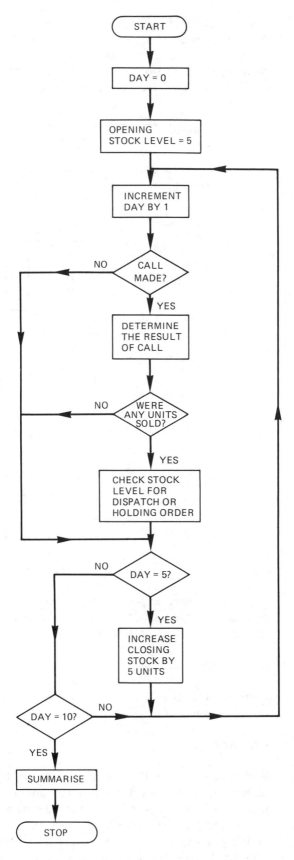

Figure 8.3

The final section of the chart shows the cumulative depletion of stock from the initial level of 5 units and the restocking of 5 units at the start of day 6. It will be noted that each delivery was followed 3 days later by a stock-out. We may conclude from this section of the chart that there would have been no stock-outs if the initial stock level had been set at 8 units.

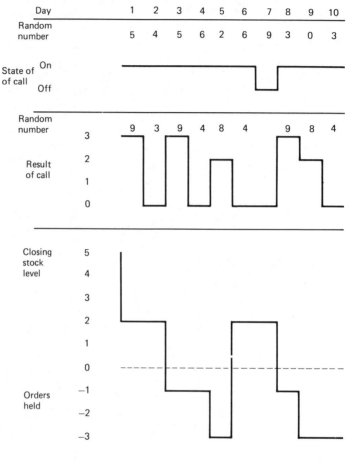

Figure 8.4

A further very important factor to be considered is that only two delivery periods have been simulated. It is essential to repeat the simulation many more times before useful conclusions can be drawn.

Exercise 8.3.1

Carry out the chart simulation requested in example 8.3.1 using a new sequence of random numbers.

Exercise 8.3.2

Following a review of the holding of stock and the expected orders a firm proposed to have an opening stock level of 12 units of a particular product. An order was placed for 6 units to be delivered for the start of the fifth week and a further order was placed for 6 units to be delivered at the start of the ninth week. Previous indications suggest that only 30 per cent of deliveries are on time while 20 per cent are 1 week late and 50 per cent are 2 weeks late. Additionally there is a variation in the requirements for stock each week as shown next:

Weekly demand (units)	Chance (%)
0	10
1	30
2	40
3	20

Use a chart simulation to cover a period of 12 weeks showing the demand each week and the level of stock held at the end of each week.

8.4 Tabular Simulation

The use of a table to record a simulation is the hallmark of tabular simulation. The table is constructed to produce a record of what has been simulated to occur and to facilitate any analysis or monitoring of the processes required. When the table is initially designed a 'pilot' run is often desirable as modification may be required. In general, an initial column would record an incremental number of events, other columns would record random numbers and the corresponding results, while others would monitor the implications of earlier columns. However, this is not an area to establish fixed rules. Rather, a creative flexible approach is more suitable.

An example is now considered in which the above guidelines are applied. However, alternative approaches may be used.

Example 8.4.1

An engineering firm has two machines A and B to produce product Z. The daily output of each machine has been specified in Table 8.1.

Table 8.1

Machine A		*Machine B*	
Daily output (units)	*Chance (%)*	*Daily output (units)*	*Chance (%)*
0	20	0	10
7	20	6	30
8	30	7	40
9	30	8	20

In addition, quality-control tests give each day's output a probability 0.95 of being accepted and a probability 0.05 of being scrapped.

Complete a tabular simulation to cover a period of 10 days, monitoring daily and cumulative output.

ANSWER

Figure 8.5 is a flowchart representing this simulation. Three look-up tables are required: one for each machine and one for the quality check (Table 8.2a, b, c).

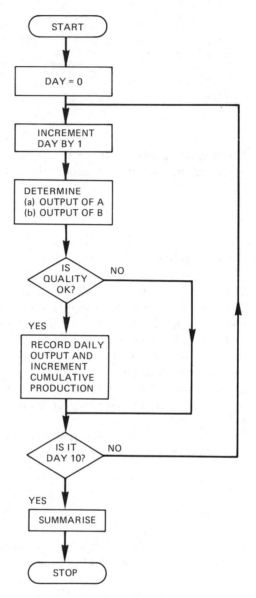

Figure 8.5

Table 8.2a

Machine A

Daily output (units)	Chance (%)	Random numbers
0	20	0, 1
7	20	2, 3
8	30	4, 5, 6
9	30	7, 8, 9

Table 8.2b

Machine B

Daily output (units)	Chance (%)	Random numbers
0	10	0
6	30	1, 2, 3
7	40	4, 5, 6, 7
8	20	8, 9

As the chances in these first two tables are all multiples of 10 per cent, only one digit from {0, 1, 2, 3, 4, 5, 6, 7, 8, 9} is required for each 10 per cent chance. But in the third table we need probabilities of 0.95 and 0.05. In this case we must use the random digits in pairs and select from the set {00, 01, 02, . . ., 98, 99}. This set contains one hundred pairs and we can assume that each pair has a 1 per cent chance of being selected. To simulate a probability 0.95 we use 95 of the pairs and to simulate a probability 0.05 we use 5. Hence we can obtain the third look-up table (Table 8.2c).

Table 8.2c

Decision	Chance (%)	Random numbers
Accept	95	00, 01, . . ., 93, 94
Reject	5	95, 96, 97, 98, 99

To carry out the simulation random-number blocks were used. Random-number tables frequently arrange the digits in blocks. A block may be selected randomly and then the digits used sequentially. The essential point is that no 'cheating' must go on. Random numbers should be used systematically in the order in which they appear and not arbitrarily selected or rejected in order to obtain hoped-for results. The blocks are shown below:

```
4  1  7  9  0      2  2  7  9  2
4  8  5  8  0      0  5  1  9  6
5  7  5  2  6      6  9  3  3  9
8  5  1  1  8      4  4  4  1  7
6  9  0  8  0      5  1  2  6  3
```

The table may now be produced (Table 8.3).

Table 8.3

Day	Machine A Random number	Output	Machine B Random number	Output	Quality test Random number	Result	Daily output	Cumulative output
1	4	8	1	6	79	✓	14	14
2	0	0	4	7	85	✓	7	21
3	8	9	0	0	57	✓	9	30
4	5	8	2	6	68	✓	14	44
5	5	8	1	6	18	✓	14	58
6	6	8	9	8	08	✓	16	74
7	0	0	2	6	27	✓	6	80
8	9	9	2	6	05	✓	15	95
9	1	0	9	8	66	✓	8	103
10	9	9	3	6	39	✓	15	118

For the first row, the first random number, 4, is looked up in Table 8.2a for machine A, the second random number, 1, is looked up in Table 8.2b for Machine B, and then the next two random numbers, 7, 9, are looked up in Table 8.2c for the Quality check. For each subsequent day a further four random digits are taken from the block of random numbers.

We note from the last entry of the final column that the cumulative output for the 10 days was 118 units and that no output was scrapped. Further simulations can be carried out and the results combined with the above to give a clearer indication of the reliability of the result.

Exercise 8.4.1

Carry out the tabular simulation requested in example 8.4.1 using a new set of random numbers. Compare your answer with that obtained for example 8.4.1.

Exercise 8.4.2

Carry out the simulation requested in example 8.3.1 using tabular simulation. You will find it helpful to include a column to indicate the opening stock-level and a column to indicate the closing stock-level for each day.

8.5 Simulation and Computers

The importance of simulation has increased considerably in recent years because of hardware and software developments in computing. The hardware has become cheaper, faster and more powerful as proliferation of mainframe, mini- and micro-computers has continued. On the software side there has been continuing development of high-level languages such as ALGOL, FORTRAN and BASIC as well as of simulation languages such as ECSL (Extended Control and Simulation Language) and the SEE-WHY system. These changes have resulted in a simplification of programming and in the facility for longer simulation runs and more repetitions of runs.

We give below a very simple example of a program in BASIC for carrying out a simulation. The reader with access to a computer is encouraged to input and run the program.

Example 8.5.1

Write a program to simulate the results of 10 calls made by a salesman, given that each call has a 50 per cent chance of success and a 50 per cent chance of failure.

ANSWER

```
100 REM X IS SET TO A RANDOM VALUE BETWEEN 0 AND 1
110 REM FOR X BETWEEN 0 AND 0.5 THE SALESMAN HAS A SUCCESSFUL CALL
120 REM FOR X BETWEEN 0.5 AND 1 THE SALESMAN HAS AN UNSUCCESSFUL CA
130 REM A SUCCESSFUL CALL IS SHOWN AS '+'
140 REM AN UNSUCCESSFUL CALL IS SHOWN AS '−'
150 REM N IS USED TO COUNT THE DAYS
200 N=0
210 N=N+1
220 X=RND(0)
230 IF X=0.5 THEN 220
240 IF X < 0.5 THEN A£='+'
250 IF X > 0.5 THEN A£='−'
260 PRINT A£:
270 IF N=10 THEN 290
280 GOTO 210
290 STOP
```

A typical outcome of running this program was the following:

$$+ + + - - - - - + +$$

The program may be run repeatedly, each time giving a set of ten +'s and −'s. Because of the simple nature of the problem, it is clear that over a large number of runs the total number of +'s and −'s should be equal.

Readers with knowledge of BASIC are recommended to attempt the following exercises. Those with access to a computer are encouraged to run their programs.

Exercise 8.5.1

Write a program in BASIC to carry out the simulation requested in example 8.3.1. Simulate ten 10-day periods and compare the results. In each case use random numbers generated by the computer.

Exercise 8.5.2

Write a program in BASIC to carry out the simulation requested in example 8.4.1. Simulate ten 10-day periods and compare the results. In each case use random numbers generated by the computer.

In computer simulation it is necessary to ensure that a repeat run uses a new set of random numbers. Otherwise a duplicate set of results will be obtained.

Specially designed simulation languages can hold many advantages over high-level languages. Thus ECSL is designed to aid management in model formulation, programming verification, validation and experimental design and analysis. However, a level of competence in the use of ECSL must be acquired initially.

The SEE-WHY system has been developed by BL Systems and has been used as an aid in the design of car production plants. The system is based on FORTRAN, which the programmer uses to call up various SEE-WHY routines. When a program has been written it may provide management with a very powerful simulation model.

In particular, a powerful colour-graphics facility may be used to depict the status of various entities. For example, the progress of car bodies in a conveyor system may be shown, or the inward and outward flows of a liquid between a set of tanks. This graphics facility also gives the programmer control over a large number of separate colour monitors which may be used to portray the interdependence of parts of a system.

A further strength of SEE-WHY is that a simulation may be stopped at any point in its progress to allow detailed study of a particular phase.

Once a simulation model has been set up in SEE-WHY, changes to it may be made interactively. For example, in a supermarket simulation queue lengths may have become too large or the check-out facilities may have become under-utilised. In such a situation the simulation may be modified by the addition or removal of check-out facilities. Also available is a full range of summary statistics which may be used to monitor the progress of a simulation. With this kind of simulation facility management can hope to learn how best to manage a system by gaining a clearer understanding of the interrelationships and 'knock-on' effects within it.

Further developments in computer systems for simulation can be expected in the future as hardware and software advances continue to be made.

Further Exercises

8.1 A company trading in motor-vehicle spares wishes to determine the levels of stock it should carry for the items in its range. Demand is not certain and there is a lead-time for stock replenishment. For one item, X, the following information is obtained:

Demand (units per day)	Probability
3	0.1
4	0.2
5	0.3
6	0.3
7	0.1

Carrying costs (per unit per day)   £0.20
Ordering costs (per order)   £5.00
Lead-time for replenishment (in days)   3
Stock on hand at the beginning of the simulation exercise was 20 units.
  You are required to:

Carry out a simulation run over a period of ten days with the objective of evaluating the following inventory rule:

Order 15 units when present inventory plus any outstanding order falls below 15 units.

The sequence of random numbers to be used is 0, 9, 1, 1, 5, 1, 8, 6, 3, 5, 7, 1, 2, 9, using the first number for day one. Your calculation should include the total cost of operating this inventory rule for ten days.

(ICMA Prof. 1)

8.2   In a simple queuing situation the following formulae may be used to calculate some of the system parameters:

average queuing time $\qquad = \dfrac{\lambda}{\mu(\mu - \lambda)}$;

average system process time
  or (time in the system) $\qquad = \dfrac{1}{\mu - \lambda}$;

average number in queue
  (including zeros) $\qquad = \dfrac{\lambda^2}{\mu(\mu - \lambda)}$;

average number in the system $\qquad = \dfrac{\lambda}{\mu - \lambda}$;

where: λ = mean (average) rate of arrivals,
       μ = mean (average) rate of service.

  You have observed a queuing system for several days and one sequence of observations had the results shown in Table 8.4.

Table 8.4

Arrival time	Time between start of observation, first and subsequent arrivals	Service time
1	41	70
2	46	12
3	38	23
4	57	36
5	87	136
6	221	55
7	20	65
8	99	4
9	3	17
10	10	17

Note: All times are expressed in units of 20 seconds.

  You are required to:

(a) calculate the four system parameters quoted above by a simulation of the system using the given data;

(b) calculate the four system parameters by using the formulae;

(c) comment on the values obtained in (a) and (b) and the use of the simulation technique.

(ICMA Prof. 1)

8.3 A large and reputable department store recently opened a special complaints counter to which customers could bring their grievances. The new service appears to be working well, except that some complaints are taken to a higher level. This invariably happens when the one and only 'Complaints Officer' is already engaged and cannot attend to a newly arrived 'serious' grievance.

As many as 40 per cent of aggrieved customers feel they have 'serious' cause for complaint and will ask to see the manager if service is not immediately available. Also, customers with complaints tend to start demanding to see the manager if they have not been attended to within five minutes.

An initial analysis of the counter's operations reveals the following arrival pattern of customers with complaints and the time which the complaints officer takes to attend to the customers concerned:

Inter-arrival time (min)	5	10	15	20	25
Probability	0.05	0.10	0.70	0.10	0.05

Service time (min)	3	5	7	9
Probability	0.1	0.4	0.4	0.1

The manager finds that too much of his time is being taken up by dealing with complaints which could easily be dealt with by more junior staff attached to the complaints counter.

Required:

Construct a simulation model to deal with the manager's problem, stating clearly the criteria used and assumptions made.

Assuming that two customers with non-serious complaints have just arrived, use the following set of random numbers to carry out a few steps in the simulation:

03	47
97	74
16	76
12	56
55	39

What would be the nature of the advice you might offer to the store manager?

(ACCA Prof. 2)

9 Dynamic Programming

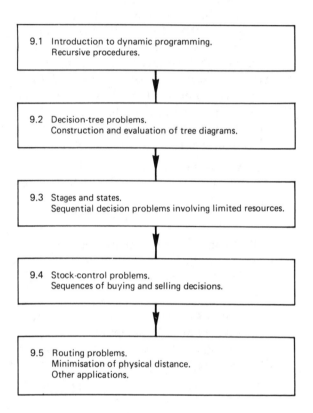

9.1 Introduction to dynamic programming. Recursive procedures.

9.2 Decision-tree problems. Construction and evaluation of tree diagrams.

9.3 Stages and states. Sequential decision problems involving limited resources.

9.4 Stock-control problems. Sequences of buying and selling decisions.

9.5 Routing problems. Minimisation of physical distance. Other applications.

9.1 Introduction

Dynamic programming is a method which has been developed to solve complex problems by using a simplifying procedure. It has many applications in business, notably to problems involving sequences of decisions in such areas as production planning, stock control, component and equipment maintenance and replacement, allocation of resources, and process design and control. The simplifying procedure significantly reduces the computational effort required.

Like simulation, considered in the previous chapter, dynamic programming is less a well-defined technique than a way of approaching certain kinds of problem. In particular, a principle known as 'embedding' is used. This enables optimal information to be retained at each stage of the solution process while non-optimal information is discarded. It is this ability to discard the non-optimal information which leads to the simplification referred to above.

A further distinctive feature of the dynamic programming approach is that it is recursive. That is to say, a solution is initially found for the last part of the problem in hand. Having found this solution, we then move back a step and seek to find a solution for the last two parts combined. This result is then used to find a solution for the last three parts, and the process is continued until we are back at the start of the whole problem and we can then obtain its solution. This chapter illustrates the principles of dynamic programming, and its recursive nature, by solving examples from various areas of application.

9.2 Decision Trees

As an initial illustration of a recursive procedure we take the example of a decision tree, with which the reader may well be familiar from studies of basic probability. In problems where this method can be applied the decision maker is faced with choosing between alternative sequences of decisions, some or all of which may have uncertain outcomes and where the outcomes of earlier decisions will affect later ones. The objective is to find the strategy which will give the best expected outcome overall.

Example 9.2.1

An oil company has recently acquired rights in a certain area to conduct surveys and test drillings to lead to lifting oil where it is found in commercially exploitable quantities. The area is already considered to have good potential for finding oil in commercial quantities. At the outset the company has the choice to conduct further geological tests or to carry out a drilling programme immediately. On the known conditions, the company estimates that there is a 70:30 chance of further tests showing a 'success'.

Whether the tests show the possibility of ultimate success or not, or even if no tests are undertaken at all, the company could still pursue its drilling programme or alternatively consider selling its rights to drill in the area. Thereafter, however, if it carries out the drilling programme, the likelihood of final success or failure is considered dependent on the foregoing stages. Thus:

if 'successful' tests have been carried out, the expectation of success in drilling is given as 80:20
if the tests indicate 'failure' then the expectation of success in drilling is given as 20:80;
if no tests have been carried out at all then the expectation of success in drilling is given as 55:45.

Costs and revenues have been estimated for all possible outcomes and the net present value of each is given in Table 9.1.

Table 9.1	Outcome	Net present value (£m)
	SUCCESS:	
	With prior tests	100
	Without prior tests	120
	FAILURE:	
	With prior tests	−50
	Without prior tests	−40
	SALE OF EXPLOITATION RIGHTS	
	Prior tests show 'success'	65
	Prior tests show 'failure'	15
	Without prior tests	45

You are required to:

(a) draw up a decision (probability) tree diagram to represent the above information;
(b) evaluate the tree in order to advise the management of the company on its best course of action.

(ICMA Prof. 1)

ANSWER

(a) The decision tree for this problem is shown as Fig. 9.1 and we consider how this diagram has been constructed. The diagram is constructed from left to right, and each decision to be made is represented by a square, while each circle represents a point of uncertainty in the process. Thus the first decision to be made is whether to sell immediately or to drill immediately or to carry out tests. (Square 1.)

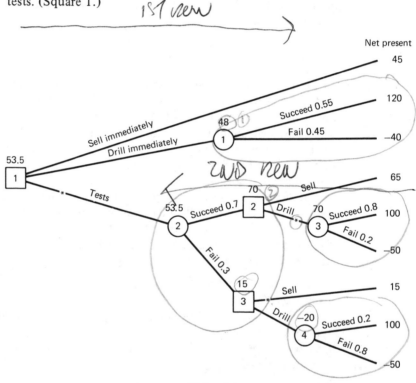

Figure 9.1

The outcome of selling immediately is certain and so the line representing this decision goes straight to the right-hand side of the diagram.

If it is decided to drill immediately, there is uncertainty about the outcome because the drilling might be either a success or a failure. This is represented by the circle in which this line ends.

Emerging from this circle there is one line for each possible outcome, representing success and failure, and on the line is noted the probability of the occurrence of that outcome.

If it is decided to carry out tests, the situation is a little more complex. The immediate outcome of the decision will be either a successful test or a failed test and this is represented by the lines, with their probabilities, emerging from circle 2. However, the result of the test having been obtained, a further decision must be made whether to sell or to drill. Hence each of these lines

138

ends in a box representing this decision. The sell decision in each case involves no uncertainty and so goes immediately to the right-hand side of the diagram. The drill decision in each case involves a further uncertainty point corresponding to successful or failed drilling, shown by circles 3 and 4.

The column of figures on the right-hand edge of the tree shows the total return achieved by reaching each of the respective end-points of the various paths through the tree. The method of evaluation now follows.

(b) Having drawn the tree we can set about evaluating it to find the best sequence of decisions by means of a procedure which works from right to left and is recursive in the sense described in section 9.1.

Suppose it had been decided to drill immediately. The expected net present value of the return from this course of action is

$$£(0.55 \times 120 + 0.45 \times (-40))m = £(66 - 18)m = £48m.$$

Hence the figure 48 shown by circle 1.

Next, suppose there were successful tests and it was decided to drill. The expected return is

$$£(0.8 \times 100 + 0.2 \times (-50))m = £(80 - 10)m = £70m.$$

Thus at the decision point following successful tests the choice is between selling for £65m or drilling for an expected return of £70m. Since £70m is the larger, the recommended decision is to drill, and this is represented by the star shown on the line and the figure of 70 by the decision box 2.

Finally, suppose there were failed tests and it was decided to drill. The expected return is

$$£0.2 \times 100 + 0.8 \times (-50)) = £(20 - 40)m = -£20m.$$

So at the decision point following failed tests the choice is between selling for a return of £15m or drilling for an expected loss of £20m.

Thus the recommended decision is to sell, and this is represented by the star shown on the sell line and the figure of 15 by the decision box 3.

Having arrived at the figures of £70m and £15m on the decision boxes following successful and failed tests respectively, we can say that the expected return following testing is

$$£(0.7 \times 70 + 0.3 \times 15)m = £(49 + 4.5)m = £53.5m.$$

This is represented by the figure 53.5 on circle 2.

We are now in a position to see which is the best initial decision by comparing the values 45, 48 and 53.5. Since 53.5 is the largest, the best decision is to carry out tests. This is represented by the star on the test line and the figure of 53.5 on the initial-decision box.

Thus we see that the best sequence of decisions is:

first carry out the tests;
if the tests succeed, proceed to drill;
if the tests fail, sell the exploitation rights.

The overall expected return from this procedure is £53.5m. Note that further information may be obtained from the decision-tree analysis beyond the optimal-expected-return policy and its value found above. For example, it may well be necessary in a given practical situation to think about the worst possible outcome of a sequence of decisions in order to avoid the risk of a severe loss. Hence in the example here management may well prefer the option of selling immediately for £45m rather than risk a possible loss of £40 m or £50m in order to obtain an additional expected gain of £3m or £8.3m respectively.

Exercise 9.2.1

In order to be able to meet an anticipated increase in demand for a basic industrial material a business is considering ways of developing the manufacturing process in order to expand capacity. After meeting current operating costs the business expects to make a net £20 000 profit in a period from its existing process when running at full capacity.

All data relate to the same period.

The research and development manager lists the following possible courses of action:

(a) adopt a process developed by another manufacturer of a similar product: this would cost £7000 in royalties and yield a net £30 000 profit (before paying the royalty);

(b) carry out one of two alternative research programmes:

   (i) the more expensive would cost £15 000 to carry out but is rated to have a 0.8 chance of success: net profit would be £40 000 (before changing the research costs) and a further income of £8000 is expected from the granting of royalties;

   (ii) the alternative research programme is less expensive, costing £12 000, but is rated to have only a 0.5 chance of successfully developing a new process: the total net return is the same as in (i) above;

(Failure of one research programme would still leave open all remaining courses of action including the other research programme.)

(c) continue to operate the existing plant and not expand to meet the new level of demand.

You are required to evaluate the above proposals to determine the most profitable course of action.

(ICMA Part IV)

9.3 Stages and States

In this section we consider further the idea of sequential-decision problems. We do so in a context which illustrates more specifically the application of dynamic programming ideas beyond the basic principle of recursive solution. The context is that each decision (referred to as a *stage*) offers several possible actions, each of which uses up a different quantity of the resource available for total implementation. The solution can be set out in the form of a grid with the stages representing the columns and the resource available representing the rows. The points of the grid representing different combinations of stage variable and resource available are the states. We use an example involving three decisions in which all outcomes are regarded as certain. However, probabilities can be introduced and dealt with using expected values (in similar manner to section 9.2) and the principles apply however large the number of decisions. Computer packages have been written for dealing with dynamic programming problems in which very large numbers of decisions can be handled, for example DYNACODE.

Problems of this type give some indication of the power of the recursive approach in that it removes the need to consider all combinations of possible actions. At each stage we can restrict attention to those actions which bring the best return from that stage onwards. This embeds optimal information and discards non-optimal information.

Example 9.3.1

An investor is offered the opportunity of participating in 3 successive investment activities, A, B and C. Activity A starts from this month (stage 1), followed by activity B and then activity C, each with a 1-month interval. Each activity requires an investment in units of £1000 (or some integer multiple). An investment activity normally lasts 6 months, with the returns given in Table 9.2. The money invested is also returned at the end of the six-month period.

If an investor has a total of £5000, how should he allocate his fund to the various activities so as to maximise his total return?

Table 9.2

Level of investment (£000)	Return on project (£)		
	A	B	C
0	0	0	0
1	80	60	70
2	180	130	140
3	310	240	220
4	480	390	290
5	540	440	340

ANSWER

The basic network for this problem is shown as Fig. 9.2. The diagram shows the states labelled in standard notation, with each initial figure denoting the stages remaining and each second figure denoting the resource still to be used.

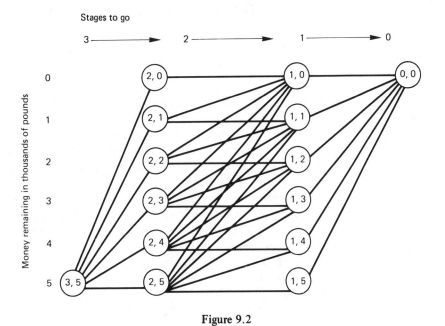

Figure 9.2

The only state which needs to be considered when there are three stages to go is the state (3, 5). This shows that 3 stages remain and that £5000 is available. Also, the only state which needs to be considered when there are no stages to go is (0, 0), as every possible investment offers the benefit of positive return and there is therefore no point in leaving any money uninvested.

As well as the nodes representing the states, the diagram shows the possible actions which can be taken as lines joining pairs of nodes. Every action which is financially possible is shown in Fig. 9.2. In the absence of dynamic programming it would be necessary to evaluate the return which could be gained from each of the twenty-one possible paths from (3, 5) to (0, 0) and identify the largest possible return. The evaluation of the network by dynamic programming is shown in Fig. 9.3, the returns from the various actions being indicated on the lines representing them.

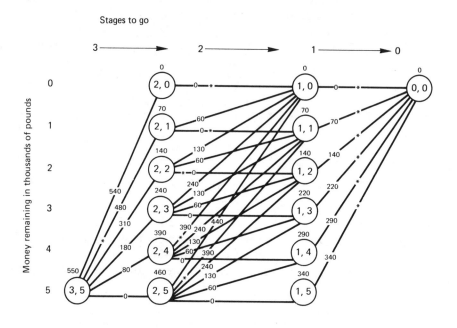

Figure 9.3

With no stages to go, no further return is possible and hence the figure 0 by node (0, 0).

From node (1, 0) onwards there is similarly no further return possible. From node (1, 1) onwards there is a return of £70 and hence the figure 70 written by this node. The same principle applies to all the other nodes corresponding to one stage remaining.

Going back a further stage, no return is possible from node (2, 0) onwards. From node (2, 1) there is a choice between investing nothing in B and going to node (1, 1) or investing £1000 in B and going to node (1, 0). The respective overall returns are £(0 + 70) and £(60 + 0). Since £70 is the larger of these, it is better to go to (1, 1). Hence a star is shown on this line and the figure 70 is written by node (2, 1). Similar choices are carried out at all the other nodes corresponding to two stages to go.

Finally, with three stages to go there is a choice between

$$540 + \quad 0 = 540,$$
$$480 + \quad 70 = 550,$$
$$310 + 140 = 450,$$
$$180 + 240 = 420,$$
$$\quad 80 + 390 = 470 \text{ and}$$
$$\quad 0 + 460 = 460.$$

Since the largest of these is 550, the best action is to invest £4000 in A, giving an overall return for the whole sequence of decisions of £550. Tracing the starred path from (3, 5) to (0, 0), we see that the best sequence of decisions is to:

first invest £4000 in A,
second invest nothing in B,
third invest £1000 in C.

Note that if we are concerned with minimising a set of values, for example maintenance costs, then the minimum value would be chosen at each step, rather than the maximum value as was used in this example concerned with maximisation of total return (see exercise 9.4.1 below).

Exercise 9.3.1

The Gassington Mineral Water Company is an old-established firm with modern ideas. At this moment three new-product proposals are being investigated by the company's market research department. Under the working titles of Perraigne, Top-Pop and Slim Fizz these minerals are to be promoted as high-class non-alcoholic party drink, teenage jet-set refresher, and slimming-aid beverage respectively. Having an extensive knowledge of rival ventures in all three fields as well as long experience of its own, the department has compiled a comprehensive table relating each product's expected contribution before advertising for the year 1977–8 to three different levels of expenditure on advertising as follows:

Product	Perraigne			Top-Pop			Slim-Fizz			
Advertising (£000)	1.0	1.5	2.0	1.0	2.0	3.0	1.0	1.5	2.0	2.5
Expected contribution 1977–8 (£000)	15	25	30	15	20	35	20	25	27.5	30

Current controls on promotional expenditure are particularly stringent, however, and the company will allocate no more than £4500 to the total advertising budget for Perraigne, Top-Pop and Slim-Fizz.

Required:
Assuming that the short-term aim is to maximise the total expected contribution before advertising of the three products, use a three-stage dynamic programming technique to determine the initial expenditure on advertising to be devoted to each.

Note: Only the expenditure given in the table should be considered and each product must receive some promotional expenditure.

(23 marks)

To what extent is your method shorter than a complete enumeration method?

(2 marks)

(ACCA Prof. 2)

DO UNE EXERCISES!

9.4 Stock-control Problems

Dynamic programming can be used in certain kinds of stock problem where we have forecasts of costs or selling prices for various times in the future or of demands for items at future times. The method can be used to determine an optimal sequence of decisions on buying, selling or manufacturing so as to achieve objectives such as maximising overall return or minimising stock costs. The time points again represent the stages for the dynamic programming formulation and the stock levels would in general correspond to the resource levels of section 9.3.

We work through an example involving purchasing and sales policy for a warehouse and leave the reader with a manufacturing problem as an exercise.

Example 9.4.1

The warehouse used by a company trading in a single line is to be either full or empty at the beginning of each month. If it is empty, the options open to the company are:

(a) Fill it up.
(b) Leave it empty for the month.

If the warehouse is full there are three options available:

(a) Sell the contents of the warehouse and leave it empty for the month.
(b) Sell the contents of the warehouse and then refill it.
(c) Leave the warehouse full for the month.

If option (c) is taken there is a stock-holding charge of £2000 for the month. The company has forecasts of the prices for buying and selling the amounts of stock held by the warehouse for the next five months as follows. The figures are in thousands of pounds.

Month	1	2	3	4	5
Buying price	20	26	36	28	22
Selling price	22	26	30	22	22

Assuming the warehouse to be full at the beginning of the first month and at the end of the fifth month, determine the optimum buying and selling policy for the five months and state the gain over the five-month period which will result from this policy.

ANSWER

The diagram for solving this problem is shown as Fig. 9.4. The nodes in the upper row represent the warehouse empty while those in the lower row represent the warehouse full.

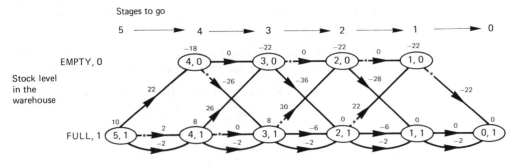

Figure 9.4

The lines between nodes represent all the options open to the company as specified in the question and the figures shown on them are obtained from the buying and selling prices given and from the stock-holding information.

Beginning the recursive process as always at the final node, we see that the maximum gain from node (0, 1) onwards is 0.

Hence from node (1, 0) onwards it is $-22 + 0 = -22$.

From node (1, 1) there is a choice between $0 + 0 = 0$ and $-2 + 0 = -2$. The larger of these is 0, so the better policy is to sell and buy. This is starred on the diagram and 0 is written by node (1, 1).

This procedure is continued on all nodes back through the diagram until we reach (5, 1). You should check that all the correct actions have been starred and the corresponding maximum-return values written by the nodes.

From the completed diagram we observe that the optimum policy is as follows:

Month	1	2	3	4	5
Action	Sell and buy	Sell and buy	Sell	Do nothing	Buy

The overall gain from this optimal sequence of decisions is £10 000.

Exercise 9.4.1

A maker of pianos has orders for pianos to be delivered at the ends of months as follows:

Month	May	June	July	August
No. of pianos	2	3	6	4

There is no stock of pianos at the beginning of May and it is not intended that there should be any surplus stock after the August delivery. If any pianos at all are built in a particular month, there is an overhead cost of £400 for that month. The building of a piano takes place completely within a calendar month.

There is a stock-holding cost of £100 per piano per month.

Determine the production schedule for pianos which will minimise total costs in meeting the given set of orders.

Notes:

(a) This is a *minimisation* problem, so in working back through the dynamic programming network you need the action which will give the *smallest* figure on the next node reached.

(b) The drawing of the network can be simplified by satisfying yourself of the following points:

  (i) Whenever pianos are made, the number produced should exactly meet the demand for a certain number of months.

  (ii) Pianos should not be made until stock is exhausted.

9.5 Routing Problems

In this section we consider using dynamic programming to find the best of several possible routes between a starting-point A and a finishing-point B. Such problems arise in areas like transportation or the laying of pipelines and the method can also be applied in cases which are not to do with physical routing at all but where relationships can be expressed in similar terms. The recurrence method of solution seen in the previous sections of this chapter can again be used. The links between nodes might carry values which represent some quantity to be minimised, such as cost or physical distance, or they might carry values representing a quantity to be maximised, such as profit.

Example 9.5.1

The diagram shown as Fig. 9.5 is a schematic representation of a map showing possible routes from town X to town Y, using main roads. The routes all pass

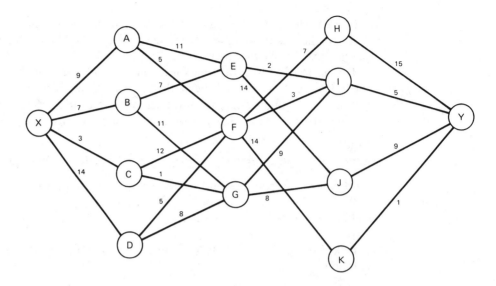

Figure 9.5

through other towns, represented by the other nodes in the diagram, and the distances between towns (in miles) are shown on the lines linking the nodes. Find the route which offers the minimum distance between the towns.

ANSWER

The solution is shown in Fig. 9.6, which is a redrawing of Fig. 9.5 showing the results of working backwards through the diagram indicating on each node the minimum distance which needs to be covered from that point on in order to reach town Y.

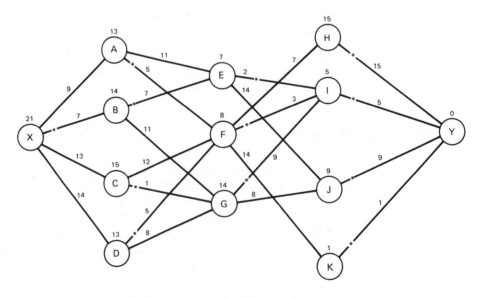

Figure 9.6

We next show an asterisk on each route back from Y to H, I, J and K. But in the case of point F we put the asterisk on route FI as FI is the minimum of FH(22), FI(8) and FK(15). This backward process is continued until the starting point X is reached where XB has an asterisk as it is the minimum of XA(22), XB(21), XC(28) and XD(27).

As in previous applications, use of the recursive approach represents a considerable saving on evaluation and comparison of every possible combination of routes.

Exercise 9.5.1

Figure 9.7 shows a set of towns through which a carrier can travel in making a journey from X to Y using the roads represented by the lines. The figures shown on the lines are the profits expected from the corresponding journeys. Find the route from X to Y which will maximise the profit which the carrier can expect to achieve.

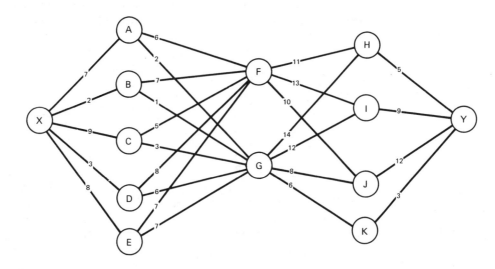

Figure 9.7

Further Exercises

PO WE EXAMPLE!

9.1 A company has £100 000 available for investment and is considering two projects A and B. Project A is equally likely to return a profit of £24 000 or a loss of £10 000, while project B is equally likely to return a profit of £36 000 or a loss of £24 000. Each project requires investment of the whole £100 000 available but if one project is undertaken immediately this amount plus the profit or minus the loss will be returned after three months. If £100 000 were available at that stage then investment in the second project could then be considered. Find the best investment policy and the expected profit associated with it.

9.2 An investor has £4000 and is faced with a sequence of three investment decisions, denoted as X, Y and Z. Investments have to be made in units of £1000 and the expected returns are as shown in Table 9.3.

Table 9.3	Investment (£000)	Expected return from X	Expected return from Y	Expected return from Z
	0	0	0	0
	1	70	80	90
	2	250	200	150
	3	300	360	190
	4	380	440	300

147

Draw a network and use dynamic programming to determine the best investment policy and the total expected return from that policy.

9.3 A piece of equipment in a factory is inspected at the end of each year and is either serviced or replaced. Both the sale value of the equipment and its servicing cost are related to its age and these are as follows:

Age of equipment (years)	1	2	3	4
Sale value (£000)	20	10	4	0
Cost of service (£000)	12	10	14	—

If a decision to replace is made, the total cost involved is £40 000. The machine currently in use has just reached the end of its third year of life. The factory as a whole has an expected life of 5 years and the machine in use at the end of that time will be sold. Find the minimum-cost schedule of servicing and replacement for the 5-year period and state the total cost of that schedule.

10 Replacement

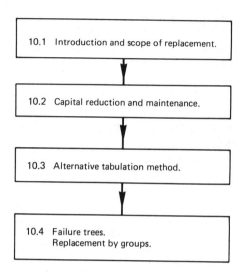

10.1 Introduction and scope of replacement.

10.2 Capital reduction and maintenance.

10.3 Alternative tabulation method.

10.4 Failure trees.
Replacement by groups.

10.1 Introduction

This chapter on replacement is concerned with the determination of an optimum policy for replacing items of equipment which wear out or otherwise lose value in course of time. The usual optimality criterion employed is that of minimising expected annual cost.

Solution of some replacement problems requires data relating to the survival probabilities of the items under consideration. Data of this nature is difficult to obtain in some industrial situations, since the determination of these probabilities may require testing. Such testing may be expensive or time consuming or both. However, such data is essential for the purpose of evaluating different possible policies.

In this chapter we consider replacement of equipment which gradually wears out and replacement of equipment which is subject to sudden failure. When the equipment gradually wears out the cost of maintenance will be increasing but the resale value will be reducing. When the equipment is subject to sudden failure, the choice will be between replacing individual items (either as they fail or at the end of each fixed period) or completely replacing *all* items at specified intervals with supplementary individual replacements as necessary.

Sections 10.2 and 10.3 are concerned with the first kind of replacement problem described above and section 10.4 with the second kind. Ideas from Chapter 9 on dynamic programming and Chapter 12 on Markov chains can also be used in the solution of replacement problems.

10.2 Replacement with Capital Reduction and Maintenance

The examples used to illustrate the points made in this section concern the determination of the optimal policy for purchase of a new cutting machine using data relating to the expected cost of initial purchase, resale value and maintenance. The general method of solution for such problems is to construct a table. The relevant data would include the cost of buying new or partly used equipment, resale or scrap value and maintenance costs. The table would show capital reduction and maintenance costs separately and then in combined form. Next, a cumulative total is obtained and divided by the number of years the equipment is held in order to determine an average price per year. This is the value which is used for comparative purposes to decide the optimal policy.

Example 10.2.1

A firm requires a cutting machine which cost £40 000 to purchase new. Table 10.1 indicates the expected annual cost of maintenance and the expected resale/scrap value assumed to apply at the end of each year of operation.

Table 10.1

Year	Expected end-of-year resale value (£000)	Expected cost of maintenance for the year (£000)
1	28	3
2	18	4
3	10	6
4	4	9

Prepare a table to determine the following:

(a) The reduction in capital.
(b) The expected combined cost of maintenance and reduction in capital.
(c) The expected cumulative combined cost of maintenance and reduction in capital.
(d) The expected annual cost of each replacement policy.

ANSWER

The required table is shown as Table 10.2.

Table 10.2

Year	Maintenance (£000)	(a) Capital reduction (£000)	(b) Combined maintenance and capital reduction (£000)	(c) Cumulative maintenance and capital reduction (£000)	(d) Average annual cost (£000)
1	3	12	15	15	15
2	4	10	14	29	14.5
3	6	8	14	43	14.3
4	9	6	15	58	14.5

The first two columns are transferred directly from Table 10.1. In column (a) the first calculated figure of £12 000 is obtained by reducing the initial value of £40 000 by the resale value of £28 000 for a 1-year-old machine. The subsequent figures in column (a) are obtained by subtracting successive values in the column of expected end-of-year resale prices. Column (b) is obtained by adding the corresponding values in the two preceding columns. Column (c) is obtained by the cumulative addition of column (b). Finally, column (d) is obtained from column (c) as a result of dividing by the number of years.

In the schedule obtained above we can compare the values in column (d) and observe that the minimum value is £14 300. This tells us that the optimal policy is to replace the machine at the end of each 3-year period.

Next we consider an extension to the above example where there exist purchasing possibilities other than buying a new machine at time zero. That is to say, it is possible to buy a used machine of various possible ages. The maintenance costs for the machine purchased in this way are related to its age in the same way as the maintenance costs for a new machine when it has reached the same age. There are now two decisions to be made. First it must be decided what age of machine should be bought, and second it must be decided how long to keep it before replacement.

Example 10.2.2

A firm requiring a cutting machine has the options of buying a new machine or a machine which is 1, 2 or 3 years old. The respective purchase costs are as shown in Table 10.3.

Table 10.3

Age at purchase	Price of machine (£000)
New	40
1 year old	31
2 years old	20
3 years old	11

Table 10.4 indicates the expected resale/scrap costs of a machine of a given age and also the expected annual cost of maintenance for a machine of that age.

Table 10.4

Age of machine (years)	Expected resale value (£000)	Expected annual cost of maintenance (£000)
1	28	3
2	18	4
3	10	6
4	4	9

Determine at what age a machine should be purchased and when it should be replaced.

ANSWER

The first policy to be considered is that of buying a new machine and this leads once more to the table seen in the answer to example 10.2.1, i.e. Table 10.2.

Table 10.2 (repeat)

Year	Maintenance (£000)	Capital reduction (£000)	Combined maintenance and capital reduction (£000)	Cumulative maintenance and capital reduction (£000)	Average annual cost (£000)
1	3	12	15	15	15
2	4	10	14	29	14.5
3	6	8	14	43	14.3
4	9	6	15	58	14.5

Thus we see that if new equipment is to be purchased it should be replaced after 3 years.

The next policy to be considered is that of purchasing a 1-year-old machine and keeping it for 1, 2 or 3 years. This leads to Table 10.5, which is similar to Table 10.2, on applying the procedures as explained in the answer to example 10.2.1.

Table 10.5

Years from purchase of the one-year-old machine	Maintenance (£000)	Capital reduction (£000)	Combined maintenance and capital reduction (£000)	Cumulative maintenance and capital reduction (£000)	Average annual cost (£000)
1	4	13	17	17	17
2	6	8	14	31	15.5
3	9	6	15	46	15.3

The initial figure of £13 000 in the capital-reduction column arises by reducing the purchase cost of £31 000 for a 1-year-old machine by the resale figure of £18 000. We see that if 1-year-old equipment is purchased it should be replaced after 3 years.

The next policy to be considered is that of purchasing a 2-year-old machine and keeping it for 1 or 2 years. This again leads to Table 10.6, which is similar to those for the policies considered previously.

Table 10.6

Years from purchase of the two-year-old machine	Maintenance (£000)	Capital reduction (£000)	Combined maintenance and capital reduction (£000)	Cumulative maintenance and capital reduction (£000)	Average annual cost (£000)
1	6	10	16	16	16
2	9	6	15	31	15.5

The initial figure of £10 000 in the capital-reduction column arises by reducing the purchase cost of £20 000 for a 2-year-old machine by the resale figure of

£10 000 for a 3-year-old machine. We see that if 2-year-old equipment is purchased it should be replaced after 2 years.

Finally, we must consider the policy of buying 3-year-old equipment and replacing it every year. Following the same procedure as for the previous policies we obtain in this case a one-line table (Table 10.7).

Table 10.7

Years from purchase of the three-year-old machine	Maintenance (£000)	Capital reduction (£000)	Combined maintenance and capital reduction (£000)	Cumulative maintenance and capital reduction (£000)	Average annual cost (£000)
1	9	7	16	16	16

The capital reduction figure of £7 000 arises by reducing the £11 000 purchase cost of a three-year-old machine by the £4 000 resale value of a 4-year-old machine.

From the four tables obtained we see that the best policy is to buy new equipment and replace it after 3 years. This has a minimum annual average cost of £14 300.

Exercise 10.2.1

A piece of mechanical equipment may be bought new or from 1 to 5 years old as follows:

Age of equipment (years)	New	1	2	3	4	5
Cost (£)	16 000	11 600	8000	5200	3200	2000

The same piece of equipment may be sold from 1 year old to 6 years old for prices as follows:

Age (years)	1	2	3	4	5	6
Selling price (£)	10 000	6600	4000	2200	1200	200

The annual costs of operating and maintaining the equipment are as follows:

Through year	1	2	3	4	5	6
Cost (£)	2000	2400	3000	4000	6000	10 000

Find the year to buy and the year to sell if the objective is to minimise the overall average cost per year. Neglect all other factors.

10.3 Alternative Tabulation Method

Problems of the type considered in section 10.2 can be solved using a more compact tabulation procedure than shown there. We shall illustrate this method by reworking example 10.2.2. Having followed that example, the reader should have no difficulty in appreciating that what is done here is exactly the same procedure in a more economical notation.

Example 10.3.1

A firm requiring a cutting machine has the options of buying a new machine or a machine which is 1, 2 or 3 years old. The respective purchase costs are shown in Table 10.8.

Table 10.8	Age at purchase	Price of machine (£000)
	New	40
	1 year old	31
	2 years old	20
	3 years old	11

Table 10.9 indicates the expected resale/scrap values of a machine of given age and also the expected annual cost of maintenance for a machine of that age.

Table 10.9	Age of machine (years)	Expected resale value (£000)	Expected annual cost of maintenance (£000)
	1	28	3
	2	18	4
	3	10	6
	4	4	9

Determine what age of machine should be purchased and when it should be replaced.

ANSWER

The first step is to draw up a table showing the purchase prices for machines of different ages and their resale values when kept for different lengths of time. The differences calculated in the cells of this table show the cumulative capital reduction figures for every combination of age at purchase and age at replacement.

For example, a machine aged 2 years at purchase costing £20 000 and aged 4 years at resale when it is worth £4000 reduces by £16 000 in value. By referring to the answer to example 10.2.2 the values in the capital-reduction columns of each of the four tables are seen to correspond to the values in Table 10.10.

Table 10.10

		Age at purchase (years)			
		New (40)	1 (31)	2 (20)	3 (11)
	1 (28)	12	—	—	—
Age at replacement (years)	2 (18)	22	13	—	—
	3 (10)	30	21	10	—
	4 (4)	36	27	16	7	(£000)

Second, we draw up a table (Table 10.11) showing the cumulative costs of maintenance for machines bought at various different ages kept for different lengths of time.

Table 10.11

		Age at purchase (years)			
		New	1	2	3
	1 (3)	3	—	—	—
Age at replacement (years)	2 (4)	7	4	—	—
	3 (6)	13	10	6	—
	4 (9)	22	19	15	9	(£000)

Finally, we obtain a table (Table 10.12) showing the cumulative combined cost of capital reduction and maintenance by adding together the corresponding figures in Tables 10.10 and 10.11. This combined figure is entered in the top left-hand corner of the cell concerned. The average annual cost is then obtained by dividing that figure by the number of years held represented by that cell. The result is entered in the bottom right-hand corner of the cell and is the basis for deciding the optimal policy.

Table 10.12

Age at purchase (years)

		New	1	2	3
Age at replacement (years)	1	15 15	—	—	—
	2	29 14.5	17 17	—	—
	3	43 14.3	31 15.5	16 16	—
	4	58 14.5	46 15.3	31 15.5	16 16

(£000)

It is convenient to average the cells working along the diagonals of the table. The cells on the leading diagonal (top left to bottom right) all represent a 1-year retention, those on the diagonal immediately below represent a 2-year retention, those on the next diagonal a 3-year retention and the final cell represents a 4-year retention.

We see from Table 10.12 that the optimal policy is to buy a new machine and replace it after 3 years. The average annual cost of this policy is £14 300. This agrees with the answer as found by the method used in example 10.2.2.

There are a number of criticisms which may be levelled at the approach to replacement problems which we have explained in sections 10.2 and 10.3. The approach as we have considered it ignores interest rates and hence the fact that the value of money becomes less the further it is into the future. This problem can be overcome by using present values of monetary amounts rather than the actual money figures. Furthermore, the data given is assumed to be relevant to future use of equipment. There may be wide variations in the maintenance costs for equipment due to such factors as variations in manufacture, changes in model specifications and variation in the use of the equipment. These matters could be incorporated into calculations by the introduction of probability distributions relating to maintenance costs based on past experience. Another criticism could be the fact that we have assumed replacement to be possible only at annual intervals. This could be overcome by using smaller time-intervals which would not change the principles of solution but would lead to larger tables.

In addition, investment decisions should give full consideration to any government incentives for depreciation of equipment or relocation of plant. There may also be taxation advantages to be gained through leasing rather than purchasing equipment.

Exercise 10.3.1

Rework exercise 10.2.1 using the alternative tabulation method explained in this section.

10.4　Probability and Failure Trees

In this section we consider the replacement of items which can be replaced either individually after they have failed or as a group at various intervals of time whether they have failed or not. This group replacement would be supplemented by individual replacement of failed items. Replacement cost per item is lower when group replacement is carried out, and so the issue is the finding of the replacement time-interval which best balances the cost of individual replacements on the one hand against the cost of wasting items which have not failed on the other. Thus we seek an optimal group-replacement time-interval.

Example 10.4.1

A set of 100 lamps is used to give warning of a series of roadworks. Each lamp is powered by a battery which is expected to fail some time during a period of 3 weeks. Replacement of failed batteries may take place only at the end of a week. This end-of-week replacement may be on an individual basis for just the batteries which have failed where the cost is £1 per battery, or it may be by replacing the whole set of 100 batteries at once (whether they have failed or not) for a group cost of £60. The following table gives data relating to the survival of batteries:

Week of use	1	2	3
Probability of failure during the week	0.2	0.5	0.3

(a) Draw a failure tree to represent the situation where batteries are replaced individually over a period of four weeks.

(b) Compare the policies of individual replacement only, and group replacement after 1, 2, 3 and 4 weeks respectively, supplemented by individual replacement at the end of each week. Which of these policies has the lowest average weekly cost of replacement?

ANSWER

(a) We may use the probability data to infer the likely failures each week if 100 batteries are used at the start. As the probabilities are 0.2, 0.5 and 0.3, we assume 20, 50 and 30 of the 100 fail by the end of week 1, 2 and 3 respectively. We are thus able to construct a 'branch' as shown in Fig. 10.1.

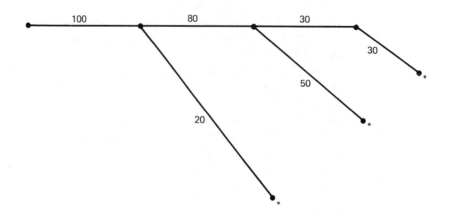

Figure 10.1

This branch may be extended to obtain a tree by linking a new branch to each of the three nodes starred. As a consequence, further nodes arise which again must be linked to new branches.

The basic convention used is to indicate the number of batteries remaining by a figure *above* a horizontal line and the number failing in a week by a figure *below* a downward sloping line. This convention simplifies the addition necessary to find weekly replacement totals.

The full failure tree is shown as Fig. 10.2 and this diagram shows also the accumulated total failures for the four weeks.

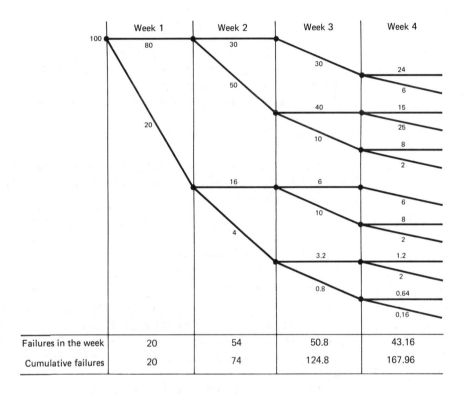

Figure 10.2

(b) We now compare the cost of individual replacement only with the cost of replacement by group at the ends of weeks 1, 2, 3 and 4 respectively.

Using individual replacement only, the mean time to replacement of a battery is

$$(0.2 \times 1 + 0.5 \times 2 + 0.3 \times 3) \text{ weeks}$$
$$= (0.2 + 1.0 + 0.9) \text{ weeks} = 2.1 \text{ weeks}.$$

Hence the expected replacement rate is $100 \div 2.1 = 47.62$ batteries per week. As each individual replacement costs £1, the expected weekly cost of this policy is £47.62.

Next, we calculate the expected weekly cost of group replacement at the end of every 1, 2, 3 or 4 weeks respectively supplemented by end-of-week replacement of failed batteries as necessary (Table 10.13).

Table 10.13 End of week	Cumulative cost of supplementary individual replacements (£)	Group replacement cost (£)	Total cost (£)	Average weekly cost (£)
1	0	60	60	60
2	20	60	80	40
3	74	60	134	44.7
4	124.8	60	184.8	46.2
5	167.96	60	227.96	45.6

Of the policies considered, the one having the lowest average weekly cost is that of group replacement at the end of each 2-week period supplemented by individual replacement as necessary.

Part of the above problem is solved by an alternative method in Example 12.4.1.

Exercise 10.4.1

An engineering company is studying a replacement strategy for its metal-cutting tools. It has collected the following data on tool life relating to normal load and operating conditions:

	Month after replacement				
	1	2	3	4	5
Percentage of original tools which have failed by the end of that month (cumulative)	10	25	50	80	100

1000 cutting tools are in use at any given time. They could be replaced by new tools on a mass-replacement basis for £1.00 per tool. Alternatively, they may be replaced individually as they fail at cost of £4 per tool. In each case, the actual cost of the tool itself is 50p, the remainder representing labour and overhead charges.

At present the company replaces tools as they fail.
You are required to:

(a) compare the costs of the current tool-replacement system with the alternative of replacing all tools at a certain fixed monthly interval together with individual replacements of those tools which have failed in the preceding interval;
(b) state the best strategy for the company to follow.

(ICMA Prof. 1)

Further Exercises

10.1 Coltel Ltd have just begun to hire out a total of 200 coloured television sets. Market research has shown that out of a hundred hirings the pattern of the length of hire is as follows:

Length of hire in years	1	2	3	4
Number of hirings	20	40	30	10

Required:

(a) Determine the number of new rentals required each year for the next 4 years to maintain Coltel's total rentals at 200 (round to nearest whole number in your calculations).   (10 marks)

(b) What is the average length of hire period? (4 marks)

(c) What is the average number of new rentals required each year? (4 marks)

(d) Coltel Ltd, in an attempt to reduce their administrative overheads, are launching an advertising campaign aimed at their existing customers to encourage them to rent for longer periods. They would regard their campaign as successful if the following pattern of hiring was achieved in the long run:

Length of hire in years	1	2	3	4	5
Number of hirings	10	30	35	15	10

If the administrative costs of arranging a hire is £20, what is the maximum amount Coltel Ltd should spend on their advertising campaign each year? (7 marks)

(ACCA Prof. 2)

10.2 A company uses complex electronic control systems in its production processes. There are 20 of these systems and each system contains 25 components which are subject to failure. The company has been recording the pattern of failure over four periods of time with the results as shown below:

Period after installation	1st	2nd	3rd	4th
Percentage of failed original components during the period	20	25	35	20

If the components are replaced as they fail it will cost £1 per component to effect the replacement. However, if all components are replaced at once, the cost is £0.50 per component.

Management is considering the following alternative replacement policies:

(a) replacement of components as they fail;

(b) replacement of components entirely at the end of a fixed number of periods together with replacement of failures during the interval.

You are required to advise management as to the most economic replacement policy. (ICMA Prof. 1)

10.3 A construction firm decided to purchase a mechanical digger and obtained the following information regarding purchase price, resale value and running costs:

Year	1	2	3	4	5
Purchase price at start of year (£000)	100	90	80	60	30

Year	1	2	3	4	5
Estimated resale value at end of year (£000)	80	70	50	20	0

Year	1	2	3	4	5
Running costs during year (£000)	20	20	30	30	40

Required:

By preparing a table of suitable values, determine the optimal time to buy and sell the digger in order to minimise the total annual costs.

11 Input–Output Analysis

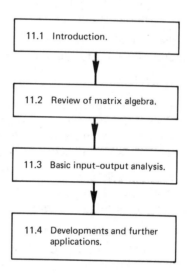

11.1 Introduction.

11.2 Review of matrix algebra.

11.3 Basic input–output analysis.

11.4 Developments and further applications.

11.1 Introduction

Input–output analysis is a tool for dealing with interactions between different business or economic entities. It can deal, for example, with interactions between departments in a factory, between firms in a group, between sectors in an economy or between whole economies. The thinking of systems underlies input–output analysis in that the interacting entities are seen as constituting a system, while everything else is part of the environment external to that system. The external environment provides a set of inputs to the system and the system provides a set of outputs to the external environment. The outputs which appear following a given set of inputs depend upon the nature of the interactions between the entities within the system.

Input–output analysis allows these interactions to be expressed and dealt with in such a way as to allow the prediction of a set of total output levels required in order to satisfy a specified set of final demand levels. We shall find that the total outputs needed from the entities will have to exceed the final external requirements because some output is used up within the system.

To illustrate the kind of problem with which input–output analysis is concerned, consider a hypothetical economy consisting of three sectors, A, B and C, with inputs and outputs for a particular period shown in the following transaction table in billions of pounds:

	Input to			External requirement	Total output
	A	B	C		
Output from A	18	30	45	15	108
Output from B	27	30	60	3	120
Output from C	54	40	60	26	180

Note that in drawing up a table like this it is assumed that all outputs can indeed be expressed in the same units. In practice, comparability of units can present a difficulty when drawing up a transaction table since output from different entities may be in totally different units. It is usual to attempt to overcome the problem by using monetary units.

Note also the convention used in the above table that output from a sector, used as input to the same sector, is shown in the table. This convention is not universally followed. If such figures are omitted then there will instead be a zero in every position on the leading diagonal in the part of the table relating to the sectors.

The basic question to be addressed is that of what outputs would be required from the sectors if the external requirements were predicted to change from £15b, £3b and £26b to something else. This is taken up in section 11.3. The method of solution depends for manageable notation on the use of matrix algebra and so we insert at this point a section reviewing basic ideas in this area. The material in section 11.2 is also prerequisite knowledge for Chapter 12. Readers familiar with matrix algebra should omit section 11.2.

11.2 Review of Matrix Algebra

A matrix is an array of numbers written in brackets. Either round or square brackets may be used.

For example, $B = \begin{pmatrix} 26 & -9 & 14 \\ 16 & 12 & -4 \end{pmatrix}$ or $B = \begin{bmatrix} 26 & -9 & 14 \\ 16 & 12 & -4 \end{bmatrix}$.

The numbers in the array are called the elements of the matrix. The example shown is referred to as a 2×3 (two-by-three) matrix since it has two rows and three columns. More generally, a matrix having r rows and c columns is an $r \times c$ matrix or a matrix of order $r \times c$. It is usual to represent a matrix by a capital letter as in the example above. A matrix having only one column is called a column vector and a matrix having only one row is called a row vector. A vector is represented by a lower-case letter which is shown underlined in handwriting or in boldface type when printed, for example, $a = \begin{pmatrix} -3 \\ 5 \\ 2.6 \end{pmatrix}$. Matrices behave according to algebraic rules which bear considerable similarity to those which govern ordinary numbers. However, there are some important differences also. We now summarise these rules.

(a) Equality

Two matrices are equal if and only if all corresponding elements are equal.

Thus if $C = \begin{pmatrix} a & b & c \\ d & e & f \end{pmatrix}$ and $D = \begin{pmatrix} 2.7 & -1.5 & 9.3 \\ 8.2 & 2.9 & -3.5 \end{pmatrix}$,

then the matrix equation $C = D$ represents six simple equations $a = 2.7$, $b = -1.5$, $c = 9.3$, $d = 8.2$, $e = 2.9$ and $f = -3.5$. Hence this apparently trivial rule is seen to be part of what makes matrices so useful, in that potentially very large numbers of equations can be expressed very concisely.

(b) Addition and Subtraction

Matrices can be added or subtracted if and only if they are of the same order.
Where addition is possible it is carried out by adding the corresponding elements
of the matrices concerned.

Thus
$$\begin{pmatrix} p & q \\ r & s \end{pmatrix} + \begin{pmatrix} t & u \\ v & w \end{pmatrix} = \begin{pmatrix} p+t & q+u \\ r+v & s+w \end{pmatrix}.$$

Similarly, for subtraction,
$$\begin{pmatrix} p & q \\ r & s \end{pmatrix} - \begin{pmatrix} t & u \\ v & w \end{pmatrix} = \begin{pmatrix} p-t & q-u \\ r-v & s-w \end{pmatrix}.$$

(c) Multiplication by a Number

Any matrix can be multiplied by a number. The procedure is simply to multiply
every element of the matrix by the number concerned.

Thus
$$a \begin{pmatrix} w & x \\ y & z \end{pmatrix} = \begin{pmatrix} aw & ax \\ ay & az \end{pmatrix}.$$

Example 11.2.1

If
$$A = \begin{pmatrix} -4 & -7 \\ 9 & 2 \\ 11 & 3 \end{pmatrix} \quad \text{and} \quad B = \begin{pmatrix} 1.5 & 4 \\ -2.5 & 7 \\ 6 & -2 \end{pmatrix}, \quad \text{find } 3A - 2B.$$

ANSWER

$$3A = 3 \begin{pmatrix} -4 & -7 \\ 9 & 2 \\ 11 & 3 \end{pmatrix} = \begin{pmatrix} -12 & -21 \\ 27 & 6 \\ 33 & 9 \end{pmatrix} \quad \text{and} \quad 2B = \begin{pmatrix} 3 & 8 \\ -5 & 14 \\ 12 & -4 \end{pmatrix}$$

Hence
$$3A - 2B = \begin{pmatrix} -12 & -21 \\ 27 & 6 \\ 33 & 9 \end{pmatrix} - \begin{pmatrix} 3 & 8 \\ -5 & 14 \\ 12 & -4 \end{pmatrix} = \begin{pmatrix} -15 & -29 \\ 32 & -8 \\ 21 & 13 \end{pmatrix}.$$

Exercise 11.2.1

If
$$X = \begin{pmatrix} 2 & -3 & 8 \\ -5 & 7 & 12 \end{pmatrix} \quad \text{and} \quad Y = \begin{pmatrix} 13 & 5 & -3 \\ 6 & -8 & 11 \end{pmatrix}, \quad \text{find } 4X + 3Y.$$

(d) Multiplication of Matrices Together

Consider two matrices, X and Y. The product XY exists if and only if the number
of columns of X is equal to the number of rows in Y. When this condition is met,
the matrices are said to be *conformable* for the product XY.

   The procedure for calculating the product when it does exist is illustrated by
the following example:

$$X = \begin{pmatrix} p_1 & p_2 & p_3 \\ q_1 & q_2 & q_3 \end{pmatrix}, \quad Y = \begin{pmatrix} a_1 & a_2 & a_3 \\ b_1 & b_2 & b_3 \\ c_1 & c_2 & c_3 \end{pmatrix}.$$

X has three columns and Y has three rows, so the matrices are conformable for
the product XY. The product XY will have order 2×3, as we will now see.

$$XY = \begin{pmatrix} p_1a_1 + p_2b_1 + p_3c_1 & p_1a_2 + p_2b_2 + p_3c_2 & p_1a_3 + p_2b_3 + p_3c_3 \\ q_1a_1 + q_2b_1 + q_3c_1 & q_1a_2 + q_2b_2 + q_3c_2 & q_1a_3 + q_2b_3 + q_3c_3 \end{pmatrix}.$$

The method is to pair the elements in each row of X with the corresponding elements in each column of Y. In the example above we see that Y has three columns but X has only two rows and so the matrices are *not* conformable for the product YX. Hence we see that it is not in general true for matrices that $XY = YX$ since only one of the products may exist. This is a respect in which matrix laws differ from those governing numbers. The technical expression for this phenomenon is to say that matrix algebra is *non-commutative*. Even if both products do exist for a pair of matrices they will, in general, be different.

In general, if X has order $r \times c$ and Y has order $c \times m$ then they are conformable for the product XY and this product has order $r \times m$. They will not be conformable for the product YX unless $m = r$. If this condition is met and YX exists, then it will have order $c \times c$.

Example 11.2.2

If $X = \begin{pmatrix} -4 & 2 \\ 2 & -14 \\ 15 & 9 \end{pmatrix}$ and $Y = \begin{pmatrix} 4 & -12 & 13 \\ -3 & 7 & 15 \end{pmatrix}$, find XY and YX.

ANSWER

$$XY = \begin{pmatrix} -16 - 6 & 48 + 14 & -52 + 30 \\ 8 + 42 & -24 - 98 & 26 - 210 \\ 60 - 27 & -180 + 63 & 195 + 135 \end{pmatrix} = \begin{pmatrix} -22 & 62 & -22 \\ 50 & -122 & -184 \\ 33 & -117 & 330 \end{pmatrix},$$

$$YX = \begin{pmatrix} -16 - 24 + 195 & 8 + 168 + 117 \\ 12 + 14 + 225 & -6 - 98 + 135 \end{pmatrix} = \begin{pmatrix} 155 & 293 \\ 251 & 31 \end{pmatrix}.$$

Exercise 11.2.2

If $X = \begin{pmatrix} -6 & 15 \\ 8 & 13 \\ 2 & -7 \end{pmatrix}$ and $Y = \begin{pmatrix} 8 & -12 \\ 4 & 20 \end{pmatrix}$, find any matrix products which exist.

(e) Transposition

If the rows and columns of a matrix X are interchanged, the resulting matrix is called the *transpose* of X and is denoted X'.

For example, $X = \begin{pmatrix} u & v & w \\ x & y & z \end{pmatrix}$ has transpose $X' = \begin{pmatrix} u & x \\ v & y \\ w & z \end{pmatrix}$.

Note that if a matrix is of order $r \times c$, then its transpose must be of order $c \times r$. A matrix which is left unaltered by transposition is called a *symmetric* matrix.

Thus, for example, $X = \begin{pmatrix} 2 & 3 & -5 \\ 3 & 7 & 9 \\ -5 & 9 & 12 \end{pmatrix}$ is a symmetric matrix because $X' = X$. We note that if a matrix is to be symmetric it must have number of rows equal to number of columns. A matrix satisfying this last condition is sometimes described as a *square* matrix.

(f) Null and Identity Matrices

A null matrix is one which has every element equal to zero. Such a matrix can be of any order. Null matrices operate in a manner very similar to the number zero in the ordinary number system:

(i) no matrix is altered by addition or subtraction of a null matrix,

(ii) multiplication of any matrix by a null matrix will always give a null matrix.

An important difference arises in the fact that two non-null matrices can be multiplied together to give a null matrix.

For example,
$$\begin{pmatrix} -2 & 4 \\ -5 & 10 \end{pmatrix} \begin{pmatrix} 6 & 14 \\ 3 & 7 \end{pmatrix} = \begin{pmatrix} 0 & 0 \\ 0 & 0 \end{pmatrix}.$$

An identity matrix is a square matrix having every element equal to zero except on the top left to bottom right diagonal (called the *leading diagonal*) where every element is equal to one. So examples of identity matrices are

$$\begin{pmatrix} 1 & 0 \\ 0 & 1 \end{pmatrix}, \quad \begin{pmatrix} 1 & 0 & 0 \\ 0 & 1 & 0 \\ 0 & 0 & 1 \end{pmatrix}, \quad \begin{pmatrix} 1 & 0 & 0 & 0 \\ 0 & 1 & 0 & 0 \\ 0 & 0 & 1 & 0 \\ 0 & 0 & 0 & 1 \end{pmatrix}.$$

Identity matrices operate in a manner similar to the number one in the ordinary number system: no matrix is altered as a result of being multiplied by an identity matrix. Thus, for example,

$$\begin{pmatrix} 8 & 5 & 7 \\ 9 & 11 & -3 \end{pmatrix} \begin{pmatrix} 1 & 0 & 0 \\ 0 & 1 & 0 \\ 0 & 0 & 1 \end{pmatrix} = \begin{pmatrix} 8 & 5 & 7 \\ 9 & 11 & -3 \end{pmatrix}$$

and
$$\begin{pmatrix} 1 & 0 \\ 0 & 1 \end{pmatrix} \begin{pmatrix} 8 & 5 & 7 \\ 9 & 11 & -3 \end{pmatrix} = \begin{pmatrix} 8 & 5 & 7 \\ 9 & 11 & -3 \end{pmatrix}.$$

The symbol I is always used to represent an identity matrix and it is left entirely to the context to show the order involved. Even within the same equation the symbol I can be used to represent matrices of different order. If in the above example the matrix

$$\begin{pmatrix} 8 & 5 & 7 \\ 9 & 11 & -3 \end{pmatrix}$$

were represented by X, the result shown there could be summarised as $IX = XI = X$.
In the first term I is a 2×2 matrix and in the second it is a 3×3 matrix.

(g) Inversion

The inverse X^{-1} of a matrix X is defined to be that matrix which when multiplied by X gives an identity matrix.
Thus $XX^{-1} = X^{-1}X = I$.
Only a square matrix can possibly have an inverse and not even every square matrix has one. A square matrix not having an inverse is described as singular.
As in the case of zero and identity matrices, it is helpful to think about inverses in terms of an anology with the ordinary number system. From the definition given above we see that an inverse operates in the same way as a reciprocal. For example, we say that 0.2 is the reciprocal of 5 because $0.2 \times 5 = 5 \times 0.2 = 1$. It is the number which when multiplied by 5 gives 1. A reciprocal could, if we wished,

be used to help us solve a simple equation. Suppose we have $5x = 7$. Multiplying both sides by the reciprocal, 0.2, would give $0.2(5x) = 0.2(7)$.

Hence
$$1.x = 1.4,$$
$$x = 1.4.$$

This may seem an extremely pedantic way of solving such a simple equation, but the method is the one which can be used for matrix equations. Suppose we have an equation $AX = B$ where A is a matrix whose elements are known and has an inverse, B is a matrix whose elements also are known, and X is an unknown matrix.

Multiplying both sides by the inverse of A we have

$$A^{-1}AX = A^{-1}B. \qquad \text{So} \qquad IX = A^{-1}B, \qquad \text{and} \qquad X = A^{-1}B.$$

(In the preceding numerical example it did not matter whether we multiplied both sides of the equation by 0.2 on the left or on the right because the order of the numbers in a product is irrelevant. In the matrix case the order is important and we must multiply both sides on the *left* by A^{-1}.)

Example 11.2.3

Given that the inverse of $\begin{pmatrix} 11 & 4 & 13 \\ 3 & 1 & 3 \\ 6 & 2 & 7 \end{pmatrix}$ is $\begin{pmatrix} -1 & 2 & 1 \\ 3 & 1 & -6 \\ 0 & -2 & 1 \end{pmatrix}$,

solve the simultaneous equations

$$11x + 4y + 13z = 64$$
$$3x + y + 3z = 15$$
$$6x + 2y + 7z = 35.$$

ANSWER

The set of equations can be written in matrix form as

$$\begin{pmatrix} 11 & 4 & 13 \\ 3 & 1 & 3 \\ 6 & 2 & 7 \end{pmatrix} \begin{pmatrix} x \\ y \\ z \end{pmatrix} = \begin{pmatrix} 64 \\ 15 \\ 35 \end{pmatrix}.$$

This matrix equation is of the form $A\mathbf{x} = \mathbf{b}$, where A and $\mathbf{b}$ are known but $\mathbf{x}$ is not.

Hence if A has an inverse it can be solved using the result above to give

$$\mathbf{x} = A^{-1}\mathbf{b}.$$

In fact, we are told that A^{-1} does exist and is equal to

$$\begin{pmatrix} -1 & 2 & 1 \\ 3 & 1 & -6 \\ 0 & -2 & 1 \end{pmatrix}.$$

Hence $\begin{pmatrix} x \\ y \\ z \end{pmatrix} = \begin{pmatrix} -1 & 2 & 1 \\ 3 & 1 & -6 \\ 0 & -2 & 1 \end{pmatrix} \begin{pmatrix} 64 \\ 15 \\ 35 \end{pmatrix} = \begin{pmatrix} -64 + 30 + 35 \\ 192 + 15 - 210 \\ 0 - 30 + 35 \end{pmatrix} = \begin{pmatrix} 1 \\ -3 \\ 5 \end{pmatrix}.$

So the solutions are $x = 1$, $y = -3$ and $z = 5$.

Exercise 11.2.3

Given that the inverse of $\begin{pmatrix} 3 & 1 \\ 3 & 4 \end{pmatrix}$ is $\frac{1}{9} \begin{pmatrix} 4 & -1 \\ -3 & 3 \end{pmatrix}$,

solve the equations
$$12x + 4y = 44$$
$$9x + 12y = 51.$$

In both the problems above the required matrix inverse was given. In reality it is necessary to be able to find matrix inverses and so we conclude this section with some comments on methods for doing this. We consider only 2×2 and 3×3 matrices. For larger matrices, a computer would be used to carry out the inversion.

First we must introduce the determinant of a 2×2 matrix.

For a matrix $\begin{pmatrix} a & b \\ b & d \end{pmatrix}$ this is denoted $\begin{vmatrix} a & b \\ c & d \end{vmatrix}$ and is calculated as $ad - bc$. Note that a determinant is a number and not a matrix.

The inverse of a 2×2 matrix can be expressed as a simple formula, arrived at by the following steps:

(a) Interchange the elements on the leading diagonal.
(b) Change the signs of the other two elements.
(c) Divide the resulting matrix by the determinant.

Thus
$$\begin{pmatrix} a & b \\ c & d \end{pmatrix}^{-1} = \frac{1}{(ad - bc)} \begin{pmatrix} d & -b \\ -c & a \end{pmatrix}.$$

Example 11.2.4

Invert the 2×2 matrix $A = \begin{pmatrix} 10 & 7 \\ 8 & 9 \end{pmatrix}$.

ANSWER

$10 \times 9 - 7 \times 8 = 90 - 56 = 34 \qquad \text{so} \qquad A^{-1} = \frac{1}{34} \begin{pmatrix} 9 & -7 \\ -8 & 10 \end{pmatrix}.$

Exercise 11.2.4

Invert the 2×2 matrix $B = \begin{pmatrix} 3 & 5 \\ 2 & 7 \end{pmatrix}$.

For a 3×3 matrix the result cannot be so simply expressed, and we explain the procedure using an example.

Example 11.2.5

Invert the matrix $\begin{pmatrix} 1 & 1 & 2 \\ 1 & 2 & 1 \\ 2 & -3 & -2 \end{pmatrix}$.

ANSWER

Step 1 Form a new 3×3 matrix whose elements are the *cofactors* of the elements of the given matrix. The cofactor of an element is obtained by eliminating the row and column containing the element and writing down the resulting 2×2 determinant multiplied by $(-1)^{r+c}$ where r is the number of the row in which the element is placed and c is the number of the column. So for this example we have the following as the matrix of cofactors:

$$\begin{pmatrix} \begin{vmatrix} 2 & 1 \\ -3 & -2 \end{vmatrix} & -\begin{vmatrix} 1 & 1 \\ 2 & -2 \end{vmatrix} & \begin{vmatrix} 1 & 2 \\ 2 & -3 \end{vmatrix} \\[2ex] -\begin{vmatrix} 1 & 2 \\ -3 & -2 \end{vmatrix} & \begin{vmatrix} 1 & 2 \\ 2 & -2 \end{vmatrix} & -\begin{vmatrix} 1 & 1 \\ 2 & -3 \end{vmatrix} \\[2ex] \begin{vmatrix} 1 & 2 \\ 2 & 1 \end{vmatrix} & -\begin{vmatrix} 1 & 2 \\ 1 & 1 \end{vmatrix} & \begin{vmatrix} 1 & 1 \\ 1 & 2 \end{vmatrix} \end{pmatrix}$$

On working out the 2 × 2 determinants this becomes

$$\begin{pmatrix} (-4+3) & -(-2-2) & (-3-4) \\ -(-2+6) & (-2-4) & -(-3-2) \\ (1-4) & -(1-2) & (2-1) \end{pmatrix} = \begin{pmatrix} -1 & 4 & -7 \\ -4 & -6 & 5 \\ -3 & 1 & 1 \end{pmatrix}.$$

Step 2 Find the determinant of the original matrix. This is done by choosing any row or column of the matrix and calculating the sum of the products

$$\text{element} \times \text{cofactor}$$

for the whole of that row or column.

For the first row here we have

$$1 \times (-1) + 1 \times 4 + 2 \times (-7) = -1 + 4 - 14 = -11.$$

Step 3 Transpose the matrix of cofactors and divide by the determinant to obtain the required inverse.

Hence $$\begin{pmatrix} 1 & 1 & 2 \\ 1 & 2 & 1 \\ 2 & -3 & -2 \end{pmatrix}^{-1} = \frac{1}{(-11)} \begin{pmatrix} -1 & -4 & -3 \\ 4 & -6 & 1 \\ -7 & 5 & 1 \end{pmatrix} = \frac{1}{11} \begin{pmatrix} 1 & 4 & 3 \\ -4 & 6 & -1 \\ 7 & -5 & -1 \end{pmatrix}.$$

The procedure used can be summed up in a formula as follows:

$$\boxed{\text{inverse of a } 3 \times 3 \text{ matrix} = \frac{\text{transposed matrix of cofactors}}{\text{determinant}}.}$$

Exercise 11.2.5

Invert the matrix $\begin{pmatrix} 1 & 2 & 1 \\ 2 & 3 & 2 \\ -3 & -4 & 1 \end{pmatrix}$ and use the results to solve the simultaneous

equations
$$\begin{aligned} 2x + 4y + 2z &= 6 \\ 10x + 15y + 10z &= 5 \\ -21x - 28y + 7z &= -14. \end{aligned}$$

11.3 Basic Input–Output Analysis

We return now to the example introduced in section 11.1 and use it to explain the fundamental ideas of input–output analysis. The problem concerns a hypothetical economy consisting of three sectors A, B and C with the following inputs and outputs (billions of pounds) shown in Table 11.1.

Table 11.1

	Input to			External requirement	Total output
	A	B	C		
Output from A	18	30	45	15	108
Output from B	27	30	60	3	120
Output from C	54	40	60	26	180

The objective at this stage is to find what outputs would be required from the sectors if the external requirements were to change from £15b, £3b and £26b to some general amounts which we shall call d_A, d_B, d_C.

In order to proceed we must first introduce the important convention underlying input–output analysis, which is that for every sector we have

$$\boxed{\text{total input = total output.}}$$

This is purely a convention and compliance with it means that balancing items need to be introduced into the table. These are shown in Table 11.2 as 'other' inputs. This item, which will be looked at further in section 11.4, includes actual inputs from the external environment such as labour and raw materials, but also includes the pure balancing item 'profit' (which may be positive or negative) in order to ensure the equality of total input and total output. The balanced transaction table has the form shown in Table 11.2.

Table 11.2

	Input to			External requirement	Total output
	A	B	C		
Output from A	18	30	45	15	108
Output from B	27	30	60	3	120
Output from C	54	40	60	26	180
Other input	9	20	15		
Total input	108	120	180		

Further progress then depends on a major assumption, namely, that as the total output of a sector changes the *proportion* of that sector's input from any given source remains constant. Within certain limits this is a reasonable assumption, but if the changes in total output are substantial then its validity becomes questionable and it is the basis of some controversy regarding the input–output approach.

Making the crucial assumption in this case leads to the following proportions:

$\frac{18}{108}$ of A's input comes from A, $\frac{30}{120}$ of B's from A, $\frac{45}{180}$ of C's from A.

$\frac{27}{108}$ of A's input comes from B, $\frac{30}{120}$ of B's from B, $\frac{60}{180}$ of C's from B.

$\frac{54}{108}$ of A's input comes from C, $\frac{40}{120}$ of B's from C, $\frac{60}{180}$ of C's from C.

These proportions, called the technical coefficients, are put in a matrix called the input–output matrix:

$$A = \begin{pmatrix} \frac{18}{108} & \frac{30}{120} & \frac{45}{180} \\ \frac{27}{108} & \frac{30}{120} & \frac{60}{180} \\ \frac{54}{108} & \frac{40}{120} & \frac{60}{180} \end{pmatrix} = \begin{pmatrix} \frac{1}{6} & \frac{1}{4} & \frac{1}{4} \\ \frac{1}{4} & \frac{1}{4} & \frac{1}{3} \\ \frac{1}{2} & \frac{1}{3} & \frac{1}{3} \end{pmatrix}.$$

Now, as stated above, we want to consider the situation where the external requirements become d_A, d_B and d_C for the products of sectors A, B and C respectively. We need to find the total outputs x_A, x_B, x_C needed from the three sectors to meet these demands.

But the convention is that total input = total output.

Therefore the total inputs to the sectors are x_A, x_B, x_C.

Now the total output needed from A is

$$x_A = d_A + \tfrac{18}{108} \times \text{input to A} + \tfrac{30}{120} \times \text{input to B} + \tfrac{45}{180} \times \text{input to C}.$$

Hence
$$x_A = d_A + \tfrac{1}{6} x_A + \tfrac{1}{4} x_B + \tfrac{1}{4} x_C$$

Similarly for B:
$$x_B = d_B + \tfrac{1}{4} x_A + \tfrac{1}{4} x_B + \tfrac{1}{3} x_C$$

and for C:
$$x_C = d_C + \tfrac{1}{2} x_A + \tfrac{1}{3} x_B + \tfrac{1}{3} x_C.$$

This set of equations can be written in matrix form as:

$$\begin{pmatrix} x_A \\ x_B \\ x_C \end{pmatrix} = \begin{pmatrix} d_A \\ d_B \\ d_C \end{pmatrix} + \begin{pmatrix} \frac{1}{6} & \frac{1}{4} & \frac{1}{4} \\ \frac{1}{4} & \frac{1}{4} & \frac{1}{3} \\ \frac{1}{2} & \frac{1}{3} & \frac{1}{3} \end{pmatrix} \begin{pmatrix} x_A \\ x_B \\ x_C \end{pmatrix}$$

or
$$\mathbf{x} = \mathbf{d} + A\mathbf{x}$$

where $\mathbf{d} = \begin{pmatrix} d_A \\ d_B \\ d_C \end{pmatrix}$ and $\mathbf{x} = \begin{pmatrix} x_A \\ x_B \\ x_C \end{pmatrix}$.

Hence
$$\mathbf{x} - A\mathbf{x} = \mathbf{d}.$$

But multiplication of any matrix by an identity leaves that matrix unchanged. So we can, if we wish, write $\mathbf{x}$ as $I\mathbf{x}$.

Hence the equation becomes
$$I\mathbf{x} - A\mathbf{x} = \mathbf{d}$$

so
$$(I - A)\mathbf{x} = \mathbf{d}.$$

Multiplying each side on the left by $(I - A)^{-1}$ gives

$$(I - A)^{-1}(I - A)\mathbf{x} = (I - A)^{-1}\mathbf{d},$$

and so we emerge with the basic equation of input–output analysis:

$$\boxed{\mathbf{x} = (I - A)^{-1}\mathbf{d}.}$$

To illustrate the use of this equation suppose in our example that the values of the new external requirements were $d_A = \pounds 10b$, $d_B = \pounds 2b$ and $d_C = \pounds 20b$.

$$I - A = \begin{pmatrix} 1 & 0 & 0 \\ 0 & 1 & 0 \\ 0 & 0 & 1 \end{pmatrix} - \begin{pmatrix} \frac{1}{6} & \frac{1}{4} & \frac{1}{4} \\ \frac{1}{4} & \frac{1}{4} & \frac{1}{3} \\ \frac{1}{2} & \frac{1}{3} & \frac{1}{3} \end{pmatrix} = \begin{pmatrix} \frac{5}{6} & -\frac{1}{4} & -\frac{1}{4} \\ -\frac{1}{4} & \frac{3}{4} & -\frac{1}{3} \\ -\frac{1}{2} & -\frac{1}{3} & \frac{2}{3} \end{pmatrix}.$$

$$\text{So } \mathbf{x} = (I - A)^{-1} \mathbf{d} = \begin{pmatrix} \frac{5}{6} & -\frac{1}{4} & -\frac{1}{4} \\ -\frac{1}{4} & \frac{3}{4} & -\frac{1}{3} \\ -\frac{1}{2} & -\frac{1}{3} & \frac{2}{3} \end{pmatrix}^{-1} \begin{pmatrix} 10 \\ 2 \\ 20 \end{pmatrix}$$

$$= \tfrac{1}{109} \begin{pmatrix} 336 & 216 & 234 \\ 288 & 372 & 294 \\ 396 & 348 & 486 \end{pmatrix} \begin{pmatrix} 10 \\ 2 \\ 20 \end{pmatrix} = \tfrac{1}{109} \begin{pmatrix} 8\,472 \\ 9\,504 \\ 14\,376 \end{pmatrix}$$

So the total outputs needed from the sectors are £77.72b from A, £87.19b from B and £131.89b from C.

Exercise 11.3.1

In preparing a budget a firm drew up the transaction table given as Table 11.3, which shows the outputs from its three departments (thousands of pounds) used as inputs to the departments and for sales and inventory.

Table 11.3

	Inputs to			Sales and inventory	Total output
	I	*II*	*III*		
Output from department I	4	0	4	12	20
Output from department II	2	3	4	21	30
Output from department III	2	3	0	35	40

The forecast sales and inventory for the next year are as follows:

Department	I	II	III
Forecast sales and inventory	211	140	70

(a) Find the matrix $I - A$ and verify that its inverse is

$$\tfrac{10}{702} \begin{pmatrix} 89 & 1 & 9 \\ 11 & 79 & 9 \\ 10 & 8 & 72 \end{pmatrix}.$$

(b) Find the vector $\mathbf{x}$ of total outputs needed from the three departments for the next year.

11.4 Developments and Further Applications

In this section we look more closely at the 'other inputs' category of the input–output table and also look at particular areas of application of input–output analysis.

Shown as Table 11.4 is a complete input–output table for a firm with the 'other' inputs explained as raw materials, labour, overhead and profit.

Table 11.4

| | Inputs to production departments | | | Sales and inventory | Total output |
	I	II	III		
Output from I	0	40	50	210	300
Output from II	30	0	50	320	400
Output from III	60	40	0	400	500
Raw materials	60	80	100	0	
Labour	30	80	50	0	
Overhead	30	40	50	0	
Profit	90	120	200		
	300	400	500		

The information in Table 11.4 can be represented in the 'T' accounts shown below. This is more or less conventional accounting notation except that in the input–output approach the balancing item, profit, is treated in the same way (by receiving reward or payment) as the actual factors of production.

Cost Factors

Raw materials

	Dept I	£60
	Dept II	80
	Dept III	100

Labour

	Dept I	£30
	Dept II	80
	Dept III	50

Overheads

	Dept I	£30
	Dept II	40
	Dept III	50

Profit

	Dept I	£90
	Dept II	120
	Dept III	200

Work-in-progress (w.i.p.)

Dept I

from Dept II	30	to Dept II	40
from Dept III	60	to Dept III	50
from Raw Materials	60	to Inventory	210
from Labour	30		
from Overhead	30		
from Profit	90		
	£300		£300

Dept II

Dept I	40	to Dept I	30
Dept III	40	to Dept III	50
Raw Materials	80	to Inventory	320
Labour	80		
Overhead	40		
Profit	120		
	£400		£400

Dept III

Dept I	50	to Dept I	60
Dept II	50	to Dept II	40
Raw Materials	100	to Inventory	400
Labour	50		
Overhead	50		
Profit	200		
	£500		£500

Finished-goods Inventory

from Dept I	210	(Note that some finished goods are
from Dept II	320	transferred to other departments'
from Dept III	400	w.i.p., not to finished-goods
		inventory.)

Suppose the forecast sales and inventory for I, II and III are 2871, 3828 and 4785 respectively.

The input–output matrix is
$$A = \begin{pmatrix} \frac{0}{300} & \frac{40}{400} & \frac{50}{500} \\ \frac{30}{300} & \frac{0}{400} & \frac{50}{500} \\ \frac{60}{300} & \frac{40}{400} & \frac{0}{500} \end{pmatrix}$$

$$= \tfrac{1}{10} \begin{pmatrix} 0 & 1 & 1 \\ 1 & 0 & 1 \\ 2 & 1 & 0 \end{pmatrix}.$$

Hence
$$I - A = \begin{pmatrix} 1 & 0 & 0 \\ 0 & 1 & 0 \\ 0 & 0 & 1 \end{pmatrix} - \tfrac{1}{10} \begin{pmatrix} 0 & 1 & 1 \\ 1 & 0 & 1 \\ 2 & 1 & 0 \end{pmatrix} = \tfrac{1}{10} \begin{pmatrix} 10 & -1 & -1 \\ -1 & 10 & -1 \\ -2 & -1 & 10 \end{pmatrix}.$$

The inverse of this can be found using the method of section 11.2 to be

$$(I - A)^{-1} = \tfrac{10}{957} \begin{bmatrix} 99 & 11 & 11 \\ 12 & 98 & 11 \\ 21 & 12 & 99 \end{bmatrix}.$$

Hence the total outputs needed, according to section 11.3, are

$$\mathbf{x} = (I - A)^{-1}\, \mathbf{d} = \tfrac{10}{957} \begin{bmatrix} 99 & 11 & 11 \\ 12 & 98 & 11 \\ 21 & 12 & 99 \end{bmatrix} \begin{bmatrix} 2871 \\ 3828 \\ 4785 \end{bmatrix} = \begin{bmatrix} 3960 \\ 4830 \\ 6060 \end{bmatrix}.$$

Going on from here, we want also to know what are the effects of these changes in total output on the labour, raw materials and overhead costs and on the profit.

We can approach this problem by looking at the proportions of total inputs to the departments which come from these sources in the same way as we looked at the proportions from the sectors when forming the matrix A in section 11.3.

Thus we see that $\frac{60}{300}$ of I's input is raw materials, $\frac{80}{400}$ of II's input is raw materials and $\frac{100}{500}$ of III's input is raw materials; also $\frac{30}{300}$ of I's input is labour, $\frac{80}{400}$ of II's input is labour and $\frac{50}{500}$ of III's input is labour and so on.

Thus in the same way as we formed matrix A in section 11.3 we can form matrix B as follows:

$$B = \begin{pmatrix} \frac{60}{300} & \frac{80}{400} & \frac{100}{500} \\ \frac{30}{300} & \frac{80}{400} & \frac{50}{500} \\ \frac{30}{300} & \frac{40}{400} & \frac{50}{500} \\ \frac{90}{300} & \frac{120}{400} & \frac{200}{500} \end{pmatrix} = \tfrac{1}{10} \begin{bmatrix} 2 & 2 & 2 \\ 1 & 2 & 1 \\ 1 & 1 & 1 \\ 3 & 3 & 4 \end{bmatrix}$$

whose elements are the proportions of input to the departments from the respective external sources.

Hence when the total outputs, and therefore inputs, change the new inputs needed from these external sources can be found by multiplying the new total inputs by this matrix of proportions. So in this example where we have found the new total outputs to be 3960, 4830 and 6060 respectively, it follows that the new total inputs needed from the respective external sources are

$$\begin{pmatrix} \text{Raw material input} \\ \text{Labour input} \\ \text{Overhead} \\ \text{Profit} \end{pmatrix} = \tfrac{1}{10} \begin{bmatrix} 2 & 2 & 2 \\ 1 & 2 & 1 \\ 1 & 1 & 1 \\ 3 & 3 & 4 \end{bmatrix} \begin{bmatrix} 3960 \\ 4830 \\ 6060 \end{bmatrix} = \begin{bmatrix} 2970 \\ 1968 \\ 1485 \\ 5061 \end{bmatrix}$$

In general, when we have found a new total output vector x we can proceed to find the new vector, c, of external inputs (including profit) by using

$$\boxed{c = Bx}$$

Note that this analysis may be continued to reconstruct the entire forecast transaction table (Table 11.5).

Table 11.5

	Input to production department			Sales and inventory	Total output
	I	II	III		
Output from I	0	483	606	2871	3960
Output from II	396	0	606	3828	4830
Output from III	792	483	0	4783	6060
Raw Materials	792	966	1212	0	
Labour	396	960	606	0	
Overhead	396	483	606	0	
Profit	1188	1449	2424	0	
Total inputs	3960	4830	6060		

If a computer is available it is helpful to use a program to assist calculation of a repetitive nature which may arise in the case of modifications which may be necessary in budget proportions. Such a program may first require the input of a transaction table followed by the demand vector, d, which should be sufficient to enable a full printout of the forecast transaction table.

Exercise 11.4.1

A firm prepared the transactions table shown as Table 11.6 for departments R and S.

Table 11.6

	Input to R	Input to S	External requirement	Total output
Output from R	1	4	5	10
Output from S	2	2	16	20
Labour and raw materials	1	4		
Overheads	2	2		
Profit	4	8		

Find the total output needed from each of the departments if external requirements change to 40 and 32 from R and S respectively. Find also the cost of labour and raw materials, the overhead and the profit if these new total outputs are achieved, and hence construct the new transactions table.

A further application of the input–output analysis approach is to problems involving the apportionment of service department overheads in situations where such departments receive service from each other. Use of the method for such a problem is illustrated by the following example.

Example 11.4.1

Consider the data in Table 11.7.

Table 11.7

	Service department		Production department	
	Maintenance	Electricity	Machining	Assembly
Man-hours of maintenance time	–	3 000	16 000	1 000
Units of electricity consumed	20 000	–	130 000	50 000
Department costs before any allocation of service departments	£50 000	£4 000	£140 000	£206 000

You are required to:

Calculate the total costs to be allocated to the production departments using matrix algebra (formulate the problem and show all workings).

(*ICMA Prof. 1*)

ANSWER

To apply input–output analysis to this kind of problem we need to treat the units of maintenance and electricity used as *inputs* to maintenance and electricty. The transaction table is shown as Table 11.8.

Table 11.8

	Input to maintenance	Input to electricity
Output from maintenance	0	20 000
Output from electricity	3 000	0
Machining	16 000	130 000
Assembly	1 000	50 000
Total input	20 000	200 000

$$\text{Hence} \qquad A = \begin{pmatrix} 0 & \frac{20\,000}{200\,000} \\ \frac{3\,000}{20\,000} & 0 \end{pmatrix} = \begin{pmatrix} 0 & \frac{1}{10} \\ \frac{3}{20} & 0 \end{pmatrix}$$

$$\text{and} \qquad B = \begin{pmatrix} \frac{16\,000}{20\,000} & \frac{130\,000}{200\,000} \\ \frac{1\,000}{20\,000} & \frac{50\,000}{200\,000} \end{pmatrix} = \begin{pmatrix} \frac{4}{5} & \frac{13}{20} \\ \frac{1}{20} & \frac{1}{4} \end{pmatrix}.$$

Thus we have all the proportions involved.

Next we treat the direct costs to maintenance and electricity as new *final demands*. The full actual costs, to be found for maintenance and electricity, are treated as *total outputs* and hence found as

$$\mathbf{x} = (I - A)^{-1}\,\mathbf{d} = \left[\begin{pmatrix} 1 & 0 \\ 0 & 1 \end{pmatrix} - \begin{pmatrix} 0 & \frac{1}{10} \\ \frac{3}{20} & 0 \end{pmatrix} \right]^{-1} \begin{pmatrix} 50\,000 \\ 4\,000 \end{pmatrix}$$

$$= \begin{pmatrix} 1 & -\frac{1}{10} \\ -\frac{3}{20} & 1 \end{pmatrix}^{-1} \begin{pmatrix} 50\,000 \\ 4\,000 \end{pmatrix}.$$

$$\text{Hence} \qquad \mathbf{x} = \frac{1}{(1 - \frac{3}{200})} \begin{pmatrix} 1 & \frac{1}{10} \\ \frac{3}{20} & 1 \end{pmatrix} \begin{pmatrix} 50\,000 \\ 4\,000 \end{pmatrix}$$

$$= \frac{200}{197} \begin{pmatrix} 50\,000 + 400 \\ 7\,500 + 4\,000 \end{pmatrix} = \frac{200}{197} \begin{pmatrix} 50\,400 \\ 11\,500 \end{pmatrix} = \begin{pmatrix} 51\,167.51 \\ 11\,675.13 \end{pmatrix}$$

We can now use the result arrived at earlier in this section to find out what is needed from machining and assembly to achieve these total outputs from maintenance and electricity.

$$\text{These are} \quad B\mathbf{x} = \begin{pmatrix} \frac{4}{5} & \frac{13}{20} \\ \frac{1}{20} & \frac{1}{4} \end{pmatrix} \begin{pmatrix} 51\,167.51 \\ 11\,675.13 \end{pmatrix} = \begin{pmatrix} 40\,934 & + 7\,588.84 \\ 2\,558.38 & + 2\,918.78 \end{pmatrix}$$

$$= \begin{pmatrix} 48\,522.84 \\ 5\,477.16 \end{pmatrix}.$$

Hence total to be assigned to machining is

$$£140\,000 + £48\,523 = \underline{£188\,523}$$

and to assembly is

$$£206\,000 + £5\,477 = \underline{£211\,477}.$$

Exercise 11.4.2

A manufacturing plant has two service departments, S_1 and S_2, and two production departments, P_1 and P_2. The overhead amounts clearly identifiable with each department were:

S_1	S_2	P_1	P_2
£6000	£10 000	£8000	£17 000

On the basis of use the services of S_1 are to be allocated:

$$30\% \text{ to } S_2 \qquad 25\% \text{ to } P_1 \qquad 45\% \text{ to } P_2,$$

and of S_2:

$$40\% \text{ to } S_1 \qquad 33\% \text{ to } P_1 \qquad 27\% \text{ to } P_2.$$

You are required to state in matrix notation the expression for I, A and $\mathbf{b}$ to obtain the most accurate allocation of the service departments' overhead to the production departments, where $S = (I - A)^{-1} \cdot \mathbf{b}$ and $S = \begin{bmatrix} S_1 \\ S_2 \end{bmatrix}$.

(ICMA Prof. 1)

Further Exercises

11.1 An employee profit-sharing scheme entitles the employees to share 10 per cent of the profit after tax. The payment made to the employees under this scheme is tax deductible. Tax is to be taken at 50 per cent. In the year to 31 March 1977 the pre-tax profit was £100 000 before charging the employees' share of the profit.

You are required to calculate the amount to which the employees are entitled, using matrix algebra. Formulate the problem and show all workings.

(ICMA Prof. 1)

11.2 An economy consisting of three sectors, A, B and C, is represented in Table 11.9 (millions of pounds of production).

Table 11.9

	User			Final demand	Total output
	A	B	C		
Producer A	8	4	2	2	16
B	4	10	2	4	20
C	4	4	2	0	10

Find the total outputs required from the three industries if final demand changes to £2m of A's output, £3m of B's output and £2m of C's output.

11.3 In order to co-ordinate the libraries of Roedene, Soedene, and Toedene more effectively, an input–output transactions matrix (Table 11.10) was formulated for the model $A\mathbf{x} + \mathbf{d} = \mathbf{x}$.

Table 11.10

Input	Library			Output		
	R	S	T	Intermediate $A\mathbf{x}$	Final $\mathbf{d}$	Total $\mathbf{x}$
Library R	0	40	50	90	210	300
Library S	30	0	50	80	320	400
Library T	30	40	0	70	430	500
Other	240	320	400			
	300	400	500			1200

Required:

(a) Find the value of $\mathbf{x}$ for the new final demand $\mathbf{d} = [440 \quad 528 \quad 704]'$.

   Hint: (i) You may assume $\mathbf{x} = (I - A)^{-1} \cdot \mathbf{d}$.

   (ii) You may assume $\begin{bmatrix} 1 & -0.1 & -0.1 \\ -0.1 & 1 & -0.1 \\ -0.1 & -0.1 & 1 \end{bmatrix}^{-1} = \frac{10}{88}\begin{bmatrix} 9 & 1 & 1 \\ 1 & 9 & 1 \\ 1 & 1 & 9 \end{bmatrix}$.

(b) Given that the 'other' category of the old transactions table may be modified to

	R	S	T
Costs	120	200	200
Social gain	120	120	200

calculate a new modified transactions table to include the new demand of part (a), a section on costs and a section on social gain.

(c) Comment on the use of the input–output technique and any benefit which may be obtained from a suitable computer program.

12 Markov Chains

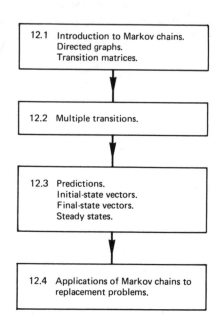

```
12.1  Introduction to Markov chains.
      Directed graphs.
      Transition matrices.
```

```
12.2  Multiple transitions.
```

```
12.3  Predictions.
      Initial-state vectors.
      Final-state vectors.
      Steady states.
```

```
12.4  Applications of Markov chains to
      replacement problems.
```

12.1 Introduction, Directed Graphs, Transition Matrices*

Andrei Andreavich Markov (1856–1922) is recognised as the 'inventor' of Markov chains. His teaching career at St Petersburg University commenced in 1880, and in 1905 he retired as a distinguished Professor of Mathematics.

Markov chains are included in operational research, as well as being part of mathematical statistics. They are concerned with the analysis of processes involving changes between various categories. The many areas of application include prediction of share prices as well as manpower planning. Predictions of this nature may be used to forecast trends, to guide managers in the formulation of a recruitment policy or to guide investment analysts in the management of funds.

An essential part of Markov chains is the specification of the particular 'states' of a system. The states referred to may be geographical boundaries, occupations, states of the weather, the prospects of a company, or even the state of the world!

When the particular set of states has been specified it is necessary to record the probability of change from one state to another during a unit of time. This information is conveniently shown in a 'directed graph' and recorded in a 'transition matrix'. A simple example is now shown to introduce the two terms.

*This chapter assumes a knowledge of matrix multiplication: a review of matrix algebra was presented in section 11.2.

Example 12.1.1

Present a directed graph and a transition matrix of the following situations:

(a) An agriculturalist observed that various weather conditions and pest popula-
tions influenced the success or failure of a crop. In particular, a successful
year was followed next year by success with probability 0.7 and by failure
with probability 0.3; however, a year of failure was followed next year by
success with probability 0.6 and by failure with probability 0.4.

(b) A stock-market analyst rated each share in a particular sector in terms of
(i) improving, (ii) steady and (iii) worsening, for each trading account. An
improving share had probability 0.8 of remaining an improving share and
probability 0.2 of changing to steady. A steady share had probability 0.2 of
changing to improving, probability 0.7 of remaining a steady share, and prob-
bility 0.1 of changing to worsening. A worsening share had probability 0.2 of
changing to steady and probability of 0.8 of remaining worsening.

ANSWER

(a) The two states of each year are success and failure.
Let success = state E_1 and failure = state E_2.
Therefore the probabilities of changes are as follows:

$$E_1 \rightarrow E_1 = 0.7, \qquad E_1 \rightarrow E_2 = 0.3,$$
$$E_2 \rightarrow E_1 = 0.6, \qquad E_2 \rightarrow E_2 = 0.4.$$

In the directed graph the states are shown as the points E_1, E_2 and the probability of possible transitions are shown on the linking lines; see Fig. 12.1.

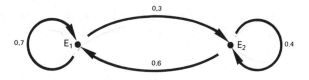

Figure 12.1

The transition matrix P is of order 2×2 as two states E_1 and E_2 are specified. Each element p_{ij} of P indicates the probability of changing from state E_i
to E_j. Hence $p_{11} = 0.7$ and $p_{12} = 0.3$ for the probability of the changes
$E_1 \rightarrow E_1$ and $E_1 \rightarrow E_2$ respectively; and $p_{21} = 0.6$ and $p_{22} = 0.4$ for the probability of changes $E_2 \rightarrow E_1$ and $E_2 \rightarrow E_2$ respectively.

Therefore, $$P = \begin{bmatrix} p_{11} & p_{12} \\ p_{21} & p_{22} \end{bmatrix} = \begin{bmatrix} 0.7 & 0.3 \\ 0.6 & 0.4 \end{bmatrix}.$$

(b) The three states for each trading account are (i) improving, (ii) steady, (iii)
worsening.
Let improving = state E_1, steady = state E_2 and worsening = state E_3.
Therefore, the probabilities of changes are

$$E_1 \rightarrow E_1 = 0.8, \qquad E_1 \rightarrow E_2 = 0.2, \qquad E_1 \rightarrow E_3 = 0,$$
$$E_2 \rightarrow E_1 = 0.2, \qquad E_2 \rightarrow E_2 = 0.7, \qquad E_2 \rightarrow E_3 = 0.1,$$
$$E_3 \rightarrow E_1 = 0, \qquad E_3 \rightarrow E_2 = 0.2, \qquad E_3 \rightarrow E_3 = 0.8.$$

In the directed graph the states are shown as the points E_1, E_2 and E_3 and the
probabilities of possible transitions are shown by linking lines. Where proba-

bility equals zero then the line is omitted, as in the cases of $E_1 \to E_3$ and $E_3 \to E_1$; see Fig. 12.2.

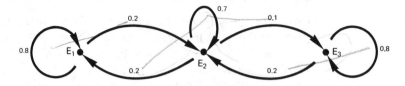

Figure 12.2

In this case the transition matrix P is 3×3 as three states are specified: E_1, E_2 and E_3. As element p_{ij} indicates a change of state $E_i \to E_j$ the elements of P correspond to the layout above.

Hence
$$P = \begin{bmatrix} p_{11} & p_{12} & p_{13} \\ p_{21} & p_{22} & p_{23} \\ p_{31} & p_{32} & p_{33} \end{bmatrix} = \begin{bmatrix} 0.8 & 0.2 & 0 \\ 0.2 & 0.7 & 0.1 \\ 0 & 0.2 & 0.8 \end{bmatrix}.$$

Note the sum of all the probabilities of transition *from* each particular state add up to one, i.e.

$$\sum_{j=1}^{j=n} p_{ij} = 1 \text{ for all rows } i.$$

This may be checked by reference to each directed graph and each row of the transition matrices, for instance in the matrix above

$$p_{31} + p_{32} + p_{33} = 0 + 0.2 + 0.8 = 1.$$

An exercise is now included so that you can gain familiarity with showing the interrelationships and recording the probabilities.

Exercise 12.1.1

Present a directed graph and a transition matrix for the following situations:

(a) Two competing television companies, TV1 and TV2, conducted a survey which revealed that when TV1 had the higher rating then for the next week TV1 would have the higher rating with probability 0.8 and TV2 would have the higher rating with probability 0.2. However, when TV2 had the higher rating then the next week TV1 would have the higher rating with probability 0.1 and TV2 would have the higher rating with probability 0.9.

(b) The safety performance of three factories, F1, F2 and F3, was reviewed each year, and the results showed that when F1 had the best safety record then for the following year F1 would have the best safety record with probability 0.4, F2 would have the best safety record with probability 0.3, and F3 would have the best safety record with probability 0.3. However, when F2 had the best safety record then for the following year F1 would have the best safety record with probability 0.3, F2 would have the best safety record with probability 0.4, and F3 would have the best safety record with probability 0.3. When F3 had the best safety record then for the following year F1 would have the best safety record with probability 0.3, F2 would have the best safety record with probability 0.3, and F3 would have the best safety record with probability 0.4.

(*Note:* It may be found more convenient to arrange the three points in the directed graph in a triangular arrangement instead of in a linear arrangement as shown in the answer to example 12.1.1(b) (Fig. 12.2).)

12.2 Multiple Transitions

In this section we shall consider the transition probabilities over two or more time units.

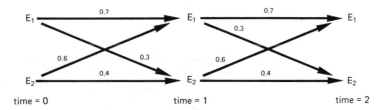

Figure 12.3

In order that we may analyse the changes over two transitions, Fig. 12.3 relates to the situation at time = 0, 1 and 2. Observe that for whatever state the system is in at time = 0 then there are two possible routes (via E_1 or E_2 at time = 1) to reach each possible state at time = 2. For instance, starting at E_1 for time = 0 we may reach E_2 at time = 2 by the two routes $E_1 \rightarrow E_1 \rightarrow E_2$ and $E_1 \rightarrow E_2 \rightarrow E_2$. The probabilities for these transitions are calculated as follows:

Probability route $E_1 \rightarrow E_1 \rightarrow E_2 = (0.7)(0.3) = 0.21$.

Probability route $E_1 \rightarrow E_2 \rightarrow E_2 = (0.3)(0.4) = 0.12$.

Hence, probability $E_1 \rightarrow E_2$ in two transitions is

$$P(E_1 \rightarrow E_1 \rightarrow E_2) + P(E_1 \rightarrow E_2 \rightarrow E_2) = 0.21 + 0.12 = 0.33.$$

This method applies in the three remaining cases for two transitions.

While it may be helpful to present the alternatives in the above diagram, the concise method is to use matrix multiplication. We use the notation P_2 to refer to the transition matrix for two time units and in general we use P_n to refer to the transition matrix for n time units.

In the above example we now find P_2 from P times P.

$$P_2 = P \cdot P = \begin{bmatrix} 0.7 & 0.3 \\ 0.6 & 0.4 \end{bmatrix} \begin{bmatrix} 0.7 & 0.3 \\ 0.6 & 0.4 \end{bmatrix}$$

$$= \begin{bmatrix} (0.7)(0.7) + (0.3)(0.6) & (0.7)(0.3) + (0.3)(0.4) \\ (0.6)(0.7) + (0.4)(0.6) & (0.6)(0.3) + (0.4)(0.4) \end{bmatrix}$$

$$= \begin{bmatrix} 0.67 & 0.33 \\ 0.66 & 0.34 \end{bmatrix}$$

The elements of P_2 are given the notation $p_{ij}^{(2)}$; hence

$$p_{11}^{(2)} = 0.67, \qquad p_{12}^{(2)} = 0.33, \qquad p_{21}^{(2)} = 0.66, \qquad p_{22}^{(2)} = 0.34.$$

In the case of n transitions we find that P_n is the matrix recording the probabilities and

$$P_n = P \cdot P \ldots P = P^n.$$

The elements of P_n are given the notation $p_{ij}^{(n)}$.

Example 12.2.1

The higher weekly ratings of two television companies, TV1 and TV2, were assumed to follow the transition matrix $P = \begin{bmatrix} 0.8 & 0.2 \\ 0.1 & 0.9 \end{bmatrix}$. Present a diagram for two transitions and calculate P_n for $n = 2$ and $n = 3$.

ANSWER

See Fig. 12.4.

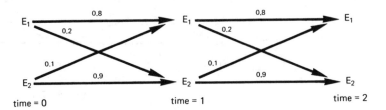

Figure 12.4

$$P_2 = P \cdot P = \begin{bmatrix} 0.8 & 0.2 \\ 0.1 & 0.9 \end{bmatrix} \begin{bmatrix} 0.8 & 0.2 \\ 0.1 & 0.9 \end{bmatrix}$$

$$= \begin{bmatrix} 0.64 + 0.02 & 0.16 + 0.18 \\ 0.08 + 0.09 & 0.02 + 0.81 \end{bmatrix}$$

$$= \begin{bmatrix} 0.66 & 0.34 \\ 0.17 & 0.83 \end{bmatrix}.$$

$$P_3 = P \cdot P \cdot P = P^2 \cdot P = \begin{bmatrix} 0.66 & 0.34 \\ 0.17 & 0.83 \end{bmatrix} \begin{bmatrix} 0.8 & 0.2 \\ 0.1 & 0.9 \end{bmatrix}$$

$$= \begin{bmatrix} 0.562 & 0.438 \\ 0.219 & 0.781 \end{bmatrix}.$$

Note again that the elements of each row add to give 1. Note also that element $p_{22}^{(3)} = 0.781$ refers to a change from state E_2 at time = 0 to a state E_2 at a time $t = 3$ with probability 0.781 and that four routes are possible.

Exercise 12.2.1

The best safety record of three factories F1, F2 and F3 for each year was assumed to follow the transition matrix below (derived from Exercise 12.1.1(b)).

$$P = \begin{bmatrix} 0.4 & 0.3 & 0.3 \\ 0.3 & 0.4 & 0.3 \\ 0.3 & 0.3 & 0.4 \end{bmatrix}.$$

Present a diagram for three transitions and calculate P_n for $n = 2$ and $n = 3$.

12.3 Predictions

To make predictions with the assumption of the probabilities of a transition matrix, further information is needed concerning the situation initially at time = 0. For example, in the prediction of crop yields the most recent crop yield outcome would be required; and in the prediction of the rating of shares in a sector the latest rating is needed.

To record this information it is convenient to use an initial-state vector for which the notation $\mathbf{p}^{(0)}$ is used.

$\mathbf{p}^{(0)} = [1 \quad 0]$ would show that a system had probability 1 it was in state E_1 and probability 0 it was in state E_2, i.e. that it was in state E_1.

To show the system was in state E_2 initially, we write

$\mathbf{p}^{(0)} = [0 \quad 1]$.

To record that all four states of an initial situation were equally likely we may write

$\mathbf{p}^{(0)} = [0.25 \quad 0.25 \quad 0.25 \quad 0.25]$.

The elements of this vector have notation

$p_1^{(0)} = 0.25, \quad p_2^{(0)} = 0.25, \quad p_3^{(0)} = 0.25, \quad p_4^{(0)} = 0.25.$

In the case where there are m initial states we use the notation

$\mathbf{p}^{(0)} = [p_1^{(0)} \quad p_2^{(0)} \quad p_3^{(0)} \quad \ldots \quad p_m^{(0)}]$.

To record a prediction after one transition we have a final state matrix of $\mathbf{p}^{(1)}$.

For example, if a prediction after one transition indicates state E_1 had probability 1 and state E_2 had probability 0 then we would write

$\mathbf{p}^{(1)} = [1 \quad 0]$.

If a prediction after four transitions indicated that state E_1 had probability 0.5, state E_2 had probability 0.3 and state E_3 had probability 0.2, then we would write

$\mathbf{p}^{(4)} = [0.5 \quad 0.3 \quad 0.2]$.

In general, after n transitions with m states we have a final state vector $\mathbf{p}^{(n)}$ where

$\mathbf{p}^{(n)} = [p_1^{(n)} \quad p_2^{(n)} \quad p_3^{(n)} \quad \ldots \quad p_m^{(n)}]$.

We may now make predictions using the formula

$\mathbf{p}^{(n)} = \mathbf{p}^{(0)} P_n$

which has an alternative expression $\mathbf{p}^{(n)} = \mathbf{p}^{(0)} P^n$.

The formula incorporates the diagrammatic approach used earlier.

Example 12.3.1

The success (E_1) or failure (E_2) of a crop each year is assumed to follow the transition matrix $P = \begin{bmatrix} 0.7 & 0.3 \\ 0.6 & 0.4 \end{bmatrix}$.

Obtain a prediction of success and failure after one transition and after two transitions in the following cases:

(a) initially in state E_1;
(b) initially in state E_2;
(c) assumed to be in state E_1 probability 0.5 and in state E_2 probability 0.5.

ANSWER

(a) We are given $\mathbf{p}^{(0)} = [1 \quad 0]$.

$$\mathbf{p}^{(1)} = \mathbf{p}^{(0)} P = [1 \quad 0] \begin{bmatrix} 0.7 & 0.3 \\ 0.6 & 0.4 \end{bmatrix} = [0.7 \quad 0.3].$$

Therefore a successful crop has probability 0.7.

$$\mathbf{p}^{(2)} = \mathbf{p}^{(0)}P_2 = \mathbf{p}^{(0)}P^2 = \mathbf{p}^{(0)}P \cdot P = (\mathbf{p}^{(0)}P) \cdot P = \mathbf{p}^{(1)}P.$$

Note above: $\mathbf{p}^{(1)} = [0.7 \quad 0.3]$.

Therefore $\mathbf{p}^{(2)} = \mathbf{p}^{(1)}P = [0.7 \quad 0.3] \begin{bmatrix} 0.7 & 0.3 \\ 0.6 & 0.4 \end{bmatrix} = [0.67 \quad 0.33]$.

Therefore a successful crop has probability 0.67.

(b) We are given $\mathbf{p}^{(0)} = [0 \quad 1]$

$$\mathbf{p}^{(1)} = \mathbf{p}^{(0)}P = [0 \quad 1] \begin{bmatrix} 0.7 & 0.3 \\ 0.6 & 0.4 \end{bmatrix} = [0.6 \quad 0.4].$$

Therefore a successful crop has probability 0.6.

$$\mathbf{p}^{(2)} = \mathbf{p}^{(1)}P = [0.6 \quad 0.4] \begin{bmatrix} 0.7 & 0.3 \\ 0.6 & 0.4 \end{bmatrix} \text{ using above result}$$

$$= [0.66 \quad 0.34].$$

Therefore a successful crop has probability 0.66.

(c) We are given $\mathbf{p}^{(0)} = [0.5 \quad 0.5]$

$$\mathbf{p}^{(1)} = \mathbf{p}^{(0)}P = [0.5 \quad 0.5] \begin{bmatrix} 0.7 & 0.3 \\ 0.6 & 0.4 \end{bmatrix}$$

$$= [0.65 \quad 0.35].$$

Therefore a successful crop has probability 0.65.

$$\mathbf{p}^{(2)} = \mathbf{p}^{(1)}P = [0.65 \quad 0.35] \begin{bmatrix} 0.7 & 0.3 \\ 0.6 & 0.4 \end{bmatrix}$$

$$= [0.665 \quad 0.335].$$

Therefore a successful crop has probability 0.665.

Exercise 12.3.1

A stock-market analyst rated each share in a particular sector in terms of improving (E_1), steady (E_2) and worsening (E_3), for each trading account. The following transition matrix was assumed to describe the situation:

$$P = \begin{bmatrix} 0.4 & 0.3 & 0.3 \\ 0.3 & 0.4 & 0.3 \\ 0.3 & 0.3 & 0.4 \end{bmatrix}.$$

Obtain the initial-state vector, the final-state vector after one transition, and the final-state vector after two transitions in each case:

(a) Ten shares held in category E_1.
(b) Ten shares held in category E_3.
(c) Thirty shares held in category E_1, forty shares held in category E_2, and thirty shares held in category E_3.

Steady States

We may find that in some cases when the initial state vector has to be multiplied by the transition matrix, then the final state vector produced is equal to the initial state vector. In such cases a steady state has occurred. Referring to the preceding example, 12.3.1, we observe that from three distinct initial states, after two transitions the final-state vectors had become similar, namely [0.67 0.33], [0.66 0.34] and [0.665 0.335]. We now consider an example to determine the steady-state vector for the transition matrix of example 12.3.1.

Example 12.3.2

The success (E_1) or failure (E_2) of a crop each year is assumed to follow the transition matrix $P = \begin{bmatrix} 0.7 & 0.3 \\ 0.6 & 0.4 \end{bmatrix}$. Determine the steady-state vector.

ANSWER

Assume a steady-state vector $\mathbf{p}^{(s)} = [p_1^{(s)} \quad p_2^{(s)}] = [x \quad y]$ exists.

such that $\mathbf{p}^{(s)} = \mathbf{p}^{(s)} . P$, where $x = p_1^{(s)}$, $y = p_2^{(s)}$ and $x + y = 1$.

Hence
$$[x \quad y] = [x \quad y] \begin{bmatrix} 0.7 & 0.3 \\ 0.6 & 0.4 \end{bmatrix}.$$

Therefore,
$$[x \quad y] = [0.7x + 0.6y \quad 0.3x + 0.4y].$$

$x = 0.7x + 0.6y$, therefore $x = 2y$, and as $x + y = 1$, $2y + y = 3y = 1$; $y = \frac{1}{3}$, $x = \frac{2}{3}$.

Hence $\mathbf{p}^{(s)} = [\frac{2}{3} \quad \frac{1}{3}]$.

Exercise 12.3.2

Determine the steady-state vector for the transition matrix in Exercise 12.3.1.

12.4 Applications to Replacement

The basic methodology we have developed so far can now be applied to replacement. However, care must be taken to specify the states of each system.

It is convenient to refer to example 10.4.1 concerning replacement. Referring to Fig. 10.1, which showed a failure branch, and Fig. 10.2, which showed a failure tree, difficulties can arise as the number of branches continues to increase. The next example uses the data of example 10.4.1 and applies the concise method of Markov chains to calculate the failures for each week.

Example 12.4.1

It is assumed that the batteries for a set of 100 lamps are replaced at the end of each week in which they fail, and that the probability of failure during each week is given by the following table:

Week	1	2	3
Probability of failure during each week	0.2	0.5	0.3

Required

(a) Identify three states and show the transitions on a directed graph.
(b) Obtain a transition matrix from the directed graph and hence predict the number of replacement batteries required at the end of each week for the first 4 weeks.

(a) Three states which may be identified are:

E_1: state that a lamp starts a week with a new battery;
E_2: state that a lamp starts a week with a 1-week-old battery;
E_3: state that a lamp starts a week with a 2-week-old battery.

To complete a directed graph all transition probabilities are required.

If a new battery starts a week there is probability 0.2 that it is replaced and probability 0.8 that it starts the next week as a week-old battery:

$$P(E_1 \rightarrow E_1) = 0.2, \qquad P(E_1 \rightarrow E_2) = 0.8.$$

Now of the 0.8 which start week 2, 0.5 fail and 0.3 start week 3 as a 2-week-old battery. Hence the probability a *1-week-old battery* will fail at the end of week 2 is $\dfrac{0.5}{0.8} = \dfrac{5}{8} = 0.625$ and the probability a *1-week-old battery* will work at the end of week 2 is $\dfrac{0.3}{0.8} = \dfrac{3}{8} = 0.375$.

Therefore, $\qquad P(E_2 \rightarrow E_2) = 0.625, \qquad P(E_2 \rightarrow E_3) = 0.375.$

However, batteries which work at the start of week 3 all fail during this week with probability 1.0.

Therefore, $\qquad\qquad\qquad P(E_3 \rightarrow E_1) = 1.0.$

All other transition probabilities = 0.
See Fig. 12.5.

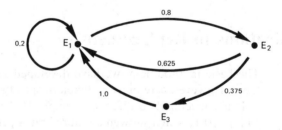

Figure 12.5

(b) Transition matrix P may be obtained from the directed graph:

$$P = \begin{bmatrix} 0.2 & 0.8 & 0 \\ 0.625 & 0 & 0.375 \\ 1 & 0 & 0 \end{bmatrix}.$$

To predict the replacements required we need an initial-state vector. An assumption is made that a battery commences in a new state E_1. Hence the initial-state vector is given by

$$\mathbf{p}^{(0)} = [1 \quad 0 \quad 0].$$

In order to determine the distribution at the end of the first week we calculate $\mathbf{p}^{(0)}P$ which gives $\mathbf{p}^{(1)}$.

Therefore, $\quad \mathbf{p}^{(1)} = \mathbf{p}^{(0)}P = [1 \quad 0 \quad 0] \begin{bmatrix} 0.2 & 0.8 & 0 \\ 0.625 & 0 & 0.375 \\ 1 & 0 & 0 \end{bmatrix}$

$$= [\underline{0.2} \quad 0.8 \quad 0].$$

Note that the first element of $\mathbf{p}^{(1)}$ is underlined as it indicates the replacement probability. Subsequently, similar elements of $\mathbf{p}^{(2)}$, $\mathbf{p}^{(3)}$ and $\mathbf{p}^{(4)}$ are underlined as they are calculated.

$$\mathbf{p}^{(2)} = \mathbf{p}^{(1)}P = \begin{bmatrix} 0.2 & 0.8 & 0 \end{bmatrix} \begin{bmatrix} 0.2 & 0.8 & 0 \\ 0.625 & 0 & 0.375 \\ 1 & 0 & 0 \end{bmatrix}$$

$$= [\underline{0.54} \quad 0.16 \quad 0.3].$$

$$\mathbf{p}^{(3)} = \mathbf{p}^{(2)}P = \begin{bmatrix} 0.54 & 0.16 & 0.3 \end{bmatrix} \begin{bmatrix} 0.2 & 0.8 & 0 \\ 0.625 & 0 & 0.375 \\ 1 & 0 & 0 \end{bmatrix}$$

$$= [\underline{0.508} \quad 0.432 \quad 0.06].$$

$$\mathbf{p}^{(4)} = \mathbf{p}^{(3)}P = \begin{bmatrix} 0.508 & 0.432 & 0.06 \end{bmatrix} \begin{bmatrix} 0.2 & 0.8 & 0 \\ 0.625 & 0 & 0.375 \\ 1 & 0 & 0 \end{bmatrix}$$

$$= [\underline{0.4316} \quad 0.4064 \quad 0.162].$$

We note the first elements of $\mathbf{p}^{(1)}$, $\mathbf{p}^{(2)}$, $\mathbf{p}^{(3)}$, $\mathbf{p}^{(4)}$ are 0.2, 0.54, 0.508 and 0.4316 respectively. Hence by multiplication by 100 we are able to determine the expected number of replacement batteries at the end of the first, second, third and fourth weeks respectively as 20, 54, 50.8 and 43.16. These values should be compared with those achieved by the failure-tree approach in example 10.4.1 (Fig. 10.2, p. 157).

Exercise 12.4.1

An engineering company is studying a replacement strategy for its metal-cutting tools. It has collected the following data on tool life relating to normal load and operating conditions:

	Month after replacement				
	1	2	3	4	5
Percentage of original tools which have failed by the end of that month (cumulative)	10	25	50	80	100

Required:

(a) Identify five states and show the transitions on a directed graph.
(b) Obtain a transition matrix from the directed graph and hence predict the number of replacement tools required at the end of each month for the first 3 months, given that initially there are 1000 new cutting tools and failures are replaced at the end of each month.

Further Exercises

12.1 If $P = \begin{pmatrix} 0.5 & 0.5 & 0 \\ 0 & 0.5 & 0.5 \\ 0.5 & 0 & 0.5 \end{pmatrix}$, find P^2 and P^3.

If $\mathbf{p}^{(0)} = (0.5, 0.25, 0.25)$, find $\mathbf{p}^{(1)}$, $\mathbf{p}^{(2)}$ and $\mathbf{p}^{(3)}$, interpreting your answer in each case.

12.2 An accounting office assigned trainees to three tasks T_1, T_2 and T_3. At the end of each week they were observed to be switched between tasks according to the following transition matrix:

$$P = \tfrac{1}{6} \begin{bmatrix} 1 & 2 & 3 \\ 2 & 1 & 3 \\ 2 & 2 & 2 \end{bmatrix}.$$

Required:

(a) If a trainee started with task T_1 during the first week, determine the probability that a trainee would be assigned to tasks T_1, T_2 and T_3,
 (i) at the end of week 1,
 (ii) at the end of week 2.

 You may assume an initial state vector $[1 \quad 0 \quad 0]$.

(b) The situation was considered stable when it was found that $\mathbf{p}^{(t)} = \mathbf{p}^{(t+1)}$ where $\mathbf{p}^{(t)}$ is the state vector after time t. By considering the product $\mathbf{p}^{(t)} \cdot P$ where $\mathbf{p}^{(t)} = [p \quad q \quad r]$ find values of p, q and r for a stable situation, and comment upon whether you consider that a trainee would expect to gain the same experience at each task.

12.3 By examination of employee work records, a firm obtains indications of staff turnover. Employees are taken on for type A work and for type B work, and the firm finds that employees in type A work will transfer to type B work with probability 0.1 at the end of each month; also, that they will leave at the end of each month with probability 0.1; while the probability is 0.8 that they will continue with type A for a further month. However, persons doing type B work for one month have a probability of 0.9 of continuing with the same work for a further month, but have a probability of 0.1 of leaving. Persons who have left the firm have not sought re-employment there.

Required:

(a) Represent the situation as a directed graph.
(b) Represent the situation as a transition matrix.
(c) If 100 employees are doing type A work at the start of the first month, find the expected number of employees in each type of employment at the start of the second, third, and fourth months.
(d) If the firm pays £100 each month for type A employees and £150 each month for type B employees during the first and the second months, but £110 and £160 for A and B respectively during the third and fourth months, find the expected value of the wages during the first four months.

13 Forecasting Methods

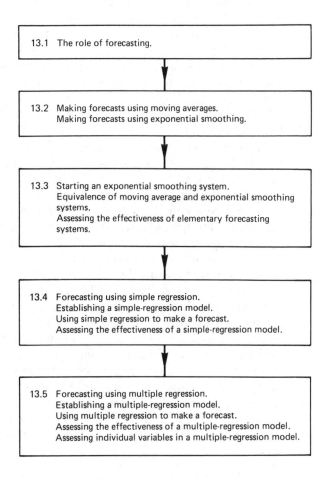

13.1 The role of forecasting.

13.2 Making forecasts using moving averages.
Making forecasts using exponential smoothing.

13.3 Starting an exponential smoothing system.
Equivalence of moving average and exponential smoothing systems.
Assessing the effectiveness of elementary forecasting systems.

13.4 Forecasting using simple regression.
Establishing a simple-regression model.
Using simple regression to make a forecast.
Assessing the effectiveness of a simple-regression model.

13.5 Forecasting using multiple regression.
Establishing a multiple-regression model.
Using multiple regression to make a forecast.
Assessing the effectiveness of a multiple-regression model.
Assessing individual variables in a multiple-regression model.

13.1 The Role of Forecasting

In any business situation it is necessary to be able to make some predictions about the future in order to plan the business operations. Arriving at such an estimate of the future is the purpose of the process of forecasting and we look in this chapter at some forecasting methods.

In the service sector a forecast of demand for the service being offered will be necessary in order to determine how many staff will need to be employed to provide the service and to decide what quantities of materials will be needed.

In the retailing sector, forecasts of sales will be needed to decide staffing levels and also to determine what quantities of stock should be purchased. For the reasons discussed in Chapter 6, stock control is a very important issue in retail business. Excessive levels of stock tie up working capital and storage space and incur further expenses through such processes as theft, insurance and, possibly, deterioration. On the other hand, inadequate reorder quantities and reorder levels lead to other problems through high ordering costs and the inability to meet orders from customers.

In the manufacturing sector too it is essential to have forecasts of sales of the products being made in order to decide how much should be produced. This affects manpower requirements, plant-purchasing decisions and again issues relating to stock. In the manufacturing situation the stock-control question manifests itself in two ways. First, decisions have to be taken on what quantities of raw materials or components should be stocked in order to keep the processes going; and second, it is necessary to decide what levels of finished goods should be held in stock.

The above-mentioned stock-control considerations apply to both types of stock, and good forecasts of sales levels are essential to maintaining such levels of stock as are in the best interests of the company. In reality no method can give a perfect insight into what the future will be and any forecast arrived at must be subject to limits of error.

From the above paragraphs it will be seen that the topic being considered in this final chapter is in a sense fundamental to much that has gone before in the book. We begin with some simple forecasting methods which assume demand to be constant apart from random fluctuations, and we look at the question of measuring how well the forecasts accord with subsequently observed values. We then proceed to simple regression as a forecasting method. This takes into account a linear trend in the data values as well as random variations. It also permits the calculation of statistical measures and the carrying out of tests to determine how well the regression model fits the data on which it is based and hence how reliable the forecasts obtained from it are likely to be. The testing method is explained.

Finally, the chapter looks at multiple-regression methods, where the forecast for the variable of interest is obtained from a knowledge of a number of other variables. The processes for establishing the model and for testing it are based on the same principles as those for simple regression, but one or two additional considerations arise. Multiple regression is considered using two explanatory variables to make the forecasts and this size of model brings in all the considerations of multiple regression. For larger numbers of explanatory variables the amount of calculation involved in multiple regression becomes very substantial and problems of this type would not normally be tackled without the aid of a computer.

13.2 Introduction to Moving Averages and Exponential Smoothing

Moving averages and exponential smoothing are forecasting methods used, particularly in a marketing context, where past data shows no discernable trend upwards or downwards but consists of values which are constant apart from random variations. An example of such data would be that represented by the graph shown in Fig. 13.1, which shows demand for a particular type of item at a series of points in time.

In making a forecast from such data as this all we can hope to do is smooth out the random variations in some way in order to predict what the next value will be. The method of moving averages does this in a very simple way by just taking the last few items and using their mean as the forecast of the next value.

In general terms, if an N-step moving average is to be used to give us a forecast F_t for the value at time t, we merely find the mean of the previous N data values $X_{t-1}, X_{t-2}, X_{t-3}, \ldots, X_{t-N}$.

i.e.

$$F_t = \frac{X_{t-1} + X_{t-2} + X_{t-3} + \ldots + X_{t-N}}{N}.$$

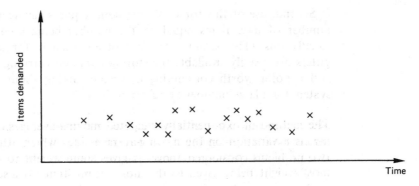

Figure 13.1

Example 13.2.1

The following figures represent the numbers of items of a particular type demanded in each of 7 months:

Month	1	2	3	4	5	6	7
Number demanded	32	40	30	38	34	42	50

Use a 3-month moving-average forecast system to obtain a series of forecasts of demand for months 4 to 8 inclusive.

ANSWER

Using the moving-average formula above we see that:

The forecast for period 4 is $\dfrac{30 + 40 + 32}{3} = \dfrac{102}{3} = 34.$

The forecast for period 5 is $\dfrac{38 + 30 + 40}{3} = \dfrac{108}{3} = 36.$

The forecast for period 6 is $\dfrac{34 + 38 + 30}{3} = \dfrac{102}{3} = 34.$

The forecast for period 7 is $\dfrac{42 + 34 + 38}{3} = \dfrac{114}{3} = 38.$

The forecast for period 8 is $\dfrac{50 + 42 + 34}{3} = \dfrac{126}{3} = 42.$

Summary:

Month	1	2	3	4	5	6	7	8
Actual demand	32	40	30	38	34	42	50	
Forecast				34	36	34	38	42

The method of moving averages provides a simple way of trying to smooth out random variations to give forecasts from data of the kind we are considering. However, the method is open to certain criticisms.

First, there is an arbitrariness about the number of values used in calculating the average. In example 13.2.1, for instance, there is no very good reason why the average of three values should be used to make the forecast rather than the average of four or five or any other number. The chosen number of items are all given equal weight — there is no attempt, for instance, to give more weight to the more recent values — and no earlier items are taken into account in any way at all.

191

Second, use of this forecasting system requires having available at every stage a number of data items equal to the number being used in the moving-average calculations. (This is much less a problem than in former days, now that computers are readily available for storing data and carrying out calculations, but is still a point worth considering if we are talking about operating a forecasting system for a large number of different lines.)

The method of exponentially weighted moving averages, or exponential smoothing, is a variation on the moving-averages idea which attempts to cope with the two problems considered above. It gives some weight to all past data items, with most weight being given to the most recent items. It also allows forecasts to be made using just two pieces of information. Denoting the forecast for time t by F_t and data items at respective time points by $X_{t-1}, X_{t-2}, X_{t-3}, \ldots$, an exponentially weighted moving-average forecast can be *defined* as

$$F_t = \alpha X_{t-1} + \alpha(1 - \alpha)X_{t-2} + \alpha(1 - \alpha)^2 X_{t-3} + \alpha(1 - \alpha)^3 X_{t-4} + \ldots \quad (1)$$

where α is a constant between 0 and 1 called the smoothing constant. Although mathematically it is permissible for α to have any value in the range 0 to 1 it has been found in practice that most meaningful forecasting systems need to use a value in the range 0.1 to 0.3 to give realistic forecasts. We will say more below on the effect of different values of α and also on measuring the effectiveness of forecasting systems. Although equation (1) above is the definition of an exponentially weighted moving average and demonstrates that all data items are taken into account with most weight being given to the most recent ones, it does not provide a useful way for actually calculating forecasts. To arrive at a better formula for this purpose, let us move back one step in time (i.e. reduce all the time values by 1) and write down the forecasting formula for time $t - 1$. This is

$$F_{t-1} = \alpha X_{t-2} + \alpha(1 - \alpha) X_{t-3} + \alpha(1 - \alpha)^2 X_{t-4} + \alpha(1 - \alpha)^3 X_{t-5} + \ldots \quad (2)$$

If we then multiply equation (2) through by $(1 - \alpha)$ we obtain

$$(1 - \alpha)F_{t-1} = \alpha(1 - \alpha)X_{t-2} + \alpha(1 - \alpha)^2 X_{t-3} + \alpha(1 - \alpha)^3 X_{t-4} + \alpha(1 - \alpha)^4 X_{t-5} + \ldots \quad (3)$$

Then subtracting (3) from (1) gives:

$$F_t - (1 - \alpha) F_{t-1} = \alpha X_{t-1}.$$

Hence the *calculation* formula:

$$\boxed{F_t = \alpha X_{t-1} + (1 - \alpha)F_{t-1}}$$

Thus we see that each forecast is a weighted average of the most recent data-value and the forecast for the previous time point. Only these two pieces of information are needed each time we want to make a forecast.

The calculating formula also makes clear the effect of different α values on the forecasting system. If α is close to 0, we see that we have a 'very smooth' forecasting system, with each forecast being similar to the previous forecast and little account being taken of new data. If α is close to 1, we have the opposite effect with forecasts tending to follow the data values around. (Some cynics have been known to suggest that the latter method is sometimes used in weather forecasting – today's weather will be the same as yesterday's weather.)

Let us now consider a numerical example on exponentially weighted moving averages.

Example 13.2.2

The following figures represent the numbers of items of a particular type demanded in each of 7 months:

Month	1	2	3	4	5	6	7
Number demanded	32	40	30	38	34	42	50

Assuming a forecast value of 32 for month 1, use exponential smoothing to obtain forecasts of numbers demanded in months 2 to 8 inclusive. Use smoothing constant $\alpha = 0.2$.

ANSWER

$\alpha = 0.2$ so $1 - \alpha = 0.8$.

$X_1 = 32$ and $F_1 = 32$ so $F_2 = 0.2 \times 32 + 0.8 \times 32 = 32.$

$X_2 = 40$ and $F_2 = 32$ so $F_3 = 0.2 \times 40 + 0.8 \times 32 = 33.6.$

$X_3 = 30$ and $F_3 = 33.6$ so $F_4 = 0.2 \times 30 + 0.8 \times 33.6 = 32.88.$

$X_4 = 38$ and $F_4 = 32.88$ so $F_5 = 0.2 \times 38 + 0.8 \times 32.88 = 33.90.$

$X_5 = 34$ and $F_5 = 33.90$ so $F_6 = 0.2 \times 34 + 0.8 \times 33.90 = 33.92.$

$X_6 = 42$ and $F_6 = 33.92$ so $F_7 = 0.2 \times 42 + 0.8 \times 33.92 = 35.54.$

$X_7 = 50$ and $F_7 = 35.54$ so $F_8 = 0.2 \times 50 + 0.8 \times 35.54 = 38.44.$

Summary:

Month	1	2	3	4	5	6	7	8
Actual demand	32	40	30	38	34	42	50	
Forecast	32	32	33.6	32.88	33.90	33.92	35.54	38.44

Exercise 13.2.1

You are given the following sales figures relating to 6 periods:

Period	1	2	3	4	5	6
Sales	55	75	50	70	60	80

You are required to find:

(a) Simple moving-average forecasts for periods 5, 6 and 7 using a 4-period moving average.
(b) Exponentially weighted moving average forecasts for periods 2 to 7, inclusive assuming a forecast of 55 for period 1 and using smoothing constant 0.25.

13.3 Further Considerations in Elementary Forecasting

In example 13.2.2 and exercise 13.2.1 we assumed knowledge of a forecast for period 1 in order to begin use of the exponential-smoothing formula. For situations involving such small amounts of data as those problems there is really no alternative to simply using the first actual data value as also the first forecast.

However, in situations where exponential smoothing is to be used for any serious forecasting purposes there would be a much longer run of past data available and this can be used to give a better starting forecast. What is done in practice is to first take the mean of the first one-third of the past data-values. Then, using this as the initial forecast, run the calculation formula through the remaining two-thirds of the past data-values. Then, when the first time-point is reached for which a real forecast is needed, inaccuracies resulting from using the mean initially will have been 'forgotten' by the system and we can hope for reliable forecasts. This procedure is equivalent to applying the definition formula (equation (1)) to the final two-thirds of the past data, with the X value in the final term being the mean of the first third. Because it is multiplied by a high power of $(1 - \alpha)$, any inaccuracies it contains will have little effect on the forecast.

We have seen that moving averages and exponential smoothing are based on very similar ideas in that they use the mean of past data-items to attempt to smooth out random variations and give a forecast of future values. The differences are in the number of items used and whether or not different weights are applied to different items. In view of this fundamental similarity, it is sometimes helpful to think about *equivalent* simple moving-average and exponentially weighted moving-average systems. What is meant by the word in this context is that two systems are equivalent if they make their forecast by using data of the same average age relative to the period for which the forecast is to be made.

For an N-step moving-average system we saw that

$$F_t = \frac{X_{t-1} + X_{t-2} + X_{t-3} + \ldots + X_{t-N}}{N},$$

so the average age of the data in periods relative to the time for which the forecast is being made is

$$A = \frac{1 + 2 + 3 + \ldots + N}{N} = \frac{\frac{1}{2}N(N+1)}{N} = \frac{N+1}{2}. \tag{4}$$

Returning to the definition formula (equation (1)) for an exponentially weighted moving average, we have that

$$F_t = \alpha X_{t-1} + \alpha(1 - \alpha)X_{t-2} + \alpha(1 - \alpha)^2 X_{t-3} + \alpha(1 - \alpha)^3 X_{t-4} + \ldots$$

Hence the average age of the data used, weighting the age of each item by its weight in the forecasting formula, is

$$A = \alpha \times 1 + \alpha(1 - \alpha) \times 2 + \alpha(1 - \alpha)^2 \times 3 + \alpha(1 - \alpha)^3 \times 4 + \ldots \tag{5}$$

Multiplying through in (5) by the factor $(1 - \alpha)$ gives:

$$(1 - \alpha)A = \alpha(1 - \alpha) + \alpha(1 - \alpha)^2 \times 2 + \alpha(1 - \alpha)^3 \times 3 + \ldots \tag{6}$$

Subtracting (6) from (5):

$$\alpha A = \alpha + \alpha(1 - \alpha) + \alpha(1 - \alpha)^2 + \alpha(1 - \alpha)^3 + \ldots \tag{7}$$

The right-hand side of (7) must be 1, as it is the sum of the weights in the exponentially weighted moving-*average* formula. We can confirm this by summing it as a geometric series to obtain

$$\alpha A = \alpha \left(\frac{1}{1 - (1 - \alpha)} \right) = \alpha \times \frac{1}{\alpha} = 1.$$

Hence,

$$A = \frac{1}{\alpha}. \tag{8}$$

So two systems are equivalent if $\dfrac{N+1}{2} = \dfrac{1}{\alpha}$. This can be thought of in two ways.

If we have a simple moving average based on N periods, then the smoothing constant α for the equivalent exponentially weighted moving average is

$$\alpha = \frac{2}{N+1}.$$

If we have an exponentially weighted moving-average system with smoothing constant α, then the number of periods N needed in a simple moving-average system in order for it to be equivalent is

$$N = \frac{2}{\alpha} - 1.$$

Example 13.3.1

Obtain 9-step simple moving-average forecasts for periods 10, 11 and 12 for the sales data given below.

Obtain also exponentially weighted moving-average forecasts for periods 2 to 12 using the equivalent exponential-smoothing system and the starting forecast suggested.

Period	1	2	3	4	5	6	7	8	9	10	11
Items sold	25	28	27	34	28	25	29	30	26	34	28
Forecast	29										

ANSWER

9-step forecast for period 10 is

$$\frac{25 + 28 + 27 + 34 + 28 + 25 + 29 + 30 + 26}{9} = \frac{252}{9} = 28.$$

9-step forecast for period 11 is

$$\frac{28 + 27 + 34 + 28 + 25 + 29 + 30 + 26 + 34}{9} = \frac{261}{9} = 29.$$

9-step forecast for period 12 is

$$\frac{27 + 34 + 28 + 25 + 29 + 30 + 26 + 34 + 28}{9} = \frac{261}{9} = 29.$$

We have used $N = 9$ in our simple moving average so the smoothing constant for the equivalent smoothing is

$$\alpha = \frac{2}{N+1} = \frac{2}{9+1} = \frac{2}{10} = 0.2.$$

Hence we can obtain exponentially weighted forecasts for periods 2 to 12 as shown in Table 13.1.

Table 13.1

Period	1	2	3	4	5	6	7	8	9	10	11	12
Items sold	25	28	27	34	28	25	29	30	26	34	28	
0.2 × items sold	5	5.6	5.4	6.8	5.6	5	5.8	6	6.2	6.8	5.6	
0.8 × previous forecast		23.2	22.56	22.53	22.34	23.21	23.13	22.50	22.64	22.91	22.49	23.43
Forecast	29	28.2	28.16	27.93	29.14	28.91	28.13	28.30	28.64	28.11	29.29	29.03

In order to measure how well a simple forecasting system is working it is common practice to look at the actual and forecast values at all the time-points for which we have both and then average the differences in terms of either their absolute values or their squares. The figures that result do not have statistical properties that allow us to readily give a direct interpretation to their values, but the measures are useful for purposes of comparing the effectiveness of one set of forecasts relative to another. The measures are illustrated in the following example.

Example 13.3.2

In examples 13.2.1 and 13.2.2 we saw the sets of observed values, simple 4-step moving-average forecasts and exponentially weighted moving-average forecasts using smoothing constant $\alpha = 0.2$ given in Table 13.2.

Table 13.2

Month	1	2	3	4	5	6	7	8
Observed value	32	40	30	38	34	42	50	
Simple moving-average forecast				34	36	34	38	42
Exponential smoothing forecast	32	32	33.6	32.88	33.90	33.92	35.54	38.44

For each of the two forecasting systems calculate the mean of the absolute deviations of the forecasts from the observed values and also calculate the mean square of the deviations.

ANSWER

For the simple moving average we have only 4 time-points for which both actual and forecast values are available (Table 13.3).

Table 13.3

Month	4	5	6	7	
Observed value, O	38	34	42	50	
Forecast value, F	34	36	34	38	
Difference, $O - F$	4	−2	8	12	
Absolute difference, $\lvert O - F \rvert$	4	2	8	12	$\Sigma \lvert O - F \rvert = 26$
Squared difference, $(O - F)^2$	16	4	64	144	$\Sigma (O - F)^2 = 228$

$$\text{Mean absolute difference (MAD)} = \frac{\Sigma \lvert O - F \rvert}{n} = \frac{26}{4} = 6.5$$

$$\text{Mean squared difference} = \frac{\Sigma (O - F)^2}{n} = \frac{228}{4} = 57$$

For the exponentially weighted moving-average system we have seven pairs of values (Table 13.4).

Table 13.4

Month	1	2	3	4	5	6	7	
Observed value, O	32	40	30	38	34	42	50	
Forecast value, F	32	32	33.6	32.88	33.90	33.92	35.54	
Difference, $O - F$	0	8	−3.6	5.12	0.10	8.08	14.46	
Absolute difference, $|O - F|$	0	8	3.6	5.12	0.10	8.08	14.46	$\Sigma |O - F| = 39.36$
Squared difference, $(O - F)^2$	0	64	12.96	26.21	0.01	65.29	209.09	$\Sigma (O - F)^2 = 377.56$

$$\text{Mean absolute difference} = \frac{\Sigma |O - F|}{n} = \frac{39.36}{7} = 5.6$$

$$\text{Mean squared difference} = \frac{377.56}{7} = 53.9$$

For the data in example 13.3.1 both forecasting systems give similar results on both the routine measures used. In both cases the largest differences are in the last two forecasts where there is a suggestion of an upward trend taking place. In such circumstances the assumptions for elementary forecasting are violated and we need to move on to look at regression methods. This is done in the following sections.

Exercise 13.3.1

(a) For the sales data given below obtain exponentially weighted moving-average forecasts of sales in periods 2 to 13 using a smoothing constant $\alpha = 0.25$ and the starting forecast suggested.
(b) Obtain simple moving-average forecasts for as many periods as possible using the equivalent simple moving-average system.
(c) For each of the sets of forecasts in (a) and (b) above find the mean absolute deviation of the forecasts from the subsequent actual values and find the mean-square deviation of the forecasts from the subsequent actual values.

Period	1	2	3	4	5	6	7	8	9	10	11	12
Items sold	40	46	44	58	46	40	48	50	42	58	46	44
Forecast	48											

13.4 Forecasting Using Simple Regression

The assumptions required in order for the simple forecasting systems of the preceding sections to be appropriate are very restrictive and in most situations where forecasting is required they will not apply. In particular there will usually be some sort of trend in the values and when this is the case the results of the simple forecasts become very unreliable. For the data used in examples 13.2.1 and 13.2.2, for instance, the values given for the last two data-points suggested an upward trend and the forecasts fell well short of the actual values.

To cope with data exhibiting a trend we need to consider the method of regression and the burden of the current section will be *simple regression*.

Regression is concerned with relationships between variables and the idea is that if we can explain one variable y in terms of other variables then we can obtain a forecast for y if we know particular values for the other variables. There can be any number of explanatory variables and the relationship we are looking for can, in principle, have any functional form.

However, it is important to realise that regression will not tell us which functional form to use. Rather when we have specified the functional form regression will tell us what is the best relationship (to be defined below) of that form for the data we have. In simple regression, we concern ourselves with just one explanatory variable, usually called x, and with a straight-line (or *linear*) form of relationship. Most of the principles of regression can be gleaned from a consideration of this case. The one explanatory variable can be time, so allowing regression to be applied to data such as we considered in section 13.2.

We now explain the regression ideas using the following example.

Example 13.4.2

A manufacturer wishes to establish a procedure to estimate direct-labour costs for small-batch production orders. He has obtained a random sample of recorded actual direct labour costs for a sample of 10 batches as shown in Table 13.5.

Table 13.5

Batch size in units (x)	Direct labour hours (£) (y)
15	200
18	240
18	260
21	290
23	300
23	320
26	380
28	370
32	400
37	470
$\Sigma x = 241$	$\Sigma y = 3230$
$\Sigma xy = 82\,780$ $\quad \Sigma x^2 = 6225$	$\Sigma y^2 = 1\,103\,900$

You are required to:

(a) calculate the least-squares regression line relating labour costs to batch size;
(b) provide the manufacturer with a forecast of direct-labour cost for an order for a batch of 25 items.

(*ICMA Prof. 1*)

ANSWER

The most elementary step we can take in looking for a simple regression relationship between two variables is to plot a graph showing variable x on the horizontal axis and variable y on the vertical axis. Such a graph is called a *scatter diagram*. The scatter diagram for the data in this example is shown in Fig. 13.2. Finding the simple regression relationship then amounts to finding the straight line which passes 'closest' to the data points, in some sense, and then obtaining its equation.

Specifically, we are looking for the 'regression of y on x' since we see the cost variable y being explained by the size of batch rather than vice versa. (It is possible to find also a regression of x on y by interchanging the roles of the two variables if we want to forecast x given the value of y. The regression relationships are different and the regression of y on x we are finding here should never be used to forecast x from y.)

To see how the line which is the regression of y on x is defined consider Fig. 13.3. It is the line such that the sum of squares of the y-direction deviations

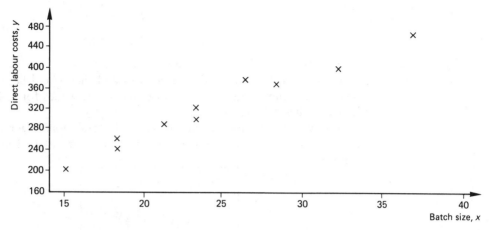

Figure 13.2

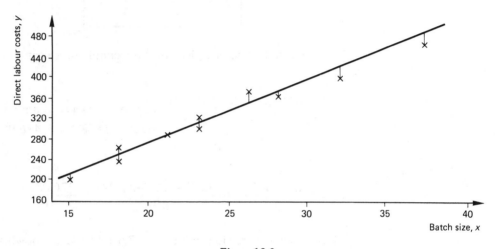

Figure 13.3

of the data-points from it is as small as possible. Hence the name 'least-squares' regression line. The general equation of such a line is

$$y = a + bx,$$

where a and b are constants. We have to find a and b so as to minimise the sum of squares of the y-direction deviations. For this example it means we have to find a and b so as to minimise

$$(a + b \times 15 - 200)^2 + (a + b \times 18 - 240)^2 + (a + b \times 18 - 260)^2$$
$$+ (a + b \times 21 - 290)^2 + (a + b \times 23 - 300)^2 + (a + b \times 23 - 320)^2$$
$$+ (a + b \times 26 - 380)^2 + (a + b \times 28 - 370)^2 + (a + b \times 32 - 400)^2$$
$$+ (a + b \times 37 - 470)^2$$

In general we need a and b so as to minimise

$$\Sigma \, (a + bx - y)^2,$$

where the summation is over all the pairs of data values.

The minimisation procedure is a straightforward exercise in differentiation which leads to the following pair of simultaneous equations for a and b:

$$na + b\Sigma x = \Sigma y$$

$$a\Sigma x + b\Sigma x^2 = \Sigma xy,$$

where n is the number of pairs of data values.

These are called the *normal equations* and they could be used in a particular instance to find a and b by substituting in the values for n, Σx, Σy, Σx^2 and Σxy and then solving.

However, it is more usual to solve the equations algebraically to give an explicit formula for b and a formula for a in terms of b. These formulae are as follows:

$$b = \frac{\Sigma xy - \dfrac{(\Sigma x)(\Sigma y)}{n}}{\Sigma x^2 - \dfrac{(\Sigma x)^2}{n}},$$

$$a = \frac{\Sigma y - b\Sigma x}{n}.$$

The appropriate sums are given in this example so we can proceed to find b and a.

$$b = \frac{82\,780 - \dfrac{241 \times 3230}{10}}{6225 - \dfrac{241^2}{10}} = \frac{82\,780 - 77\,843}{6225 - 5808.1} = \frac{4937}{416.9} = 11.842,$$

$$a = \frac{\Sigma y - b\,\Sigma x}{n} = \frac{3230 - 11.842 \times 241}{10} = \frac{376.0375}{10} = 37.6.$$

The least-squares regression line is $y = 37.6 + 11.842x$. Knowing this equation we can obtain the required forecast of the cost of a batch of 25 items by substituting $x = 25$ into it. We obtain

$$y = 37.6 + 11.842 \times 25 = 37.6 + 296.05 = 333.65.$$

The forecast direct-labour cost for a batch of 25 items is £333.65.

In order to measure the effectiveness of a regression line for forecasting purposes we again use a method based on the sum of squares of deviations of the actual values from those predicted by regression. That is to say, we use the value of $\Sigma(a + bx - y)^2$ when this has been minimised. However, it is not usual in this situation to use the 'residual' sum of squares in its raw form but to use statistics derived from it. Not only can these statistics be used for comparative purposes in the way we saw the measures for elementary forecasting methods being used, but they have also an objective meaning and tests of statistical significance can be carried out on them.

One measure which can be used is the coefficient of determination. This is obtained by expressing the residual sum of squares as a proportion of the total variation of the y values about their mean and subtracting from one. It is denoted by the symbol r^2.

Thus

$$r^2 = 1 - \frac{\Sigma(a + bx - y)^2}{\Sigma(y - \overline{y})^2}.$$

The formula can be rewritten

$$r^2 = \frac{\Sigma(y - \overline{y})^2 - \Sigma(a + bx - y)^2}{\Sigma(y - \overline{y})^2}.$$

In this form the numerator which is the difference between the total sum of squares and the residual is called the explained sum of squares and is denoted SSEx. It represents the sum of squares of the vertical distances between $\overline{y}$ and points on the regression line for the x values in the data.

Thus $\qquad$ SSEx $= \Sigma(a + bx - \overline{y})^2.$

But the regression formula for a is $a = \overline{y} - b\overline{x}.$

Hence $\qquad$ SSEx $= \Sigma(\overline{y} - b\overline{x} + bx - \overline{y})^2$
$$= \Sigma[b(x - \overline{x})]^2 = b^2 \Sigma(x - \overline{x})^2.$$

Replacing one b in this product by the regression formula then gives

$$\text{SSEx} = b \cdot \frac{\Sigma(x - \overline{x})(y - \overline{y})}{\Sigma(x - \overline{x})^2} \cdot \Sigma(x - \overline{x})^2.$$

Hence $\qquad$ $$\boxed{\text{SSEx} = b \cdot \Sigma(x - \overline{x})(y - \overline{y}) = b \cdot \left[\Sigma xy - \frac{(\Sigma x)(\Sigma y)}{n}\right].}$$

This is the expression generally used to evaluate the explained sum of squares. It is usual to represent the total sum of squares by SST.

So $\qquad$ $$\boxed{\text{SST} = \Sigma(y - \overline{y})^2 = \Sigma y^2 - \frac{(\Sigma y)^2}{n}.}$$

The residual sum of squares, denoted SSU, is then normally found in practice by subtracting the explained sum of squares from the total:

$$\boxed{\text{SSU} = \text{SST} - \text{SSEx.}}$$

The coefficient of determination can be written as $r^2 = \dfrac{\text{SSEx}}{\text{SST}}.$

Referring to the solution to example 13.3.2, we have

$$b = 11.842 \qquad \text{and} \qquad \Sigma(x - \overline{x})(y - \overline{y}) = 4937$$

so $\qquad$ SSEx $= 11.842 \times 4937 = 58\,463.954,$

$$\text{SST} = \Sigma y^2 - \frac{(\Sigma y)^2}{n} = 1\,103\,900 - \frac{3230^2}{10} = 1\,103\,900 - 1\,043\,290 = 60\,610.$$

Hence, $\qquad$ $$r^2 = \frac{\text{SSEx}}{\text{SST}} = \frac{58\,463.954}{60\,610} = 0.965.$$

This tells us that 96.5 per cent of the variation in the figures for direct labour costs is explained by the regression relationship on batch size. This proportion seems quite large and suggests that the regression is very effective in explaining the variation in the direct-labour-costs figures. However, we can go further and carry out a test of statistical significance to decide whether the value for r^2 is sufficiently close to 1 for the model to be regarded as significant in explaining the variation. If it is found to be so, then we can have confidence in the forecasts obtained for y by inserting values of x into the regression model.

The test using the coefficient of determination for the simple regression model involves calculating the statistic $\dfrac{(n-2)r^2}{(1-r^2)}$ and comparing its value with the F distribution table for 1 degree of freedom in the numerator and $n-2$ degrees of freedom in the denominator. The reason for this somewhat mysterious statistic will become clearer when we carry out another test procedure below.

For the moment we carry out the test for the data in example 13.4.2:

$$\frac{(n-2)r^2}{(1-r^2)} = \frac{8 \times 0.965}{1-0.965} = \frac{7.72}{0.035} = 220.$$

The table for the F distribution shows the 0.1 per cent point of $F_{1,8}$ to be 25.42. As the statistic value greatly exceeds this, we can certainly conclude that the regression model is highly significant in explaining the variation in the direct-labour costs.

Note that the square root of the coefficient of determination is called the *coefficient of correlation* between x and y. It is denoted by the symbol r.

A second method for testing the significance of a regression model uses the technique of *analysis of variance*. This method uses the same sums of squares as we have seen above for the coefficient of determination. The statistic which is ultimately tested is the same as that used above, as we shall see. However, the approach, using a table format, is considerably different and the test statistic arises this way in a more natural manner. The table has columns showing the sources of variation, the sum of squares associated with each source of variation, the degrees of freedom (explained below) for each source and the mean square per degree of freedom for each source.

The test involves looking at the ratio of the mean square per degree of freedom for the explained variation (MSEx) to the mean square per degree of freedom for the residual variation (MSU). If this ratio is large, as decided by comparing with the F table, then we can conclude that the explained variation is large compared with what is left over and hence say that the regression model is significant. The degrees of freedom for the total sum of squares are the number of *independent* contributions to that sum from the data. Now we have

$$\text{SST} = \Sigma (y - \bar{y})^2 = (y_1 - \bar{y})^2 + (y_2 - \bar{y})^2 + (y_3 - \bar{y})^2 + \ldots + (y_{n-1} - \bar{y})^2$$
$$+ (y_n - \bar{y})^2.$$

But, by definition of the mean, we know that

$$(y_1 - \bar{y}) + (y_2 - \bar{y}) + (y_3 - \bar{y}) + \ldots + (y_{n-1} - \bar{y}) + (y_n - \bar{y}) = 0.$$

Hence if we know $n-1$ of these brackets, the remaining one can be found by subtraction from zero.

So the number of independent contributions to SST is $n-1$. This is the number of degrees of freedom of SST.

The most helpful way to think about the number of degrees of freedom for the explained sum of squares SSEx is in terms of the physical freedom of the regression line (for the simple model) or plane (as it would be for a multiple-regression model). The way the line for the simple-regression model is defined constrains it to pass through the point $x = \bar{x}$, $y = \bar{y}$. This being the case, the only freedom the line has is in respect of its slope and hence the number of degrees of freedom is 1.

Having established the degrees of freedom for the total sum of squares and for the explained sum of squares, the degrees of freedom for the residual can be found by subtraction. So for simple regression the degrees of freedom for the residual sum of squares is

$$(n-1) - 1 = n - 2.$$

Hence the general form of the analysis of variance table for testing a simple-regression model is shown in Table 13.6.

Table 13.6	Source of variation	Sum of squares	Degrees of freedom	Mean square	Variance ratio
	Regression	SSEx	1	$MSEx = \dfrac{SSEx}{1}$	$VR = \dfrac{MSEx}{MSU}$
	Residual	SSU	$n - 2$	$MSU = \dfrac{SSU}{n - 2}$	
	Total	SST	$n - 1$		

The significance of the variance ratio is tested by comparing it with the table of the F distribution having 1 degree of freedom in the numerator and $n - 2$ degrees of freedom in the denominator.

For the data in example 13.3.2 we saw that

$$SST = 60\,610 \qquad \text{and} \qquad SSEx = 58\,463.954,$$

so
$$SSU = 60\,610 - 58\,463.954 = 2\,146.046.$$

Using these figures we can complete the analysis of variance table as Table 13.7.

Table 13.7	Source of variation	Sum of squares	Degrees of freedom	Mean square	Variance ratio
	Regression	58 463.954	1	58 463.954	218
	Residual	2 146.046	8	268.356	
	Total	60 610	9		

The figure 218 is then compared with the F distribution table. The 0.1 per cent point of $F_{1,8}$ is at 25.42 and the value 218 greatly exceeds this so we can conclude that the regression model is highly significant in explaining the variation in direct labour costs.

The numerical difference between the analysis of variance statistic above and the value of $\dfrac{(n - 2)r^2}{1 - r^2}$ in the preceding test has occurred only because of rounding error in using $r^2 = 0.965$ in the first test. The two statistics are actually identical, as can be easily demonstrated in the following way:

$$\frac{(n - 2)r^2}{1 - r^2} = \frac{(n - 2)\dfrac{SSEx}{SST}}{1 - \dfrac{SSEx}{SST}} = \frac{(n - 2)\dfrac{SSEx}{SST}}{\dfrac{SST - SSEx}{SST}} = \frac{(n - 2)\,SSEx}{SSU}$$

$$= \frac{\dfrac{SSEx}{1}}{\dfrac{SSU}{n - 2}} = \frac{MSEx}{MSU}.$$

Exercise 13.4.1

A company having a large number of machines wants to investigate the relationship between the number of machines to be serviced at a particular time and the average service time required by the mechanics. (It is suspected that the mechanics work faster when there are more machines to be serviced.) So records have been compiled showing for days on which various different numbers of breakdowns occurred the average service time per machine on that day. The records are as shown in Table 13.8.

Table 13.8

Number of reported breakdowns, x:	8	9	10	11	12	13	14	15	16	17	18	19	20
Average service time in minutes, y:	61.5	56.0	56.5	46.5	51.5	44.5	46.0	44.5	43.0	37.5	39.5	32.0	31.0

You are required to:

(a) Find the least-squares regression line of the form $y = a + bx$.
(b) Forecast average service time on a day when 17 machines break down.
(c) Calculate the coefficient of determination and use it to test the significance of the regression model.
(d) Test the significance of the model using analysis of variance.

13.5 Forecasting Using Multiple Regression

In section 13.4 we looked at regression forecasting for the case where variation in a variable of interest was explained by means of a regression on one explanatory variable. In this section we extend this to the case where the regression is on several explanatory variables. For the purposes of exposition we limit ourselves to the case of just two explanatory variables, but this case illustrates all the principles of multiple regression. Certainly in practice it is hard to imagine anybody attempting a regression on more than two variables without a computer, and even for a regression on two variables a computer or programmed calculator would normally be used.

Again we explain the ideas using an example.

Example 13.5.1

A firm making fastenings used in the construction industry wishes to assess the effectiveness of its advertising. To do this it decides to fit a regression model using sales values as the dependent variable and using previous quarters' advertising expenditure and a production index for the construction industry as the explanatory variables. The quarterly data for the last three years are as shown in Table 13.9.

Table 13.9

Sales, y (£000)	Previous quarter's advertising, x_1 (£000)	Construction index, x_2
381	2.066	94.8
426	2.190	99.6
440	2.230	99.8
586	2.232	99.9
589	2.284	102.1
618	2.348	105.5
620	2.468	106.3
645	2.502	107.0
651	2.550	108.5
741	2.854	109.2
842	2.940	110.5
925	3.792	110.8

You are required to:

(a) Determine the least-squares regression model.
(b) Make a forecast of the sales in a quarter when the previous quarter's advertising was £3000 and the construction index was 110.
(c) Test the significance of the least-squares regression model.
(d) Test the significance of the regression coefficient for advertising expenditure and hence comment on the effectiveness of the advertising.

ANSWER

(a) The model we are seeking to establish here is

$$y = b_0 + b_1 x_1 + b_2 x_2$$

where b_0, b_1 and b_2 are constants.

Following the same approach as for the simple regression model in section 13.4 we need to find these so as to minimise

$$\Sigma (b_0 + b_1 x_1 + b_2 x_2 - y)^2$$

where the summation is over all triplets of data values. Differentiating the above expression with respect to each of b_0, b_1 and b_2 separately and equating the result to zero gives the following set of normal equations for this model:

$$n b_0 + b_1 \Sigma x_1 + b_2 \Sigma x_2 = \Sigma y \qquad (1)$$

$$b_0 \Sigma x_1 + b_1 \Sigma x_1^2 + b_2 \Sigma x_1 x_2 = \Sigma x_1 y \qquad (2)$$

$$b_0 \Sigma x_2 + b_1 \Sigma x_1 x_2 + b_2 \Sigma x_2^2 = \Sigma x_2 y. \qquad (3)$$

These could be used directly by inserting values for the sums and then solving the resulting equations. However, it is more usual to work in terms of formulae obtained by manipulating the equations algebraically.

Multiplying through in equation (1) by $\dfrac{\Sigma x_1}{n}$ and subtracting the result from equation (2) gives

$$b_1 \left[\Sigma x_1^2 - \frac{(\Sigma x_1)^2}{n} \right] + b_2 \left[\Sigma x_1 x_2 - \frac{(\Sigma x_1)(\Sigma x_2)}{n} \right] = \Sigma x_1 y - \frac{(\Sigma x_1)(\Sigma y)}{n}.$$
$$(4)$$

Multiplying through in equation (1) by $\dfrac{\Sigma x_2}{n}$ and subtracting the result from equation (3) gives

$$b_1 \left[\Sigma x_1 x_2 - \frac{(\Sigma x_1)(\Sigma x_2)}{n} \right] + b_2 \left[\Sigma x_2^2 - \frac{(\Sigma x_2)^2}{n} \right] = \Sigma x_2 y - \frac{(\Sigma x_2)(\Sigma y)}{n}.$$
$$(5)$$

The two equations (4) and (5) can then be more tidily written as follows:

$$b_1 \Sigma (x_1 - \overline{x}_1)^2 + b_2 \Sigma (x_1 - \overline{x}_1)(x_2 - \overline{x}_2) = \Sigma (x_1 - \overline{x}_1)(y - \overline{y}),$$

$$b_1 \Sigma (x_1 - \overline{x}_1)(x_2 - \overline{x}_2) + b_2 \Sigma (x_2 - \overline{x}_2)^2 = \Sigma (x_2 - \overline{x}_2)(y - \overline{y}).$$

These can then, if we wish, be written in matrix form as

$$\begin{pmatrix} \Sigma (x_1 - \overline{x}_1)^2 & \Sigma (x_1 - \overline{x}_1)(x_2 - \overline{x}_2) \\ \Sigma (x_1 - \overline{x}_1)(x_2 - \overline{x}_2) & \Sigma (x_2 - \overline{x}_2)^2 \end{pmatrix} \begin{pmatrix} b_1 \\ b_2 \end{pmatrix} = \begin{pmatrix} \Sigma (x_1 - \overline{x}_1)(y - \overline{y}) \\ \Sigma (x_2 - \overline{x}_2)(y - \overline{y}) \end{pmatrix}$$

Hence

$$\begin{pmatrix} b_1 \\ b_2 \end{pmatrix} = \begin{pmatrix} \Sigma(x_1 - \overline{x}_1)^2 & \Sigma(x_1 - \overline{x}_1)(x_2 - \overline{x}_2) \\ \Sigma(x_1 - \overline{x}_1)(x_2 - \overline{x}_2) & \Sigma(x_2 - \overline{x}_2)^2 \end{pmatrix}^{-1} \begin{pmatrix} \Sigma(x_1 - \overline{x}_1)(y - \overline{y}) \\ \Sigma(x_2 - \overline{x}_2)(y - \overline{y}) \end{pmatrix} \tag{6}$$

For the two-explanatory-variable case the benefit from using matrix notation is marginal but it is worth considering because it provides a compact notation for expressing the most general kind of multiple-regression situation.

For the two-variable case if we let

$$A = \begin{pmatrix} x_{11} - \overline{x}_1 & x_{21} - \overline{x}_2 \\ x_{12} - \overline{x}_1 & x_{22} - \overline{x}_2 \\ x_{13} - \overline{x}_1 & x_{23} - \overline{x}_2 \\ x_{14} - \overline{x}_1 & x_{24} - \overline{x}_2 \\ \cdot & \cdot \\ \cdot & \cdot \\ \cdot & \cdot \\ x_{1n} - \overline{x}_1 & x_{2n} - \overline{x}_2 \end{pmatrix}, \quad \mathbf{b} = \begin{pmatrix} b_1 \\ b_2 \end{pmatrix}, \quad \mathbf{y} = \begin{pmatrix} y_1 \\ y_2 \\ y_3 \\ y_4 \\ \cdot \\ \cdot \\ \cdot \\ y_n \end{pmatrix}, \quad \overline{\mathbf{y}} = \begin{pmatrix} \overline{y} \\ \overline{y} \\ \overline{y} \\ \overline{y} \\ \cdot \\ \cdot \\ \cdot \\ \overline{y} \end{pmatrix}$$

then equation (6) can be written $(A'A)\mathbf{b} = A'(\mathbf{y} - \overline{\mathbf{y}})$.

Hence the regression coefficient can be found by solving the matrix equation to obtain $\mathbf{b} = (A'A)^{-1} A'(\mathbf{y} - \overline{\mathbf{y}})$.

This is valid for a multiple regression of any size with suitable redefinition of matrix A to include a column for each explanatory variable. The coefficient b_0 is found by substituting the values of the other coefficients into equation (1), or its equivalent for larger models. For the present case we have

$$b_0 = \frac{\Sigma y - b_1 \Sigma x_1 - b_2 \Sigma x_2}{n}. \tag{7}$$

For the data in this example we have sums, sums of squares and sums of cross-products as follows.

$\Sigma y \quad = 7464, \qquad \Sigma x_1 \quad = 30.456, \qquad \Sigma x_2 \quad = 1254,$

$\Sigma y^2 = 4\,930\,374, \quad \Sigma x_1^2 = 79.770\,648, \quad \Sigma x_2^2 = 131\,334.38,$

$\Sigma x_1 y = 19\,707.472, \quad \Sigma x_2 y = 788\,340.4, \quad \Sigma x_1 x_2 = 3\,203.8398.$

So $\quad \Sigma(x_1 - \overline{x}_1)^2 = 79.770\,648 - \dfrac{30.456^2}{12} = 2.473\,320.$

$\Sigma(x_1 - \overline{x}_1)(x_2 - \overline{x}_2) = 3\,203.8398 - \dfrac{30.456 \times 1254}{12} = 21.1878,$

$\Sigma(x_2 - \overline{x}_2)^2 = 131\,334.38 - \dfrac{1254^2}{12} = 291.38,$

$\Sigma(x_1 - \overline{x}_1)(y - \overline{y}) = 19\,707.472 - \dfrac{30.456 \times 7464}{12} = 763.84,$

$\Sigma(x_2 - \overline{x}_2)(y - \overline{y}) = 788\,340.4 - \dfrac{1254 \times 7464}{12} = 8352.4.$

Using equation (6) we thus have $\begin{pmatrix} b_1 \\ b_2 \end{pmatrix} = \begin{pmatrix} 2.473\,320 & 21.1878 \\ 21.1878 & 291.38 \end{pmatrix}^{-1} \begin{pmatrix} 763.84 \\ 8352.4 \end{pmatrix}.$

Then inverting the 2×2 matrix as shown in Chapter 11 gives

$$\begin{pmatrix} b_1 \\ b_2 \end{pmatrix} = \frac{1}{271.753\,12} \begin{pmatrix} 291.38 & -21.1878 \\ -21.1878 & 2.473\,320 \end{pmatrix} \begin{pmatrix} 763.84 \\ 8352.4 \end{pmatrix} = \begin{pmatrix} 167.795 \\ 16.463 \end{pmatrix}.$$

Substituting these values for b_1 and b_2 in equation (7):

$$b_0 = \frac{7464 - 167.795 \times 30.456 - 16.463 \times 1254}{12} = \frac{-18\,290.966}{12} = -1524.247.$$

The least-squares regression model is

$$y = -1524.247 + 167.795 x_1 + 16.463 x_2.$$

(b) A forecast of the value of the explained variables y for given values of the explanatory variables can be obtained by substituting the given values into the model.

Hence for a quarter when the previous quarter's advertising was £3000 and the construction index was 110 the sales forecast is

$$\begin{aligned} y &= -1524.247 + 167.795 \times 3 + 16.463 \times 110 \\ &= -1524.247 + 503.385 + 1810.93 \\ &= 790.068 \end{aligned}$$

The forecast value for sales is £790 000.

(c) The overall effectiveness of a multiple-regression model can be tested using the same methods as we saw for the simple-regression model in section 13.4. That is to say, we can use a coefficient of determination or we can use analysis of variance.

Either way, we begin with a total sum of squares

$$\boxed{\text{SST} = \Sigma (y - \bar{y})^2 = \Sigma y^2 - \frac{(\Sigma y)^2}{n}.}$$

The explained sum of squares this time is

$$\text{SSEx} = \Sigma (b_0 + b_1 x_1 + b_2 x_2 - \bar{y})^2,$$

and by reasoning similar to that in section 13.4 this can be shown to give

$$\boxed{\begin{aligned} \text{SSEx} &= b_1 \Sigma (x_1 - \bar{x}_1)(y - \bar{y}) + b_2 \Sigma (x_2 - \bar{x}_2)(y - \bar{y}) \\ &= b_1 \left[\Sigma x_1 y - \frac{(\Sigma x_1)(\Sigma y)}{n} \right] + b_2 \left[\Sigma x_2 y - \frac{(\Sigma x_2)(\Sigma y)}{n} \right]. \end{aligned}}$$

This method for finding SSEx can be extended to any number of explanatory variables. For the multiple-regression case it is usual to represent the coefficient of determination by capital R squared. As in the simple regression case it is found as the ratio of the explained sum of squares to the total sum of squares. Thus $R^2 = \dfrac{\text{SSEx}}{\text{SST}}$.

For this example we have

$$\text{SST} = 4\,930\,374 - \frac{7464^2}{12} = 287\,766,$$

$$\text{SSEx} = 167.795 \times 763.84 + 16.463 \times 8352.4 = 265\,674.09.$$

$$\text{Hence, } R^2 = \frac{265\,674.09}{287\,766}.$$

This tells us that 92.323 per cent of the variation in the y values is explained by the regression on x_1 and x_2. This seems large, but, again as in the simple regression case, we can carry out a test of significance to decide whether R^2 is close to 1. The test statistic, for reasons which will become clear when we consider analysis of variance below, is

$$\frac{(n-3)R^2}{2(1-R^2)}.$$

Its significance is tested by comparing it with the F distribution table for 2 degrees of freedom in the numerator and $n-3$ degrees of freedom in the denominator.

For the data in the example we have

$$\frac{(n-3)R^2}{2(1-R^2)} = \frac{9 \times 0.923\,23}{2 \times 0.076\,77} = \frac{8.309\,07}{0.153\,54} = 54.1.$$

The table for the F distribution shows the 0.1 per cent point of $F_{2,9}$ to be at 16.39. As the statistic value greatly exceeds this, we can conclude that the regression model is highly significant in explaining the variation in the sales. Note that the square root of the coefficient of multiple determination is called the multiple-correlation coefficient. It is denoted by the symbol R. In the analysis of variance method the residual sum of squares can again be found by subtracting the explained sum of squares from the total:

$$SSU = SST - SSEx.$$

The degrees of freedom for the total sum of squares are $n-1$, exactly as we saw for the simple-regression case. In geometrical terms the regression model for explanatory variables is a plane in three-dimensional space. The plane passes through the point $(\bar{x}_1, \bar{x}_2, \bar{y})$ and thus has two degrees of freedom; it can rotate about each of two perpendicular axes. In general, the number of degrees of freedom for the explained sum of squares in a multiple-regression model is equal to the number of explanatory variables.

The number of degrees of freedom for the residual sum of squares can again be found by subtraction and so for the two-explanatory-variable model it is

$$(n-1) - 2 = n - 3.$$

Hence for the example being considered here the analysis of variance table is as shown in Table 13.10.

Table 13.10	Source of variation	Sum of squares	Degrees of freedom	Mean square	Variance ratio
	Regression	265 674.09	2	132 837.04	54.1
	Residual	22 091.91	9	2 454.6566	
	Total	287 766	11		

The figure 54.1 is then compared with the F table for 2 degrees of freedom in the numerator and 9 in the denominator. The 0.1 per cent point of $F_{2,9}$ is 16.39 and the value 54.1 greatly exceeds this, so the model is seen to be significant in explaining the variation in sales.

Using the same argument as for the simple model in section 13.4, you should confirm that the variance ratio in this analysis of variance table must always be the same as the test statistic obtained when the coefficient of multiple determination method is used.

(d) When considering *simple* regression the significance of the model implies that the only explanatory variable is significant in explaining the variation in the dependent variable. However, in the case of multiple regression it is necesaary in addition to considering the significance of the regression model as a whole to consider the significance of each of the explanatory variables individually.

In this particular case we are asked about the significance of advertising expenditure. A test of the significance of an individual variable is carried out as a test of whether its regression coefficient is significantly different from zero. Thus for advertising expenditure, which is variable x_1, the test to be carried out has null and alternative hypotheses: $H_0 : b_1 = 0$
$$H_1 : b_1 \neq 0.$$

The test is executed by comparing $\dfrac{b_1 - 0}{\text{standard error of } b_1}$ with the percentage points of the t distribution having $n - 3$ degrees of freedom, or, equivalently, by comparing the square of this statistic with the percentage points of the F distribution having one degree of freedom in the numerator and $n - 3$ degrees of freedom in the denominator. To carry out the required test we must, therefore, find the standard error of b_1. To do this we must take the inverse of the sum of squares and cross-products matrix, i.e.

$$\begin{pmatrix} \Sigma (x_1 - \bar{x}_1)^2 & \Sigma (x_1 - \bar{x}_1)(x_2 - \bar{x}_2) \\ \Sigma (x_1 - \bar{x}_1)(x_2 - \bar{x}_2) & \Sigma (x_2 - \bar{x}_2)^2 \end{pmatrix}^{-1}$$

and look at the elements on the leading (i.e. top left to bottom right) diagonal. Thus if the inverse is denoted

$$\begin{pmatrix} C_{11} & C_{12} \\ C_{21} & C_{22} \end{pmatrix}$$

then we must use C_{11} and C_{22} to find the standard errors for b_1 and b_2 respectively. The appropriate matrix element must be multiplied by the mean-square error MSU and then the square root taken to give the required standard error.

Thus,
$$\text{standard error of } b_1 = \sqrt{C_{11} \times \text{MSU}}$$
$$\text{standard error of } b_2 = \sqrt{C_{22} \times \text{MSU}}.$$

The principle extends to multiple regression involving any number of explanatory variables using the leading diagonal elements of $(A'A)^{-1}$ with the MSU to obtain the standard errors.

For the problem in hand we have seen that

$$\begin{pmatrix} \Sigma (x_1 - \bar{x}_1)^2 & \Sigma (x_1 - \bar{x}_1)(x_2 - \bar{x}_2) \\ \Sigma (x_1 - \bar{x}_1)(x_2 - \bar{x}_2) & \Sigma (x_2 - \bar{x}_2)^2 \end{pmatrix}^{-1}$$

$$= \frac{1}{271.753\,12} \begin{pmatrix} 291.38 & -21.1878 \\ -21.1878 & 2.473\,320 \end{pmatrix}$$

and that MSU $= 2\,454.6566$.

Hence standard error of $b_1 = \sqrt{\dfrac{291.38}{271.753\,12} \times 2454.6566}$

$$= 51.302.$$

We have seen also that $\quad b_1 = 167.795$.

So the test statistic for the t-test is $\dfrac{167.795 - 0}{51.302} = 3.27$

The 0.5 per cent points of t_9 are at ± 3.25 and 3.27 is outside this range. So on a 1 per cent two-sided test of significance the regression coefficient for advertising is shown to be significantly different from zero. We can therefore conclude that advertising is a significant variable in explaining variation in sales.

Exercise 13.5.1

For the data given in Table 13.11 relating to three variables x_1, x_2 and y you are required to do the following:

(a) Determine the least-squares regression model of the form

$$y = b_0 + b_1 x_1 + b_2 x_2.$$

(b) Forecast the value of y if $x_1 = 11.0$ and $x_2 = 0.500$.
(c) Test the significance of the multiple-regression model using both analysis of variance and the coefficient of determination.
(d) Test the significance of variable x_1 in explaining the variation in y.

Table 13.11

y	x_1	x_2
1.964	1.0	−0.266
2.137	2.0	0.016
4.955	3.0	−0.635
2.677	4.0	1.163
3.432	5.0	−0.496
4.296	6.0	−0.182
4.222	7.0	−1.249
6.298	8.0	−1.097
5.741	9.0	0.313
5.043	10.0	0.212

Further Exercises

13.1 The total sales of electricity in Great Britain during the years 1964–74 are given in Table 13.12.

Table 13.12

Year	Total sales (gigawatt hours)
1964	140 374
1965	151 071
1966	156 931
1967	161 664
1968	173 925
1969	185 423
1970	193 907
1971	199 442
1972	206 370
1973	220 591
1974	213 888

Source: *Annual Abstract of Statistics 1975*, Table 191.

(a) Find the equation of a least-square line fitting the data.
(b) Based on the information given and the equation found in (a), estimate the sales of electricity in 1977.
(c) Assuming the present trends continue, in what year would you expect 1965 sales to be doubled?

Workings for all sections of the question must be shown together with approximations used.

(*ICMA Fdn. B*)

13.2 A hop growers' association is analysing demand for its hops and has collected the data shown in Table 13.13.

Table 13.13

Year to December	Bushels of hops purchased (000 bushels)	Average price per bushel (£)
1972	500	9.00
1973	530	8.60
1974	510	11.00
1975	580	9.50
1976	600	9.30
1977	600	13.00
1978	630	11.50

The association's statistician has calculated the following regression equations and test statistics in relation to the above information:

(a) Quantity purchased (y) in relation to time (x):
$y = 475.7 + 22.14x$.
R^2 (unadjusted) $= 0.8931$; F ratio $= 41.78$;
regression coefficient t value $= 6.464$.

(b) Quantity purchased (y) in relation to price (x):
$y = 410.7 + 14.96x$
R^2 (unadjusted) $= 0.2246$; F ratio $= 1.45$;
regression t value $= 1.204$.

(c) Deviation of quantity purchased from trend (y)(as expected in (a) above) in relation to price (x):
$y = 611.2 - 0.59x$.
R^2 (unadjusted) $= 0.3300$; F ratio $= 2.46$;
regression coefficient t value $= 1.569$.

You are required to:

(i) describe the information given by the R^2, F and t statistics, using the information in the sections (a) to (c) above to illustrate your answer;

(ii) examine each equation in turn and discuss its suitability for use as a predictor of the demand for hops;

(iii) give two other factors which could be present in the the situation and exerting an influence on the demand for hops.

(ICMA Prof. 1)

13.3 The data given in Table 13.14 was collected from the Industrial Products Manufacturing Company Limited.

Table 13.14

Month	Total overhead y	Direct labour hours (DLH) x	Plant hours (PH)
January	15 000	736	184
February	14 500	800	160
March	15 750	1 008	168
April	15 250	880	176
May	16 250	1 056	176
June	15 000	840	168
	$\Sigma y = 91\,750$	$\Sigma x = 5\,320$	
	$\bar{y} = 15\,291.7$	$\bar{x} = 886.7$	

You are required to:

(a) compute a least-squares cost equation based on direct labour hours;
(b) compute the coefficient of determination (r^2) for (a);
(c) compare and discuss the relationship of your solution in (a) to the equation of:

$$\text{total overhead} = 5758 + 4.7\ \text{DLH} + 31\ \text{PH}.$$

(where DLH = direct labour hours, PH = plant hours) obtained by a regression using DLH and PH as variables and coefficient of determination $R^2 = 0.9873$;
(d) estimate the total overhead for a month with 1000 DLH and 168 PH, using the equation in (c).

(ICMA Prof. 1)

Appendix 1
Solutions to Exercises

Chapter 2

2.1.1 7 Assault and 7 Dandy. Maximum profit = £410.
2.3.1 (a) No tanks, 2000 trays, 2000 tubs.
      (b) 2000 slack hours in process Y.
      (c) Shadow price £$\frac{2}{3}$ per hour for process X.
         Shadow price £$\frac{1}{3}$ per hour for process Z.
2.3.2 (b) 30 000 cases of talcum powder, 24 000 cases of shaving foam.
         20 000 cases of hair spray, 25 000 cases of deodorant.
         The production of shaving foam is 16 000 cases below maximum expected demand.
         21 slack hours of finishing time, 2.5 slack hours of printing time, 30.5 slack hours of packaging time.
         £8230 is the maximum contribution.
         £14 is the shadow price per hour of extra production time.
         Marginal increase in contribution per extra 1000 cases of talcum powder sold is £10. Marginal increase in contribution per extra 1000 cases of hair spray sold is £39. Marginal increase in contribution per extra 1000 cases of deodorant sold is £34.
2.4.1 (a) 17$\frac{1}{2}$ hours of plant A. 3$\frac{3}{4}$ hours of plant B.
      (b) £195 is the minimum cost.
         57$\frac{1}{4}$ units is the production of product II above the minimum required.
         £1.50 is the increase in cost per additional unit of I.
         £2.00 is the increase in cost per additional unit of III.

Further Exercises

2.1 (b) 7 golf courses and 7 sports centres. Maximum income = £2.73m.
     (c) 10 golf courses and 5 sports centres. Maximum income = £2.85m.
     (d) Change in income = £120 000.
2.2 1020 of X, 30 of Y and 1060 of Z. Maximum = £19 460.
2.3 9 kg of A, no B and no C. Minimum cost = £1.80.
2.4 15 of X and 2 of Y. Maximum contribution = £169.
     Y production falls 33 short of exceeding X by 20.
     Shadow price of production time is £2.90 per hour.
     Extra revenue can be obtained at a marginal reduction of 5p contribution per £1 revenue.

Chapter 3

3.2.1   AIV, BIII, CII, DI; cost £53.
3.3.1   AIV 2, BII 1, BIII 2, CII 2, DI 1, DIII 2, DIV 1; cost £148.
3.5.1   AII 3, BI 4, CI 4, CIV 1, DI 1, DII 2, DIII 4; cost £73.
3.6.1   AIII 2, BI 0, BIV 3, CIII 2, CV 1, DI 1, DII 3, DV 0; profit £189.
3.6.2   AI, BIV, CIII, DII, profit £68.
3.7.1   *Alternative to 3.3.1:* AIV 2, BII 2, BIII 1, CI 1, CII 1, DIII 3, DIV 1. *Alternative to 3.5.1:* AII 1, AIII 2, BI 4, CI 4, CIV 1, DI 1, DII 4, DIII 2. *Alternative to 3.6.1:* AIII 1, AV 1, BI 0, BIV 3, CIII 3, DI 1, DII 3, DV 0.

Further Exercises

3.1   AI 4, AIV 2, BII 2, BIII 6, CII 5, CIV 12; cost £459.
3.2   aA 10 000, aD 10 000, bB 18 000, bC 6 000, bD 14 000, cC 16 000; cost £166 000.

Chapter 4

4.1.1   A should use II and B should use III. Value of game = 1.
4.2.1   B should never use III. Then A should never use II.
A should use I for $\frac{1}{3}$ of the time and III for $\frac{2}{3}$ of the time.
B should use I for $\frac{3}{5}$ of the time and II for $\frac{2}{5}$ of the time.
The value of the game is zero.
4.3.1   B should use I for $\frac{7}{9}$ of the time and II for $\frac{2}{9}$ of the time.
A should use only strategy III. The value of the game is 4.
4.4.1   A should use I for $\frac{78}{121}$ of the time, II for $\frac{32}{121}$ of the time and III for $\frac{32}{121}$ of the time.
B should use I for $\frac{66}{121}$ of the time, II for $\frac{16}{121}$ of the time and III for $\frac{39}{121}$ of the time.
The value of the game is $\frac{38}{121}$.

Further Exercises

4.1   B should never use III because it is dominated by I.
The resulting 2 x 2 game has a saddle point.
A should use only II. B should use only I. The value of the game is −2.
4.2   Sawfaye should use price cutting for $\frac{4}{7}$ of the time and advertising for $\frac{3}{7}$.
Scote should use price cutting for $\frac{3}{7}$ of the time and advertising for $\frac{4}{7}$.
The value of the game is a profit increase of £$\frac{5000}{7}$ for Scote at the expense of Sawfaye.
4.3   Road should never use speed because it is dominated by cost.
Rail should use speed $\frac{5}{14}$ of the time and comfort $\frac{9}{14}$ of the time. Road should use comfort $\frac{2}{7}$ of the time and cost $\frac{5}{7}$ of the time.
The value of the game is $\frac{17\,000}{7}$ customers gained by road at the expense of rail.
4.4   The company should use I for $\frac{19}{48}$ of the time, II for $\frac{15}{48}$ of the time and III for $\frac{14}{48}$ of the time.
The country should use I for $\frac{15}{48}$ of the time, II for $\frac{12}{48}$ of the time and III for $\frac{21}{48}$ of the time.
The value of the game is £4 375 000 to the company.

Chapter 5

5.1.1　(c) The critical path activities are 1, 2, 3, 4, 5, 6, 8, 9, 10, 11, 12, 13, 24, 25.

Minimum duration is 29 days.

5.2.1　Normal duration is 28 days. Normal cost is £4650.

The critical activities are a, e, f, i, j.

Optimum time is 21 days. Minimum cost is £4490.

Durations and costs of individual activities in the optimum situation are as follows:

Activity	a	b	c	d	e	f	g	h	i	j
Duration (days)	5	7	7	8	8	3	9	5	2	3
Cost (£)	550	450	380	700	800	320	800	230	450	510

5.3.1　(a) Normal time is 39 days. Associated cost is £107 000.

(b) Minimum time is 26 days. Associated minimum cost is £115 250.

(c) Minimum cost is £105 750. Associated time is 36 days.

5.4.1　(a) Normal duration is 44 days. Normal cost is £8280.

Critical path is 0–10–7–8–4–5.

(b) Number of different paths is 4.

(c) Minimum time is 21 days. For this to be achieved at least possible cost all activities are critical except 7–8.

The associated minimum cost is £13 480.

(d) Maximum number of men needed is 19 (on days 18 to 22).

5.5.1　(b) All paths are critical. Average duration is 10 days.

Variable cost is £88.

(c) Minimum time is 9 days with probability 0.35.

Maximum time is 15 days with probability 0.10.

Further Exercises

5.1　(a) The critical-path activities are A, C, E and G.

The length of the path is 14 days.

(b) Yes, the critical path will change.

The new critical path is A, C, F, G. Length is 15 days.

(c) Minimum time is 11 days. Total additional cost is £500.

F is ultimately speeded up by 1 day, and E and G each by 3 days.

5.2　(a) The critical path activities are A, C, G, H, I, J, K.

Duration is 12 weeks.

(b) B must be started no later than in week 3.

(c) With appropriate scheduling, the minimum team size is 6.

5.3　(a) The critical-path activities are D, E, F, G, I. Duration is 47 days.

(b)

Activity	A	B	C	D	E	F	G	H	I
Total float	10	10	11	0	0	0	0	12	0

(c) Minimum number of staff needed is 3.

(d) Total time increased by 1 day by doing B and C sequentially instead of together.

Chapter 6

6.1.1　(a) £121 096.　　(b) £131 000.

6.2.1　1600 tons.

6.3.1　(a) 170.　　(b) 195.

6.4.1　(a) 20 tons.　　(b) 7 tons.

6.5.1　EBQ is 1162.

Reorder level is when accumulated orders reach 516.

Further Exercises

6.1   (a) 784.
      (b) (i) +11.8 per cent,   (ii) −13.4 per cent.
6.2   (b) EBQ is 4082.
         Total cost for year using batch size 4082 is £1 881 124.
         Total cost for year using discount batch size 4500 is £1 505 478.
6.3   (b) 39.
      (c) Buy in batches of 150 items.
6.4   (b) 10 286.

Chapter 7

7.2.1 (b) £5.
7.2.2 (a) £144. (b) £160.
7.3.1 (a) 10 min for 1-channel system.
          11.11 min for 2-channel system.
          12.45 min for 3-channel system.
      (b) The 3-channel system at £147 per hour.
          (The 1-channel system costs £170 per hour,
          and the 2-channel system £156.)
      (c) £16.67 per hour.
7.3.2 (a) (i) £78,   (ii) £77.88.

Further Exercises

7.1   Slow, cheap man gives total cost of £18 per hour.
      Fast, expensive man gives total cost of £10 per hour.
      The fast expensive man should be used.
7.2   (a) 13.5 minutes.
      (b) 0.178.
      (c) 0.75.
7.3   Total 5-year cost: machine A   £52 000.
                      machine B   £10 143.
                      machine C   £6 000.
      Machine C should be installed.

Chapter 9

9.2.1 First do research programme (b) (i).
       If it fails, do research programme (b) (ii).
       If that also fails take action (a).
9.3.1 £2000 for Perraigne, £1000 for Top-Pop, £1500 for Slim-Fizz.
9.4.1 Build 5 in May, none in June, 10 in July and none in August.
9.5.1 Route is X–E–F–I–Y or X–E–F–J–Y.
       These both result in a profit of 37.

Further Exercises

9.1   Invest in A first. If it succeeds, then invest in B.
      The expected profit is £10 000.
9.2   *Either* Nothing in X, £3000 in Y, £1000 in Z.
      Or   £2000 in X, £2000 in Y, nothing in Z.
      Both policies lead to profit of £450.

9.3   Buy a new machine immediately. Keep it for three years.
       Buy another new one and keep it just one year.
       Buy another new one for the final year. Total cost is £88 000.

Chapter 10

10.2.1 Buy: 1-year-old equipment;
       Sell: 4-year-old equipment.
       Capital reduction £9400,
       Maintenance £9400,
       Average annual cost £6267.
10.3.1 Buy: 1-year-old equipment;
       Sell: 4-year-old equipment.
       Capital reduction £9400,
       Maintenance £9400,
       Average annual cost £6267.
10.4.1 (b) Replace all units at the end of two months (£1020 per month).

Further Exercises

10.1   (a) 40, 88, 94, 86.
       (b) 2.3 years.
       (c) 87.
       (d) £40.
10.2   Replace all units at the end of four periods (£235 per period).
10.3   Buy: new. Sell: after two years. Capital reduction £30 000, running cost
       £40 000, average annual cost £35 000.

Chapter 11

11.2.1 $\begin{pmatrix} 47 & 3 & 23 \\ -2 & 4 & 81 \end{pmatrix}$

11.2.2 $XY = \begin{pmatrix} 12 & 372 \\ 116 & 164 \\ -12 & -168 \end{pmatrix}$. YX does not exist.

11.2.3 $x = 3, y = 2.$

11.2.4 $\frac{1}{11} \begin{pmatrix} 7 & -5 \\ -2 & 3 \end{pmatrix}$

11.2.5 $x = \dfrac{-25}{4}, y = 5, z = \dfrac{-3}{4}.$

11.3.1 (a) $I - A = \begin{pmatrix} 0.8 & 0 & -0.9 \\ -0.1 & 0.9 & -0.1 \\ -0.1 & -0.1 & 1.0 \end{pmatrix}$

       (b) $\mathbf{x} = \begin{pmatrix} 278.5 \\ 199.5 \\ 117.8 \end{pmatrix}$

11.4.1 New transaction table:

	Input to		External	Total
	R	S	requirements	output
Output from R	5.5	9.6	40	55
Output from S	11	4.8	32	48
Labour and materials	5.5	9.6		
Overheads	11	4.8		
Profit	22	19.2		
Total input	55	48		

11.4.2 $I = \begin{pmatrix} 1 & 0 \\ 0 & 1 \end{pmatrix}$, $A = \begin{pmatrix} 0 & 0.4 \\ 0.3 & 0 \end{pmatrix}$, $\mathbf{b} = \begin{pmatrix} 6000 \\ 1000 \end{pmatrix}$, $\mathbf{s} = \begin{pmatrix} 11\,364 \\ 13\,409 \end{pmatrix}$.

Final allocations to the production departments are £15 266 to P_1 and £25 734 to P_2.

Further Exercises

11.1   £5263.

11.2   £16.84m from A, £19.47m from B, £12.63m from C.

11.3   (a) $\mathbf{x} = \begin{pmatrix} 590 \\ 670 \\ 830 \end{pmatrix}$

(b) New transactions table:

	Input to			Final	Total
	R	S	T	demand	output
Output from R	0	67	83	440	590
Output from S	59	0	83	528	670
Output from T	59	67	0	704	830
Costs	236	335	332		
Social gain	236	201	332		
Total input	590	670	830		

Chapter 12

12.1.1 (a) Let $E_1 \equiv$ TV1 higher rating, $E_2 \equiv$ TV2 higher rating.
$$P = \begin{bmatrix} 0.8 & 0.2 \\ 0.1 & 0.9 \end{bmatrix}.$$
(b) Let $E_1 \equiv$ F1 best record, $E_2 \equiv$ F2 best record, $E_3 \equiv$ F3 best record.
$$P = \begin{bmatrix} 0.4 & 0.3 & 0.3 \\ 0.3 & 0.4 & 0.3 \\ 0.3 & 0.3 & 0.4 \end{bmatrix}.$$

12.2.1 Probability of all transitions 0.3, except horizontal links which = 0.4.
$$P_2 = \begin{bmatrix} 0.34 & 0.33 & 0.33 \\ 0.33 & 0.34 & 0.33 \\ 0.33 & 0.33 & 0.34 \end{bmatrix}, P_3 = \begin{bmatrix} 0.334 & 0.333 & 0.333 \\ 0.333 & 0.334 & 0.333 \\ 0.333 & 0.333 & 0.334 \end{bmatrix}.$$

12.3.1 Observe results of 12.2.1 for P and P^2.
(a) $\mathbf{p}^{(0)} = [1\ \ 0\ \ 0]$, $\mathbf{p}^{(1)} = \mathbf{p}^{(0)}P = [0.4\ \ 0.3\ \ 0.3]$,
$\mathbf{p}^{(2)} = \mathbf{p}^{(0)}P^2 = [0.34\ \ 0.33\ \ 0.33]$.
Multiply $\mathbf{p}^{(0)}$, $\mathbf{p}^{(1)}$, $\mathbf{p}^{(2)}$ by 10 to find the expected distribution of shares.

(b) $\mathbf{p}^{(0)} = [0 \quad 0 \quad 1]$, $\mathbf{p}^{(1)} = \mathbf{p}^{(0)}P = [0.3 \quad 0.3 \quad 0.4]$,
$\mathbf{p}^{(2)} = \mathbf{p}^{(0)}P^2 = [0.33 \quad 0.33 \quad 0.34]$.
Multiply $\mathbf{p}^{(0)}, \mathbf{p}^{(1)}, \mathbf{p}^{(2)}$ by 10 to find the expected distribution of shares.

(c) $\mathbf{p}^{(0)} = [0.3 \quad 0.4 \quad 0.3]$, $\mathbf{p}^{(1)} = \mathbf{p}^{(0)}P = [0.33 \quad 0.34 \quad 0.33]$,
$\mathbf{p}^{(2)} = \mathbf{p}^{(0)}P = [0.333 \quad 0.334 \quad 0.333]$.
Multiply $\mathbf{p}^{(0)}, \mathbf{p}^{(1)}, \mathbf{p}^{(2)}$ by 100 to find the expected distribution of shares.

12.3.2 $\mathbf{p}^{(s)} = [\tfrac{1}{3} \quad \tfrac{1}{3} \quad \tfrac{1}{3}]$.

12.4.1 State E_1 = cutting tool starts the month new.
State E_2 = cutting tool starts the month one month old.
State E_3 = cutting tool starts the month two months old.
State E_4 = cutting tool starts the month three months old.
State E_5 = cutting tool starts the month four months old.

$$P = \begin{bmatrix} \tfrac{1}{10} & \tfrac{9}{10} & 0 & 0 & 0 \\ \tfrac{1}{6} & 0 & \tfrac{5}{6} & 0 & 0 \\ \tfrac{1}{3} & 0 & 0 & \tfrac{2}{3} & 0 \\ \tfrac{3}{5} & 0 & 0 & 0 & \tfrac{2}{5} \\ 1 & 0 & 0 & 0 & 0 \end{bmatrix}.$$

Replacement tools required: 100, 160, 281.

Further Exercises

12.1 $P^2 = \tfrac{1}{4}\begin{bmatrix} 1 & 2 & 1 \\ 1 & 1 & 2 \\ 2 & 1 & 1 \end{bmatrix}$, $P^3 = \tfrac{1}{8}\begin{bmatrix} 2 & 3 & 3 \\ 3 & 2 & 3 \\ 3 & 3 & 2 \end{bmatrix}$.
$\mathbf{p}^{(1)} = \tfrac{1}{8}[3 \quad 3 \quad 2]$, $\mathbf{p}^{(2)} = \tfrac{1}{16}[5 \quad 6 \quad 5]$,
$\mathbf{p}^{(3)} = \tfrac{1}{32}[10 \quad 11 \quad 11]$.

12.2 (a) (i) $\tfrac{1}{6}, \tfrac{2}{6}, \tfrac{3}{6}$ (ii) $\tfrac{11}{36}, \tfrac{10}{36}, \tfrac{15}{36}$
(b) $p = \tfrac{2}{7}, q = \tfrac{2}{7}, r = \tfrac{3}{7}$

12.3 (b) $$P = \begin{bmatrix} 0.8 & 0.1 & 0.1 \\ 0 & 0.9 & 0.1 \\ 0 & 0 & 1 \end{bmatrix}.$$
(c) 80, 10; 64, 17; 51.2, 21.7.
(d) £37 985.

Chapter 13

13.2.1 (a) 62.5, 63.75, 65.
(b) 55, 62.75, 60.2, 62.16, 61.73, 65.38.

13.3.1 (a) 46, 46, 45.5, 48.63, 47.97, 48, 48, 48.5, 46.5, 49.38, 48.53, 47.40.
(b) Forecasts for periods 8 to 13 are: 46, 47.43, 46.86, 47.14, 46.86.
(c) MAD for (i) is 5.02
RMS for (i) is 6.46
MAD for (ii) is 5.31
RMS for (ii) is 6.12.

13.4.1 (a) $y = 77.30 - 2.28x$.
(b) The forecast is 38.54 min.
(c) $R^2 = 0.923$, $\dfrac{(n-2)R^2}{1-R^2} = 132.1$, significant on $F_{1,11}$.
(d) Variance ratio = 132.1, significant on $F_{1,11}$.

13.5.1 (a) $y = 1.828\,262\,1 + 0.384\,467\,9x_1 - 0.601\,820\,8x_2$.
(b) The forecast is $y = 5.756$.

(c) Variance ratio = 9.076. Significant at 2.5 per cent level on $F_{2,7}$.

$$R^2 = 0.7217, \frac{(n-3)R^2}{2(1-R^2)} = 9.076,$$

significant at 2.5 per cent level on $F_{2,7}$.

(d) $\dfrac{b_1}{\text{standard error of } b_1} = 3.8978$.

Significant at 1 per cent level on t_7.

Further Exercises

13.1 (a) $y = 182\,144.18 + 8086.409x$.
   (b) 246 835.45 gigawatt hours
   (c) 1984
13.3 (a) $y = 11\,226.08 + 4.54x$.
   (b) $r^2 = 0.811$.
   (d) 15 666

Appendix 2
Additional Reading

We have included a selection of titles below in order to give a direction to further reading and an opportunity for further exercises. Operational research has an extensive literature, ranging from books presenting an overview of the subject to books dealing with specialist advanced topics, as well as learned journals and reports. Our choice categorises fifteen titles under a 'general' heading, one journal and a further fourteen titles related to particular chapters.

General

R. L. Ackoff and W. Sasieni, *Fundamentals of Operations Research* (New York: Wiley, 1968).

E. S. Buffa and J. S. Dyer, *Management Science/Operations Research* (Santa Barbara: Wiley, 1977).

J. S. Croucher, *Operations Research: A First Course* (Oxford: Pergamon, 1980).

H. G. Daellenbach and J. A. George, *Introduction to Operations Research Techniques* (Boston: Allyn and Bacon, 1978).

D. J. Hallett and T. Lucey, *Quantitative Techniques: A Practice and Revision Manual* (Eastleigh, Hampshire: D. P. Publications, 1983).

B. T. Houlden (ed.), *Some Techniques of Operational Research* (London: English UP, 1962).

T. Lucey, *Quantitative Techniques: An Instructional Manual*, 2nd edn (Winchester, Hampshire: D. P. Publications, 1982).

M. S. Makower and E. Williamson, *Operational Research: Problems, Techniques, and Exercises*, 2nd edn (London: Hodder and Stoughton, 1975).

F. Owen and R. H. Jones, *Modern Analytical Techniques* (Stockport: Polytech, 1973).

D. T. Phillips, A. Ravindran and J. Solberg, *Operations Research: Principles and Practice* (New York: Wiley, 1976).

B. H. P. Rivett and R. L. Ackoff, *A Manager's Guide to O.R.* (London: Wiley, 1963).

M. Sasieni, A. Yaspan and L. Friedman, *Operations Research: Methods and Problems* (New York, Wiley, 1959).

H. A. Taha, *Operations Research: An Introduction*, 3rd edn (London: Macmillan, 1983).

J. E. Ullmann, *Theory and Problems of Quantitative Methods in Management* (New York: McGraw-Hill, 1976).

F. M. Wilkes, *Elements of Operational Research* (Maidenhead: McGraw-Hill, 1980).

Journal

Journal of the Operational Research Society (Oxford).

Chapter 1   Introduction

J. W. Bryant (ed.), *Financial Modelling in Corporate Management* (Chichester: Wiley, 1982).

D. Martin (ed.), *Operational Research — The Science of Decision Making in Business, Industry, Government and Society* (Birmingham: Operational Research Society, 1985).

P. Rivett, *Model Building for Decision Analysis* (Chichester: Wiley, 1980).

B. Wilson, *Systems: Concepts, Methodologies, and Applications* (Chichester: Wiley, 1984).

Chapter 2   Linear Programming

G. Hadley, *Linear Programming* (Reading, Massachusetts: Addison-Wesley, 1962).

Chapter 4   The Theory of Games

J. von Neumann and O. Morgenstern, *Theory of Games and Economic Behaviour* (Princeton: Princeton UP, 1936).

Chapter 5   Network Analysis

A. Battersby, *Network Analysis for Planning and Scheduling*, 3rd edn (London: Macmillan, 1970).

Chapter 6   Stock Control

R. G. Brown, *Decision Rules for Inventory Management* (New York: Holt, Rinehart and Winston, 1967).

G. Hadley and T. M. Whitin, *Analysis of Inventory Systems* (Englewood Cliffs, NJ: Prentice-Hall, 1963).

Chapter 7   Queuing

A. M. Lee, *Applied Queueing Theory* (London: Macmillan, 1966).

Chapter 8   Simulation

M. Pidd, *Computer Simulation in Management Science* (Chichester: Wiley, 1984).

K. D. Tocher, *The Art of Simulation* (London: English UP, 1963).

Chapter 9   Dynamic Programming

R. E. Bellman and S. Dreyfuss, *Applied Dynamic Programming* (Princeton: Princeton UP, 1962).

Chapter 12   Markov Chains

D. J. Bartholomew, *Stochastic Models for Social Processes*, 3rd edn (Chichester: Wiley, 1982).

Index